THE REGULATIVE PRINCIPLE OF PRINCIPLE OF WORSHIP: EXPLAINED AND APPLIED

By Daniel F.N. Ritchie

PRESS

Copyright © 2007 by Daniel F.N. Ritchie

THE REGULATIVE PRINCIPLE OF WORSHIP:
Explained and Applied

by Daniel F.N. Ritchie

Printed in the United States of America

ISBN 978-1-60266-061-8

All rights reserved solely by the author. The author guarantees all contents are original and do not infringe upon the legal rights of any other person or work. No part of this book may be reproduced in any form without the permission of the author. The views expressed in this book are not necessarily those of the publisher.

Unless otherwise indicated all Scripture quotations in this work are taken from the English Standard Version (ESV) of the Holy Bible, Copyright © 2002 Collins.

Scripture quotations marked ASV are from the American Standard Version, Copyright © 1901 Thomas Nelson & Sons.

Scripture quotations marked AV are from the Authorised King James Version.

Scripture quotations marked NASB are from the New American Standard Bible: Updated Edition, Copyright © 1995 The Lockman Foundation.

Scripture quotations marked NIV are from the New International Version, Copyright © 1978 New York International Bible Society.

Scripture quotations marked NKJV are from the New King James Version, Copyright © 1982 Thomas Nelson Inc.

Scripture quotations marked RV are from the Revised Version.

Note:quotations from older authors have been slightly modernised.

www.xulonpress.com

Contents

Introduction

If someone were to ask you 'what is a Reformed Christian?' most of us would probably answer that a Reformed Christian is someone who subscribes to the doctrines commonly called the five points of Calvinism (total depravity, unconditional election, limited atonement, irresistible grace and perseverance of the saints). However, this is only part of the story. To be considered 'Reformed', in the historical sense, one is not only required to be a Calvinist in one's view of the doctrines of salvation; but one must also adhere to what is known as the 'regulative principle', which is, 'the theory of church government and worship that not only church doctrine but church practice, must be based on clear Scriptural warrant.'(A. Cairns, *Dictionary of Theological Terms*, p. 305). This is the consistent outworking of the principle that 'there is no other head of the Church, but the Lord Jesus Christ' (*Westminster Confession of Faith* Chapter 25: Section 6). If Jesus Christ alone is King and Head of

His Church, 'the church of God, which he obtained with his own blood' (Acts 20:28), then He alone has the right to stipulate how His Church should be governed and how it should worship Him. Thus when He gave the Apostles the 'Great Commission', Christ told them 'all authority in heaven and on earth has been given to me' (Matt. 28:18); this means that, as Mediator, Jesus is 'head over all things to the church' (Eph. 1:22). Consequently, the office bearers of the Church, when instructing Christ's disciples, have the duty assigned to them of 'teaching them to observe all that I have commanded you' (Matt. 28:20). Notice that not even the Apostles had the right to invent their own religious ceremonies, but were bound to adhere strictly to whatever the Lord had commanded them in His word.

Although the regulative principle also applies to the government of the Church, this book (in the will of the Lord) shall only examine how it applies to the Church's worship. Hopefully, we shall explore the historical background of the Reformed understanding of the Scriptural law of worship and its Biblical basis. Moreover, I hope to apply the regulative principle to the specific parts of worship in an effort to defend the Biblical doctrine of worship set forth in the Westminster Confession of Faith and currently practiced by the Reformed Presbyterian Church of Ireland.

CHAPTER 1:

Differences between Protestants

One of the fundamental principles of the Protestant Reformation in the 16th century was that, the Bible, and not the Church, was the sole standard and authority upon which the Christian faith is based. This principle is called Sola Scriptura (Latin for 'Scripture Alone'). Protestants therefore affirm that the Bible alone is the authoritative, complete, perfect and infallible revelation of the will of God for the Church 'unto which nothing at any time is to be added, whether by new revelations of the Spirit, or traditions of men' (*Westminster Confession of Faith* Chapter 1: Section 6). While all Protestants accepted the principle of Sola Scriptura as far as it applied to theology (i.e. the attributes of God, the Person of Christ, and the doctrines of salvation etc) a fundamental difference among the Reformers emerged concerning the application of Sola Scriptura to Church government and worship. The Lutheran wing of the Reformation (led by Martin Luther) would accept anything in worship that was not specifically condemned in the Bible; this is known as the 'normative principle'. Whereas, the Reformed wing (led by John Calvin), would only permit something in worship if it was ordained by God in the Bible; this is called the regulative principle.

Both sets of Protestants united in condemning the Roman Catholic Mass as blasphemous idolatry, (because it taught that Christ was continually re-sacrificed). Moreover, Luther could not accept the Mass because as Horton Davies observes:

> If men were justified by their faith in the right-eousness of Christ, accepting his sacrifice as the all-sufficient guarantee for the pardon of their sins, then all practice motivated by a belief in justification by works had to disappear. Such practices included attending the Mass as a good work and going on religious pilgrimages. (H. Davies, *The Worship of the English Puritans*, p. 15).

Lutherans saw that the Popish Mass was inconsistent with the doctrine of justification by faith alone in Christ's finished work; and therefore it was contrary to the gospel. Again the Reformed agreed, but they emphasised the fact that the Mass was wrong, not simply because it was contrary to the spirit of the gospel, but also due to the fact that much of what went on in the Mass had not been ordained by God in the Scriptures. Thus the Scottish Reformer John Knox said:

> The Mass is Idolatry. All worshipping, honouring, or service invented by the brain of man in the religion of God, without his own express commandment is idolatry. The Mass is invented by the brain of man, without any commandment of God; therefore it is idolatry. (Cited in B.M. Schwertley, *Sola Scriptura and the Regulative Principle of Worship*, p.32).

Notice that Knox condemned the Mass (not on the basis that it was contrary to the gospel and explicitly blasphemous) on the basis that it was an invention of men's minds which had no Scriptural warrant. While it is true that not every man made invention that has been introduced into divine worship is as heinous as the Romish Mass; nevertheless it is interesting that Knox could refute the Papists simply by pointing out that their practice had no Biblical warrant.

The Reformed Protestants believed that their doctrine of worship was the consistent outworking of the doctrines of original sin and man's total depravity and inability; since, due to the fall, man is essentially corrupt he could not worship God according to his own ideas. This is because man is sinful 'and therefore his own ideas of what constituted correct worship were initiated by his sinfulness.'(H. Davies, *The Worship of the English Puritans*, p. 19). If man was to worship God correctly he had to worship Him only in accordance with what He had revealed in

His word. Therefore, Scripture Alone was the basis upon which the Church must build its doctrine of worship.

In his magnificent book *The Necessity of Reforming the Church*, John Calvin asserts that the Regulative Principle must be adhered to if the Church is to be thoroughly reformed of all Romish corruptions and if men are to worship God 'in spirit and truth' (John 4:23). He writes:

> The rule which distinguishes between pure and vitiated worship is of universal application, in order that we may not adopt any device which seems fit to ourselves, but look to the injunctions of Him who alone is entitled to prescribe. Therefore if we would have him to approve our worship, this rule, which he enforces with the utmost strictness, must be carefully observed. For there is a twofold reason why the Lord, in condemning and prohibiting all fictitious worship, requires us to give obedience only to His own voice. First it tends to establish His authority that we do not follow our own pleasures, but depend entirely on His sovereignty; and, secondly, such is our folly, that when we are left at liberty, all we are able to do is go astray. And then when <u>once we have turned aside from the right path, there is no end to our wanderings, until we get buried under a multitude of superstitions</u>. Justly, therefore, does the Lord, in order to assert his full right of dominion,

strictly enjoin what he wishes us to do, and at once reject all human devices which are at variance with his command. Justly, too, does he, in express terms, define our limits, that we may not, by fabricating perverse modes of worship, provoke his anger against us. (p. 128)

Calvin regarded strict adherence to the regulative principle as the only way of safeguarding the worship of God from a mass of superstitious and man-made inventions. If the normative principle were to be adopted there would be no end to what men would impose on the Church's worship. After all, how large would the Bible have to be if it were to explicitly forbid everything in worship that man could invent which would be displeasing to the God of Holiness? I doubt that the whole world could contain what would have to be written. Moreover, Calvin recognised that when men worship according to the Scriptural law they show their dependence on the Sovereignty of God. However, when men worship God according to their own ideas, they express a desire to be independent of God. Hence, the normative principle could justly be described as Arminianism in worship. Whereas a consistent application of Calvinistic doctrine, that man cannot please God by his own efforts but is entirely dependent on His Sovereign grace, will lead one to accept that the regulative principle of worship is the logical outworking of the principles of God's Sovereignty and man's depravity.

At the Reformation, the Reformed Church of Scotland accepted Calvin's position, while the Episcopalian (Anglican/Prelatic) Church of England accepted Luther's. A significant number of English Protestants agreed (to a greater or lesser extent) with their Scottish brethren; these were known as the Puritans who sought to further reform the English Church believing that it was still too close to Rome. They had serious problems with the authority that the *Thirty Nine Articles* of the Church of England gives to the Church to invent religious ceremonies independent of what God had revealed in Scripture. Article 20 – 'Of the Authority of the Church' reads:

> The Church has power to decree Rites or Ceremonies and authority in Controversies of Faith: and yet it is not lawful for the Church to ordain anything that is contrary to God's Word written... (Cited in P. Schaff (ed), *The Creeds of Christendom*, p. 500).

Sadly the English Church at the Reformation had basically adopted Roman Catholic logic concerning what is permissible in the worship of God. With the Church of England taking such power to itself independent of the word of God, it was hardly surprising when Archbishop William Laud in the 1630s sought to bring the Anglican Church's worship closer to that of Roman Catholic ritualism and replace its Calvinistic theology with Arminianism. Thus the English Church of Laud's day had a man-made system of Church government (Episcopalianism: government by

Bishops), a man-pleasing view of worship (the normative principle) and a man-centred view of salvation
(Arminianism). The earlier abuses in Church government and worship had clearly left the door open for
Arminianism to infect the English Church – totally
undermining the Sovereignty of God.

Despite the Stuart Kings (James I and Charles
I) attempts to enforce Episcopalian government
and ritualistic worship on the Church of Scotland,
following the signing of the *National Covenant of
Scotland* in 1638, Presbyterianism triumphed at
the General Assembly of that year as Prelacy was
abolished. The English Puritans looked to the Scots
for help during the Civil war against Charles I that
broke out in the 1640s. This led to the signing of the
Solemn League and Covenant in 1643 in an attempt
to reform the Church of England along the same
lines as the Presbyterian Church of Scotland. One of
the documents which flowed from the Covenanted
Reformation was the *Westminster Confession of
Faith* which was compiled by some of the most
learned Puritan theologians along with the assistance of some leading Scottish Covenanters (such
as Samuel Rutherford and George Gillespie). This
document sets forth the Reformed understanding of
the Scriptural law of worship. Hence, in chapter 21
entitled – 'Of Religious Worship and the Sabbath
Day' we read:

> The acceptable way of worshipping the true
> God is instituted by himself and so limited
> by His own revealed will, that he may not

be worshipped according to the imaginations and devices of men, or the suggestions
of Satan, under any visible representation,
or any other way not prescribed in the Holy
Scripture. (Chapter 21: Section 1)

The *Westminster Confession* leaves no room open
for the Church to invent and enforce the observation
of religious ceremonies which are not set down in
Scripture. A.A. Hodge summarized the Confession's
teaching on the regulative principle when he said that
'God in His Word has prescribed for us how we may
worship Him acceptably; and that it is an offence to
him and a sin in us...to worship and serve him in
any way not prescribed.' (*The Confession of Faith*, p.
270). The Westminster Divine's view of worship was
simply the outworking of their doctrine that the Holy
Scripture is the infallible and complete rule of faith
and practice. Thus the Confession states in Chapter 1:
Section 6 'The whole counsel of God concerning all
things necessary for His own glory, man's salvation,
faith, and life, is either expressly set down in Scripture,
or by good and necessary consequence may be
deduced from Scripture.' Therefore for something to
be a regulative principle of worship, according to our
Confession, it either must be explicitly commanded
in Scripture or by approved historical examples in the
Bible (such as synagogue attendance by Christ and
the Apostles) or by good and necessary consequence
be inferred from many passages of Scripture (such
as infant baptism and Sunday Sabbath observance).
Regretfully, the Scriptural law of worship has been

rejected not only by Lutherans and Episcopalians but also by many Fundamentalist Evangelicals who determine what is acceptable in worship on a pragmatic basis. Often rites are introduced into worship, such as solo singers, music groups, uninspired song, testimony times, altar calls, drama, dance, comedy etc, on the basis that they will draw in the crowds and so more people will get saved. The question is rarely asked whether or not God approves of such things in His worship; ultimately the end justifies the means. Even more disturbing has been the wholesale abandonment or re-interpretation of the regulative principle (to the point that it is rendered meaningless) by many people in denominations bearing the name 'Presbyterian' or 'Reformed' throughout the world. Consequently, it is imperative that we can prove our present position has a sound Biblical and theological basis if we are to call other Christian Churches back to the regulative principle and away from Romanism and Arminianism in worship.

CHAPTER 2:

The Biblical Basis for the Regulative Principle of Worship

The analysis of the Biblical basis for the regulative principle shall be divided into two sections; the first will seek to give an overview of the Biblical theology of worship, the second, on the other hand, will examine particular texts of Scripture individually.

A Biblical Theology of Worship

My Church's Testimony states 'Christian worship is the response of the believer to the revelation of God's saving grace in Jesus Christ.' (*The Testimony of the Reformed Presbyterian Church of Ireland*, p.37).

Holy Scripture makes it abundantly clear that the worship of the Lord is a solemn duty, to be given to God (Father, Son and Holy Spirit) alone, that is why Jesus refused to worship Satan telling him 'You shall worship the Lord your God and him only shall you serve' (Luke 4:8). Moreover, in the first commandment God claims for Himself the exclusive rights of worship 'I am the LORD your God...You shall have no other gods before me' (Ex. 20:2-3). If man is to know how to worship the Most High God correctly what must he do? Is natural revelation (the creation) enough to instruct us as to how we are to worship the Lord? While the creation does tell us something about what God is like 'The heavens declare the glory of God, and the sky above proclaims his handiwork' (Psalm 19:1) it is not enough to give men a saving knowledge of God (Rom. 10:17). Nor can natural revelation instruct us as to how we are to worship the Lord. Even though the heathen know enough about God from creation to be 'without excuse' (Rom. 1:20) this couldn't guide them into true worship 'For although they knew God, they did not honour him as God...Claiming to be wise, they became fools, and exchanged the glory of the immortal God for images resembling mortal man and birds and animals and reptiles' (Rom. 1:21-23). Man clearly needs something additional to creation if he is going to worship God correctly, or else he will be like the Athenian Philosophers that Paul addressed at the Areopagus who worshipped 'the unknown god' (Acts 17:23).

So if natural revelation cannot teach us how we are to worship God, where should the Christian turn to for guidance? Because 'those former ways of God's revealing His will unto His people' such as prophecy, tongue speaking, visions, dreams etc. has 'now ceased' (*Westminster Confession of Faith* Chapter 1: Section 6) with the completion of the Biblical Canon (the 66 books which make up our Bible); thus we read in 1 Cor. 13:8-10 'As for prophecies they will pass away; as for tongues, they will cease; as for knowledge, it will pass away...but when the perfect comes, the partial will pass away', the Christian can now only turn to his Bible if he is to know how to worship the Lord correctly. This is why the *Shorter Catechism* tells us (in the answer to question 2) that 'the Word of God...is the only rule to direct us how we may glorify and enjoy him.' Furthermore, the Apostle Paul when writing to Timothy, said 'All Scripture is breathed out by God and profitable for teaching, for reproof, for correction, and for training in right-eousness, that the man of God may be competent, equipped for every good work' (2 Tim. 3:16). If the Christian is to be suitably equipped for worshipping the Lord, then he has no option but to turn to God's Word and receive instruction from the Old and New Testament as to how, and by what means, he should worship the God of his salvation. For this reason, the Puritan theologian Dr. John Owen concluded that God has given His word unto the Church, 'that thereby it might be instructed in his mind and will as to what concerns the worship and obedience that he requires of us.' (*A Brief Instruction in the Worship of God and Discipline of the Churches of the New Testament*, Works: 15, p. 450) Therefore, if God has given us His Word, Owen comes to the logical conclusion that 'it supposes, it declares, that of ourselves we are ignorant how God is, |and| how he ought to be worshipped.'(Ibid.). Since God repeatedly forbids us to add to His Word 'You shall not add to the word that I command you, nor take from it' (Deut. 4:2), 'Do not add to his words, lest he rebuke you and you be found a liar' (Prov. 30:6), and 'I warn everyone who hears the words of the prophecy of this book: if anyone adds to them, God will add to him the plagues described in this book' (Rev. 22:18); then one must assume that Scripture alone is the sufficient guide for the Christian in matters of faith and worship.

Moreover, John Owen further observes 'All acceptable devotion in them that worship God is the effect of faith, which respects the precepts and promises of God alone. And no devotion is acceptable unto him, but what proceeds from faith and is an effect of faith; for "without faith it is impossible to please |God|" (Heb. 11:6).'(Ibid., p. 467). Thus Abel's sacrifice was accepted by the Lord because it was based on faith in God's command; whereas Cain's was rejected for being faithless, self devised worship (Genesis 4). Consequently, if our acts of religious devotion are to be acceptable to God they must be in accordance to what has been revealed in the Scriptures, for 'faith in all things respects the commands and authority of God.'(Ibid.). Since it would be idolatry to put our faith in the commandments of men (Matt. 15:9) the Christian can only worship God in faith by obeying what He has said in His Word concerning how He is to be worshipped.

Worship not based on faith in what is set down in the word of God is therefore not Biblical worship as it cannot please God. Although some may complain that this seems highly restrictive (which in a positive sense it is), such objections to the regulative principle are but a sinful expression of man's desire to be independent of God's sovereign authority. Due to the fact that purity of worship is not merely a trivial issue, such people need to consider these questions:

> Is God the sovereign Lord of all? Is His revealed will to be accepted as the infallible guide of human conduct? Has He the right to rule in His own house? Has He a right to prescribe the way by which He may be approached and worshipped? (W.H. Vincent, *The Scriptural Law of Worship* in The Psalms in Worship by J. McNaughter (ed), p.23).

If the answer to these questions is 'yes', then God's rights in these matters are exclusive. No man or Church may dare to dictate the manner in which God is to be worshipped, without a solid foundation in Scripture. Only God Himself has the right to decide how He is to be approached, otherwise how can He be Sovereign if men may decide how He is to be worshipped? The acceptance of the normative principle would mean that the creature could tell the Creator how He is to be worshipped! However, if we believe that God is Sovereign then we must acknowledge this by submitting, in dependence upon Him, to the Scriptural law of worship. Any other approach detracts from His Sovereignty and is thus rightly described as Arminianism in worship (Arminianism is the view man has an independent free-will outside of God's control) as the normative principle (whatever is not condemned in the Bible is permissible in worship) is best suited to this type of theology.

If Scripture alone is our guide in worship, then human inventions (which are not appointed in the Bible) are automatically prohibited. Commenting on human devices in worship John Owen remarks 'for although they are not in particular and expressly forbidden, - for it was simply impossible that all instances wherein the wit of man might exercise its invention in such things should be reckoned up and condemned, - yet they fall directly under those severe prohibitions which God has recorded to secure his worship from all such additions unto it, of what sort soever.' (J. Owen, *A Brief Instruction in the Worship of God and Discipline of the Churches of the New Testament*, Works: 15, p. 470). The Roman Catholic view that whatever is not forbidden is permissible is simply not sustainable, because taken to its logical conclusion it would mean that man could worship God acceptably without the guidance of Scripture, thus making the need for special revelation redundant. Moreover, if Lutherans, Episcopalians and modern Evangelicals are going to be consistent in denying the regulative principle of worship, then what is to stop them from following Rome in denying the sufficiency of Scripture in the formulation of doctrine? Why can't the Church formulate its own doctrines, just so long as they are not explicitly forbidden in

Scripture? On this line of reasoning one could accept purgatory, Papal infallibility and the immaculate conception of Mary, as none of these doctrines are explicitly condemned in the Word of God. For this reason, William H. Vincent perceived the danger of Evangelicals defending the use of uninspired hymns in worship on the basis that they are not forbidden in Holy Scripture:

> When you have made an opening in the door of God's house large enough to admit songs of praise which God has not authorized, that same hole will admit the worship of the Virgin Mary, prayers to St. Peter, confession to the priest, holy water, kissing the Pope's toe, and the whole brood of pollutions and monstrosities from which the Church escaped in the tremendous revolution and reformation of the sixteenth century. (*The Scriptural Law of Worship* in The Psalms in Worship by J. McNaughter (ed), p. 28).

Also it would appear reasonable to assume that when something is commanded by the Lord, that whatever is opposed to this command is forbidden. Therefore, when God commands us 'You shall not murder' (Ex. 20:13), He obviously forbids us to engage in practices that would endanger our own lives or those of others, even though these practices may not be explicitly condemned in Scripture. So, one must conclude that when God commands us to worship Him in a certain way, for example with the inspired Psalms;

then He forbids us from worshipping Him in any other way, such as with uninspired songs.

If one denies the regulative principle, how then does one explain the fact that the construction of the Old Testament Tabernacle, right down to the most minute details, was prescribed by the Lord in Exodus 25-28? This seems a little over the top if the regulative principle is not Biblical; why couldn't the people of Israel just build the Tabernacle whatever way they liked? Clearly they were dependant upon God's revealed will if their worship was to be acceptable. When we come to the construction of the Temple in Solomon's day the same principle applied. All the details for the building of the Temple that David passed on to Solomon were revealed to him by God himself. So David told Solomon 'All this he made clear to me in writing from the hand of the LORD, all the work to be done according to the plan' (1 Chron. 28:19). Yet this all seems a bit pointless if God will accept anything in worship that He hasn't explicitly forbidden! Therefore we must conclude that God can only be worshipped in the manner that He has revealed in His Word and in no other way. Indeed the books of 1 and 2 Chronicles read like a historical commentary on how faithful (or unfaithful) God's people were to the regulative principle. While the worship of both the Tabernacle and the Temple have passed away - with the completion of Christ's work of redemption (Eph. 2:15-16; Col. 2:14-17); the regulative principle 'that God reserves to Himself the right to appoint the ordinances and manner of His own worship stands forever.' (W.H. Vincent, *The Scriptural Law of*

Worship in The Psalms in Worship by J. McNaughter (ed), p. 25). This is demonstrated by the fact that the Lord Jesus Christ, the King and Head of the Church, established and authorised the ordinances distinct to the New Covenant; namely Baptism (Matt. 28: 19) and the Lord's Supper (Matt. 26:26-29). So, even though New Testament worship is much simpler than that of the Old Covenant, it still falls under the regulative principle that whatever is not authorised in the word of God is forbidden. In light of this overview of the Biblical theology of worship, one must conclude that the normative principle (whatever is not forbidden is allowed) is highly un-Scriptural. Moreover, it has been sufficiently demonstrated that the Reformed conception of the Scriptural Law of worship is clearly the teaching of the word of God. Nevertheless it may be useful to examine some specific texts to further establish the principle; this will be done (D.V.) in the following pages.

Old Testament Basis For the Regulative Principle of Worship

Whereas previously we sought to demonstrate the Scriptural nature of the regulative principle by a general overview of Biblical theology; in this section shall seek to further prove the truthfulness of the Scriptural law of worship (that only what God commands in worship is acceptable) from specific Biblical texts.

Analysis of some Scriptural texts relating to the Regulative Principle

Exodus 20:4-6

The first Biblical text to be analysed, the second commandment, is perhaps central to understanding the reasoning behind the regulative principle of worship. We read in Exodus 20:4-6:

You shall not make for yourself a carved image, or any likeness of anything that is in heaven above, or that is in the earth beneath, or that is in the water under the earth. You shall not bow down to them or serve them, for I the LORD your God am a jealous God, visiting the iniquity of the fathers on the children to the third and the fourth generation of those who hate me, but showing steadfast love to the thousands of those who love me and keep my commandments.

The opening words provide the key to understanding this passage. When God says 'You shall not make' all human invention in divine worship is automatically prohibited. Only the Lord Himself has the right to appoint how He is to be approached in worship, any divergence from this rule is (to a greater or lesser extent) idolatry. So it is not simply the more extreme forms of idolatry which God condemns; the making of carved images 'is the archetype of all man's attempts to worship God through the work of his own hands. Idolatry and the introduction of unwarranted practices into services of worship are illegitimate children of the same father.' (M. Bushell, *The Songs of Zion*, p. 145). Both work on the assumption that what God has ordained is insufficient in His own worship, thus undermining God's Sovereign authority. The Reformed view of worship is the only one that can be faithful to this commandment, as it alone recognises the sinfulness of human nature. Therefore, G.I. Williamson writes:

> When a man has little appreciation of this truth, he may feel that he can invent something that will add value to Christian worship. He may feel, for example, that he can write a hymn that will improve the worship service by expressing a thought that he feels has been neglected. But when a man understands his own unworthiness before God, he will not imagine for one moment that he can improve on the inspired psalms of God. (*The Westminster Shorter Catechism: For Study Classes*, p. 203).

It should not come as a surprise to us if those who reject the regulative principle of worship also go on to undermine the Sovereign grace of God in the salvation of sinners. The acceptance of the normative principle (that man can please God by his own inventions) by the 'Church' of Rome has no doubt contributed to her view that the salvation of sinners is by grace plus meritorious works. After all, if man isn't so fallen as to forbid him from worshipping God by his own ideas, then why can't he contribute to his own salvation? Hence, the Reformed Christian realises that adherence to the regulative principle is a vital acknowledgement of sinful man's dependence on God for salvation, and thus helps to safeguard the gospel of grace from Romish and Arminian errors. For these reasons the Westminster Divines concluded that 'the second commandment forbids the worshipping of God by images, or any other way not appointed in his Word' (*Shorter Catechism* answer to question 51).

Leviticus 10:1-3

The next passage to be examined is one of the most fearful in the whole Bible, yet it provides us with irrefutable proof of the Scriptural law of worship. Leviticus 10:1-3 reads:

Now Nadab and Abihu, the sons of Aaron, each took his censer and put fire in it and laid incense on it and offered unauthorized fire before the LORD, which he had not commanded them. And fire came out from before the LORD and consumed them, and they died before the LORD. Then Moses said to Aaron, "This is what the LORD has said, 'Among those who are near me I will be sanctified, and before all

**the people I will be glorified.'" And Aaron
held his peace.**

This passage displays the zeal that God has
for His own glory and His concern about the way
in which He is worshipped. Prof. David McKay
observes from this text that, in the worship of the
Lord in the Old Testament, 'additions made without
divine sanction brought dramatic retribution.' (*The
Bond of Love*, p. 229). What great sin did Nadab and
Abihu commit that provoked the Lord to such anger?
It was quite simply because they took it upon themselves to offer 'unauthorized fire before the LORD,
which he had not commanded them.' Note carefully
that they were not consumed for doing something
that God had expressly forbidden them to do, but
rather for doing something in divine worship that
the Lord 'had not commanded them'; in other words
they were killed for violating the regulative principle
of worship. Thus for this reason, William H. Vincent
commented on the passage that 'the fire which they
used would perhaps burn as brightly and consume
incense just as well, and doubtless many would say
"it is just as good": but it lacked this peculiar mark of
sanctity – it was not of God's appointment; it was not
divine fire.' (Cited in J. McNaughter (ed) The Psalms
in Worship, p. 29). The judgement that God poured
out upon Nadab and Abihu for their sinful presumption, demonstrates to us, in the clearest possible
terms, how much He abominates human inventions
in divine worship. In light of this text dare we intrude

merely human devices into the worship of God on the pretext that Scripture does not prohibit them?

Leviticus 22: 31-33

God made clear His concern that His worship be kept holy when He said to Moses:

So you shall keep my commandments and do them: I am the LORD. And you shall not profane my holy name, that I may be sanctified among the people of Israel. I am the LORD who sanctifies you, who brought you out of the land of Egypt to be your God I am the LORD.

In this context, where the rules for acceptable offerings are being laid down, when the Lord tells the people of Israel 'you shall not profane my holy name' He forbids them from corrupting, adding to or detracting from His sacred worship. The French Reformer John Calvin, when explaining this text wrote:

They hallow God's name who turn not away from its rightful and sincere worship. Let this be carefully observed, that whatever fancies men devise, are so many profanations of God's name; for although the superstitions may please themselves by their imaginations, yet is all their religion full of sacrilege, whereby God complains that His holiness is profaned. (Cited in B.M. Schwertley, *Sola Scriptura and the Regulative Principle of Worship*, p. 146).

What Calvin appears to be saying is that since God's name is holy (by God's 'name' he means all by which God is revealed) human addition in divine worship profanes (that is make common or unclean) the holy name of the Lord. Therefore, we are required to receive, observe and keep 'pure and entire, all such worship and ordinances as God has appointed in his Word' (*Shorter Catechism* answer to question 50) without any human inventions, whether explicitly condemned in the Bible or not.

Numbers 15:39

God commanded the people of Israel to make tassels on the corners of their garments throughout their generations. He then explains to Moses the rationale behind this command:

And it shall be a tassel for you to look at and remember all the commandments of the LORD, to do them, not to follow after your own heart and your own eyes, which you are inclined to whore after.

It is obvious from this passage that the commandments of the Lord are a sufficient guide for His people in the worship of their King. Here God forbids His Church from following the sinful desires of their own hearts which they were 'inclined to whore after' and orders His people to only follow His commandments in worship. This leaves no door open for merely human inventions, and this text proves that such devices are but an example of man's sinfulness. Thus, Calvin writes:

> He shows that He would have His people contented with that rule which He prescribes, without the admixture of any of their own imaginations; and again He denounces the vanity of whatever men invent for themselves, and however pleasing any human scheme may appear to them, He still repudiates and condemns it. And this is still more clearly expressed in the last word, when He says that men "go a whoring" whenever they are governed by their own counsels. This declaration is deserving of our especial observation, for whilst they account their zeal to be very good and very right they do nothing else but pollute themselves by spiritual adultery. (Ibid., p. 46)

Calvin perceives that while men may be zealous in the performance of religious ceremonies, that are merely of man's devising, this supposed enthusiasm is but 'a zeal for God but not according to knowledge' (Rom. 10:2) which, far from increasing religious devotion, is in reality, spiritual adultery. True zeal for the Lord's worship will be guided only by what He has revealed in His Word. Often one meets a

Christian who is an enthusiastic solo-singer or loves nothing better than to give their testimony in Church or to play in a worship band; yet they never stop to think whether or not God approves of their acts of devotion, they are persuaded that because they can't find a verse which explicitly condemns their practice God must be pleased with their service. However, this verse on its own is enough to expose the foolishness of such reasoning.

Deuteronomy 4:2

In this text the Lord explains to His people the sufficiency of His Word as the only rule of faith and worship. It is written:

You shall not add to the word that I command you, nor take from it, that you may keep the commandments of the LORD your God that I command you.

This verse exposes the folly of the Romanists, who claim that they are free to invent doctrines and religious ceremonies. While Roman Catholics may protest that their additions do not directly contradict the word of God, this verse, beyond all reasonable doubt, proves that to add to God's word is in fact to contradict it. Dr John Gill, the great Reformed Baptist theologian, points out that here the Lord forbids His people to 'make laws of their own, and join them to the law of God, and set them on a level with it, or prefer them before it: as the Scribes and Pharisees did in Christ's time, who by their traditions made the word of God of none effect, as do the Papists also by their unwritten traditions.' (*An Exposition of the Old Testament*, p. 720) Less consistent Protestants, who hold to the normative principle, are also rebuked by this text. The fact of the matter is that to add to what God commands in worship is to high-handedly sin against this verse.

Deuteronomy 12:28-32

Here God lays out directives for His people to safeguard them from the idolatry of the heathen nations who the children of Israel were about to dispossess from the land:

> **Be careful to obey all these words that I command you, that it may go well with you and with your children after you for ever, when you do what is good and right in the sight of the LORD your God. When the LORD your God cuts off before you the nations whom you go in to dispossess, and you dispossess them and dwell in their land, take care that you are not ensnared to follow them, after they have been destroyed before you, and that you do not enquire about their gods, saying, 'How did these nations serve their gods? – that I also may do the same.' You shall not worship the LORD your God in that way, for every abominable thing that the LORD hates**

they have done for their gods, for they even burn their sons and their daughters in the fire to their gods. Everything that I command you, you shall be careful to do. You shall not add to it or take from it.

In order to keep them from the abominations of the heathen nations, which were so extreme that it even included them sacrificing their own children to their false gods (v.31), God's people must not add or detract from His word. Therefore the Church's worship can only be pure when it is carried out specifically according to the manner prescribed in the Bible; to depart from Scripture alone is to open a door for all kinds of pagan idolatry to enter the Church. A Biblical example of this is found in 1 Kings 12 when Jeroboam the king of Israel decided to set golden calves in Dan and Bethel, created his own priesthood, and appointed his own holy-day which 'he had devised from his own heart' (1 Kings 12:33). This also explains why the worship of Roman Catholicism is little more than Christianised heathenism; Popery has simply taken ceremonies from pagan Greece and Rome and incorporated them into divine worship, and this is a blasphemous abomination in the sight of God. To a lesser extent modern Evangelicals do a similar thing when they introduce country and western music, drama, solo-singers and other forms of entertainment into God's worship; they are simply following the precepts of the world rather than the commandments of the Lord. For this reason Matthew Henry writes 'we may then hope in our religious worship to obtain the divine acceptance when we observe the divine appointment. God will have his own work done in his own way.' (*Commentary on the Whole Bible*, vol. 1, p. 607).

1 Samuel 13:8-14

The prophet Samuel had instructed King Saul to 'go down before me to Gilgal. And behold, I am coming to you to offer burnt offerings and to sacrifice peace offerings. Seven days you shall wait, until I come to you and show you what you shall do' (1 Sam. 10:8). However, we read that Saul was not obedient to this command:

He waited for seven days, the time appointed by Samuel. But Samuel did not come to Gilgal, and the people were scattering from him. So Saul said, "Bring the burnt offering here to me, and the peace offerings." And he offered the burnt offering. As soon as he had finished offering the burnt offering, behold, Samuel came. And Saul went out to meet him and greet him. Samuel said "What have you done?" And Saul said, "When I saw that the people were scattering from me, and that you did not come within the days appointed, and that the Philistines had mustered at Michmash, I said, 'Now the Philistines will come down against me at Gilgal, and I have not sought the favour

of the LORD.' So I forced myself, and offered the burnt offering." And Samuel said to Saul, "You have done foolishly. You have not kept the command of the LORD your God, with which he commanded you. For then the LORD would have established your kingdom over Israel for ever. But now your kingdom shall not continue. The LORD has sought out a man after his own heart, and the LORD has commanded him to be prince over his people, because you have not kept what the LORD commanded you.

As the end of the passage makes clear the reason why the Lord removed the Kingdom from Saul and gave it to David was because of Saul's unfaithfulness to the Lord in the matter of worship. This was the means by which Saul's unbelief in God, as He is revealed in His word, was exposed. Yet when we analyse the passage one finds that the attitude of Saul to the worship of God has much in common with modern Evangelicalism, and highlights the contemporary lack of faith in the sufficiency of God's word. Saul had been commanded by Samuel to wait in Gilgal for seven days, where Samuel (who was a priest) would offer sacrifice. However, when Saul noticed that the people were scattering from him, and that Samuel did not come within the appointed time and that the Philistines were grouping together at Mishmash; he thought that he should take it upon himself to offer sacrifice. But Saul had no warrant to offer sacrifice as he was not a priest, therefore Samuel rebuked him because he 'had not kept the command of the LORD your God which he commanded you' (v.13). Saul tried to defend his actions on a pragmatic basis, when he saw that 'the people were scattering from him' (v.8), he decided that he needed to do something which God had not commanded (offer sacrifices) in order to keep the people on board. In the same way many modern Evangelicals have justified the introduction of various forms of entertainment such as puppet shows, rock bands, drama and comedian preachers on the basis that it will attract people to the Church without any thought for what God has said. Saul also justified his actions on the basis of the Machiavellian philosophy 'that the end justifies the means.' When he saw that 'the Philistines had mustered at Michmash' (v.11) Saul reasoned to himself 'I have not sought the favour of the LORD' (v.12) so he was justified in offering sacrifice, even though he had no warrant to do this. Likewise many Evangelical Christians argue that because people have been saved through a solo-singer, or a testimony, or an altar call that these are automatically justified and God accepts them. According to this pragmatic logic God will accept something just as long as it works! However, the teaching of this passage is that to introduce unwarranted human devices into the worship of the Lord is nothing less than unbelief in the clear teaching of God's word;

1 Chronicles 13:9-11

This incident is part of a narrative describing the removal of the Ark of God from Kirjath-jearim, during David's reign, where it had lain for some seventy years since the time of its return by the Philistines:

And when they came to the threshing floor of Chidon, Uzzah put out his hand to take hold of the ark, for the oxen stumbled. And the anger of the LORD was kindled against Uzzah, and he struck him down because he put out his hand to the ark, and he died there before God. And David was angry because the LORD had broken out against Uzzah. And that place is called Perez-uzza to this day.

Humanly speaking the death of Uzza seems totally senseless, why should a man die for merely touching the ark? Yet to touch the ark (which was the visible pledge of God's presence in the midst of His people) was to profane (render unclean) its holiness and this was warned against in Numbers 4:15 'they must not touch the holy things, lest they die.' However, as Michael Bushell explains the heart of Uzzah's sin 'lies in the fact that according to Numbers 4, the Ark was supposed to be moved only by means of staves on the side of the Ark, on the shoulders of the Levites, and not on a cart.' (*The Songs of Zion*, p. 147) Moreover, God's command 'as to how the

Ark was to be moved excluded every other means.'
(Ibid.) Uzzah may have had sincere motives behind
his actions, to protect the ark of God from falling,
yet sincerity and good intentions in worship are not
enough. If something is introduced into God's worship
that He has not required, regardless of the purity of
the motives, it is still unacceptable in His sight. Often
human inventions are brought into divine worship on
the basis that they are a good idea. For example, it
would be a good idea to allow a choir to sing sepa-
rately from the congregation, or it would be a good
idea to appoint a holy-day to celebrate the incarnation, or it would be a good idea to have pictures of
Christ. Yet if these things were really good ideas then
surely God would have ordained them in His word.
The fact that human inventions are not permitted in
worship tells us that they are in fact a very bad idea
as they show a lack of faith in the means that God has
appointed. God does not need our innovations; He is
Sovereign and has appointed the precise means by
which He is to be worshipped. Dare we undermine
Him by intruding our ideas into His worship?

2 Chronicles 26: 16-19

King Uzziah is a prime example of a person who
thought that it would be a good idea to do something
that God had not commanded:

**But when he was strong, he grew proud
to his destruction. For he was unfaithful
to the LORD his God and entered the**

temple of the LORD to burn incense on the altar of incense. But Azariah the priest went in after him, with eighty priests of the LORD who were men of valour, and they withstood King Uzziah and said to him "It is not for you, Uzziah, to burn incense to the LORD, but for the priests the sons of Aaron, who are consecrated to burn incense. Go out of the sanctuary, for you have done wrong, and it will bring you no honour from the LORD God." Then Uzziah was angry. Now he had a censer in his hand to burn incense, and when he became angry with the priests, leprosy broke out on his forehead in the presence of the priests in the house of the LORD, by the altar of incense.

This portion of Holy Scripture teaches us the true source of all breaches of the regulative principle, namely, the pride of sinful man. When Uzziah was strong 'he grew proud' this caused him to be unfaithful to the LORD his God' leading him to enter into 'the temple of the LORD to burn incense' which was a job only for the priests. Keep in mind that Uzziah was a good king, unlike others he did not forsake the temple of the Lord, but his ill-informed and rash zeal for God led him to do something in worship that the Lord had not instructed him to do. Therefore Uzziah's burning of incense represented a proud disregard and unbelief in God's word. Thus Matthew Henry writes 'men's pretending to forbidden knowledge, and exercising themselves in things too high for them, are owing to the pride of their heart, and the fleshy mind they are vainly puffed up with.' (*Commentary on the Whole Bible*, vol. 2, p. 764). Furthermore, Azariah's rebuke of Uzziah shows us that Church office-bearers may reprove those who seek to violate the Scriptural law of worship. Notice that even though Uzziah was a king he was not exempt from obeying the regulative principle (this refutes the non-sensical theory of the 'divine right of kings' upon which the Stuart kings built their system of tyranny in Britain); no man, no matter how great, may presume to introduce into divine worship what the Lord has not asked for. If we rebuke other people for breaking the regulative principle (and this should be done in meekness remembering what great sinners we are ourselves) then we should not be surprised if they became angry, as Uzziah did (v.19), at having their sin exposed. However, if they later acknowledge the error of their ways it will have been well worth the pain inflicted; 'faithful are the wounds of a friend' (Prov. 27:6).

Isaiah 29:13

It is recorded in Isaiah's prophecy:

And the Lord said "Because this people draw near with their mouth and honour me with their lips, while their hearts are far from me, and their fear of me is a commandment taught by men."

The Lord, in this verse, explains to His Church that religious hypocrisy, honouring God with our lips when our hearts are far from Him, is directly linked with submitting to human inventions in worship. While it is possible to still be hypocritical while outwardly obeying the regulative principle of worship; this verse would appear to teach that religious hypocrisy flourishes when the regulative principle is abandoned. John Calvin comments:

When God is worshipped by inventions of men, he condemns this "fear" as superstitious, though men endeavour to cloak it under a plausible pretence of religion, or devotion, or reverence...To make "the commandments of men", and not the word of God, the rule of worshipping him is a subversion of order. But it is the will of the Lord, that our "fear", and the reverence with which we worship him, shall be regulated by the rule of his word; and he demands nothing so much as simple obedience, by which we shall conform ourselves and all our actions to the rule of the word, and not turn aside to the right hand or to the left. Hence it is sufficiently evident, that those who learn from the "inventions of men" how they should worship God, not only are manifestly foolish, but near themselves out by destructive toil, because they do nothing else than provoke God's anger; for he could not testify more plainly than by the tremendous severity of this chastisement, how great is the abhorrence with which he regards false worship. (Cited in B.M. Schwertley, *Sola Scriptura and the Regulative Principle of Worship*, pp 148-9)

Jeremiah 7:30-31

Through the prophet Jeremiah the Lord condemned some of the worst abominations in the Old Testament, simply on the basis that they were a violation of the regulative principle of worship:

For the sons of Judah have done evil in my sight, declares the LORD. They have set their detestable things in the house that is called by my name to defile it. And they have built the high places of Topheth, which is in the Valley of the Son of Hinnom, to burn their sons and their daughters in the fire, which I did not command, nor did it come into my mind.

The sacrificing of their children to a false god was an act of murder by the sons of Judah; yet it is condemned not on the basis that it was an unlawful taking of life (which it was) but rather on the premise that what they were doing, as an act of religious devotion, had never been commanded by the Lord their God. Just as the neglect of the regulative principle had led the Jews into horrible idolatry, so John Calvin understood its acceptance to be the basis upon which the Church must be systematically reformed. He writes upon this verse:

> God here cuts off from men every occasion for making evasions, since he condemns by this one phrase, "I have not commanded them" whatever the Jews devised. There is then no other argument needed to condemn super-stitions, than that they are not commanded by God: for when men allow themselves to worship God according to their own fancies, and attend not to his commands they pervert true religion. And if this principle was adopted by the Papists, all of those fictitious modes of worship, in which they absurdly exer-cise themselves, would fall to the ground. It is indeed a horrible thing for the Papists to seek to discharge their duties towards God by performing their own superstitions. There is an immense number of them, as it is well known, and as it manifestly appears. Were they to admit this principle, that we cannot rightly worship God except by obeying his word they would be delivered from their deep abyss of error. The Prophet's words then are very important, when he says, that God commanded no such thing, and that men assume to themselves too much wisdom, when they devise what he never required, nay, what he never knew. (Ibid., pp 150-1).

Is Calvin going a little over the top here? I don't think so; let's just imagine that the Roman Catholic 'Church' was to adopt the regulative principle (that what is not commanded is forbidden). If this were to happen then it would no longer be the anti-Christian ecclesiastical monster and 'synagogue of Satan' (Rev. 3:9) that it presently is. Take heed of the warnings both of Scripture and history; faithfulness to the regulative principle of worship is a safeguard to a Church's doctrinal integrity as it is inconsistent to be indifferent about worship and firm on other doctrines. The adoption of the normative principle on the other hand may be the first step along a Church's road to apostasy from the gospel. This is what happened to Rome, and Protestants must be careful not to follow in her footsteps.

New Testament Basis For the Regulative Principle of Worship

Some Christians have tried to get around the demands of the regulative principle by claiming that it only applied to the worship of the Old Testament and that the New Testament gives us greater 'liberty'. This section shall demonstrate however, that though the precise form of worship has changed, the moral obligation of the regulative principle still applies in the New Testament dispensation.

Matthew 15:1-2

In these verses the scribes and Pharisees declare their adherence to human traditions in religion, and criticise Christ's disciples for not observing them. Thus it is written:

Then Pharisees and scribes came to Jesus from Jerusalem and said "Why do your disciples break the tradition of the elders? For they do not wash their hands when they eat?

Notice the Pharisees do not accuse the disciples of breaking the law of God, but with not abiding by a human tradition of washing their hands before eating. It should be observed that this text is not condemning the practice of hand-washing before meals; however, it is forbidding the observance of religious traditions which have no basis in the word of God. The disciples refused to participate in washing their hands because it was merely a human invention in religion. This teaches us that we too, should not participate in religious ordinances that are not taught in the word of God (such as singing an uninspired hymn or celebrating an un-Scriptural holy day). David Dickson, the 17th century Covenanter minister, explains the motives behind the disciples' behaviour:

That which otherwise is lawful in itself while it abides within the limits of civil fashions may be left undone, and be discountenanced, when it is set up in state within the limits of religion: therefore the disciples did not wash their hands before meat, in the company of Pharisees, who made washing at that time to be a holy and religious act. (*A Brief Exposition of the Evangel of Jesus Christ According to Matthew*, p. 207)

Declension in Churches often begins with the gradual additions of human traditions; thus the 'Church' of Rome fell from being a pure Apostolic Church of Christ into the apostate body which it now is. However, this didn't happen over night, gradually tradition upon tradition was added until eventually, as John Owen remarked, the worship of God was reduced to 'a theatrical, pompous show of carnal devotion.' (*A Brief Instruction Concerning the Worship of God and the Discipline of the Churches of the New Testament*, Works: 15, p. 468). Often the same thing happens in Protestant Churches, as human traditions infiltrate the pure worship of God. Perhaps first of all a prayer-book is added, then it becomes obligatory to kneel at the Lord's Table, then the Church decides to observe holy-days outside of the Sabbath, perhaps ministers are commanded to make the sign of the cross in baptism or to wear clerical vestments, maybe preaching is replaced by a drama group or somebody giving their testimony, the Psalms are then laid aside for uninspired songs and choruses, and instrumental music is played during the service. The end result is either - the ritualistic pomp and ceremony of the Episcopalian Churches, or the man-centred entertainment which passes for worship among modern Evangelicals.

Sadly, many Christians display a Pharisaic spirit when they meet other believers who do not participate in their man-made ceremonies. Often when you try to explain to someone why the Reformed Presbyterian Church does not observe Christmas or Easter as religious holy-days, or why Covenanters only sing the divinely inspired Psalms without instrumental accompaniment, other Christians think that your part of some kind of cult! Yet they rarely come to us with Scriptural arguments; our practice is obnoxious to them because it violates their long-standing traditions. Human nature, like the spirit of the Pharisees, is often intensely conservative; people become attached to long-standing traditions, and so any attempt at reform, regardless of whether it is Biblical, often offends them. Therefore, we need to keep an open-mind like the Bereans, when Paul found them 'examining the Scriptures daily to see if these things were so' (Acts 17:11); and if our current practice in worship is found to be inconsistent with the word of God it must be dropped. George Gillespie (possibly the most learned early Covenanter minister) recognised the importance of the regulative principle, and the danger of human traditions, when he said:

> But among such things as have been the accursed means of the church's desolation, which peradventure might seem to some of you to have least harm and evil in them, are the ceremonies of kneeling in the

act of receiving the Lord's supper, cross in baptism, bishoping, holidays [he means holy days], etc. which are pressed under the name of things indifferent; yet if you survey the sundry [various] inconviences and grievous consequences of the same, you will think otherwise. The vain shows and shadows of these ceremonies have hid and obscured the substance of religion; the true life of godliness is smothered down and suppressed by the burden of these human inventions; for their sakes, many, who are both faithful servants to Christ and loyal subjects to the King, are evil-spoken of, mocked, reproached, menaced, molested. (Cited in B.M. Schwertley, *Sola Scriptura and the Regulative Principle of Worship*, p. 23)

Later Covenanter ministers, like James Guthrie, Donald Cargill and James Renwick were actually put to death by the state partly for refusing to countenance human ceremonies in God's worship. Even to this very day man-made rites are a major source of division among conservative Presbyterians. Congregations are at war as to whether or not they should only use pianos and organs or introduce drums and guitars; when, in reality, the Bible warrants neither. In one evangelical denomination, which I know of, people have actually been disciplined for refusing to give testimonies or participate in singing groups. If only the regulative principle had been heartily embraced this scandalous division among the godly could have been avoided. What will you do? Be like the Pharisees and persecute other believers for not following human traditions or accept the Bible alone as your guide in worship?

Matthew 15:7-9

The Lord Jesus Christ strongly rebuked the Pharisees for adding to the word of God (thus violating the regulative principle) by applying Isaiah 29:13 specifically to them. He said:

You hypocrites! Well did Isaiah prophesy of you when he said: "this people honours me with their lips, but their heart is far from me; in vain do they worship me, teaching as doctrines the commandments of men."

Jesus vigorously reproves the scribes and Pharisees for daring to place the commandments of men on a par with the commandments of the Lord. Therefore, acts of religious worship which have no foundation in the word of God, but are the inventions of men, are here repudiated by Christ - the King of the Church. Consequently, Michael Bushell observes that 'the passage before us teaches very clearly that worship that is regulated by human prescriptions or tradition is vain worship and is not acceptable to God.' (*The Songs of Zion*, p. 148). So if your worship, or my worship, is not based on what God has said in the word that He has 'breathed out' (2 Tim. 3:16) by His Holy Spirit, then that worship is rejected by the Lord. If we are to truly worship God, not hypo-critically like the Pharisees, then we must worship Him in the way that He has appointed in the Bible. Otherwise we are not worshipping God properly, we are merely worshipping our idea of what we want God to be like, not as He really is.

Matthew 28:18-20

When the Lord Jesus, as Head of His own Church, gave His Apostles the 'Great Commission'; He re-affirmed that the regulative principle of worship (whatever is not commanded is forbidden) is a permanent moral principle to be observed by the Church until Christ returns. Thus we read:

> **And Jesus came and said to them, "All authority in heaven and in earth has been given to me. Go therefore and make disciples of all nations, baptising them in the name of the Father and of the Son and of the Holy Spirit, teaching them to observe all that I have commanded you. And, behold, I am with you always, to the end of the age.**

The Apostles, just like ministers today, were not free to teach the converts to Christ whatever they wanted (just so long as it wasn't specifi-cally condemned in Scripture) as Lutherans and Episcopalians teach; rather they were to instruct the believers 'teaching them to observe all that I have commanded you.' Jesus does not say to them 'observe anything you want, except what ceremonies I explicitly forbid'; nor does the Lord instruct them to invent human devices in worship in order to attract people to the Church (which is the attitude adopted by many modern Evangelicals). Christ instructs His Apostles only to teach believers what He has commanded them in His word. The logical conclusion of this is that the Lord Jesus Christ does not permit the observation of human traditions that are not ordained in the word of God. Only His ordinances of worship that He has prescribed in the Scriptures are permissible. As Matthew Henry put it 'they must teach them not their own inventions, but the institutions of Christ; to them they must religiously adhere, and in the knowledge of them Christians must be trained up.' (*Commentary on the Whole Bible*, vol. 5, p. 363). Or as the learned Dr. John Gill writes, in similar vein, that ministers are to teach 'everything that Christ has commanded, be it what it will, and nothing else; for Christ's ministers are not to teach for doctrines the commandments of men; enjoin that on the churches, what is of their own, or other men's devising, and was never ordered by Christ.' (*An Exposition of the New Testament*, vol. 1, p. 306). Because what Jesus commanded is relevant 'to the end of the age'; the Church, at no time, has ever any right to add to Christ's ordinances, but must always use only the means of worship that He has appointed. David Dickson's words sum up the purpose of the 'Great Commission' brilliantly 'the ministers and rulers of the Church are limited to the commands given to them from Christ; they may not enjoin to the Church anything save the commands of Christ.' (*A Brief Exposition of the Evangel of Jesus Christ According to Matthew*, p. 416).

John 4:20-24

At the end of a conversation between Christ and the woman of Samaria, our Lord goes right to the heart of what true worship is; the woman of Samaria said to Jesus:

> **"Our fathers worshipped on this mountain, but you say that in Jerusalem is the place where people ought to worship." Jesus said to her, "Woman, believe me, the hour is coming when neither on this mountain nor in Jerusalem will you worship the Father. You worship what you do not know; we worship what we know, for salvation is from the Jews. But the hour is coming, and is now here, when the true worshippers will worship the Father in spirit and truth for the father is seeking such people to worship him. God is spirit, and those who worship him must worship in spirit and truth**.

Jesus makes it clear to the woman of Samaria that the Old Testament form of worship (in the Temple at Jerusalem) was passing away; thus adherence to the regulative principle in the New Testament frees us from the obligation to worship God in a holy place (or with sacrifices, choirs, musical instruments) as they did under the Old Covenant. Remember, that upon the death of our Lord the veil of the Temple was torn in two (Matt. 27:51) thus abolishing the ceremonial law. As Michael Bushell observes 'One could hardly imagine a clearer indication of the fact that every change or modification in the manner of worship requires a divine sanction.' (*The Songs of Zion*, p. 146). Therefore the reason why New Testament worship differs from that of the Old Testament is because God Himself has changed it. So the regulative principle still applies in the New Covenant era, even though a change has taken place in the precise patterns of worship.

The woman of Samaria's conception of worship was fundamentally flawed; she thought that the Samaritans worship was acceptable because 'Our fathers worshipped on this mountain [Mt. Gerizim]' (v.20) 'she thinks they have antiquity, tradition and succession on their side.' (M. Henry, *Commentary on the Whole Bible*, vol. 5, p. 730). However, Jesus condemns her false worship saying 'You worship what you do not know' (v.22). The fact that her worship was part of a long accepted tradition did not justify it in the eyes of our Lord. Due to the fact that her worship wasn't informed by the word of God it was condemned; whereas Christ defends the Jewish form of worship because it was Biblical 'we worship what we know for salvation is of the Jews' (v.23). The Jews truly worshipped God because their worship had been ordained by Him. Matthew Henry contrasts the ignorant worship of the Samaritans, with the informed worship of the Jews, by saying:

> Ignorance is so far from being the mother of devotion that it is the murderer of it. Those that worship God ignorantly offer the blind for sacrifice, and it is the sacrifice of fools...we [referring to the Jews] go upon sure grounds in our worship, for our people are catechised and trained up in the knowledge of God, as he has revealed himself in the Scripture. (Ibid).

Therefore, we can only truly worship God if our minds have been informed by what He has said in the Scriptures. Forms of worship which originate from outside of the word (such as that of the Samaritans) are a form of idolatry.

Furthermore, when Christ says 'God is spirit, those who worship him must worship in spirit and truth' (v.24); He teaches us that worship is dependent upon the Spirit of God because the Holy Spirit is the source of worship. Therefore to worship God in 'spirit and in truth' we must worship Him in the way that He has told us in the Scriptures that the Holy Spirit wrote (2 Peter 1:21). As Michael Bushell says 'As in salvation it is the Spirit of God who takes the initiative in the giving of life, so in worship it is the Spirit of God who through His Word takes the initiative in determining how and where and under what conditions God is to be worshipped.' (*The Songs of Zion*, p. 151). Moreover, the late Prof. John Murray saw this as foundational to understanding why the regulative principle is the only basis upon which we can worship God in 'spirit and in truth':

> How are we to worship God? 'With what shall I come before the Lord, and bow myself before the high God?" (Micah 6:6). This is the question of the regulative principle of worship. How can I know that what I bring is acceptable to him? Worship consists of the offering of 'spiritual sacrifices acceptable to God by Jesus Christ.' This will surely not be questioned. So the matter of supreme concern is: What is acceptable? What is dictated and directed by the Holy Spirit?
>
> The question is really that of 'Spiritual worship', worship authorized by the Holy Spirit, constrained by the Holy Spirit, offered in the Holy Spirit. And so we must ask: Where does the Holy Spirit give us direction respecting that which he appears and leads us to render? The answer is: only in the Scripture as the Word which he has inspired. This simply means that for all modes and elements of worship there must be authorization from the Word of God. The Reformed principle is that the acceptable way of worshipping God is instituted by himself, and so limited by his revealed will that he may not be worshipped in any other way than that prescribed in the Holy Scripture, that what is not commanded is forbidden. This is in contrast with the

view that what is not forbidden is permitted. (*Collected Writings*, vol. 1, pp 167-8).

So if our worship is to be in 'spirit and in truth' it must be carried out in the manner that the Holy Spirit has told us in His word, and not according to our own fallible and sinful ideas.

Colossians 2:20-23

The Apostle Paul tells the Colossians not to submit to the commandments of men in their religious practice:

If with Christ you died to the elemental spirits of the world, why, as if you were still alive to the world do you submit to regulations – "Do not handle, Do not taste, Do not touch" (referring to things that all perish as they are used) – according to human precepts and teachings? These have indeed an appearance of wisdom in promoting self-made religion and asceticism and severity to the body, but they are of no value in stopping the indulgence of the flesh.

Paul regarded submission to human regulations as merely promoting 'self-made religion' (ESV and NASB). The meaning of this can further be brought out by looking at some other translations; for instance 'self-imposed religion' (NKJV), 'will-worship' (AV and RV), or best of all 'self-imposed worship' (NIV). So when people invent their own ways of worshipping God, which He has not ordained, they are simply engaging in 'self-imposed worship' – forms of worship that they have imposed on themselves and others without any regard to the commands of King Jesus.

In his *Institutes of the Christian Religion*, John Calvin concludes that Paul here condemns all 'fictious modes of worship which men themselves devise or receive from others, and all precepts whatsoever which they presume to deliver at their own hand concerning the worship of God.' (p. 419). While not all human inventions in worship are as reprehensible as the asceticism of the Gnostics, which Paul is here refuting, nevertheless as mere 'human precepts and teachings' (v.22) they are of no benefit to the Christian in pursuing holiness, as 'they are of no value in stopping the indulgence of the flesh' (v.23). So if your minister decided to stop preaching a sermon on a Sabbath morning in order to let the drama group have a performance, you should not be surprised if the congregation does not grow in sanctification, as they have been denied the means of grace only to be fed with man-made entertainment. This passage also reproves the folly of many Fundamentalists who impose silly man-made rules on their congregations. Christians in these types of Churches tend to think that sanctification is a matter of not drinking alcohol (even moderately), or not going to the cinema, or not listening to popular music, their knee-jerk reaction to abuses of legitimate activities ends up becoming mere 'self-imposed religion' which Paul elsewhere condemns, in very strong terms, as 'doctrines of demons' (1 Tim. 4:1 NKJV). Having invented man-made rules of conduct, it comes as little surprise to find that many of the same Fundamentalists countenance man-made traditions in worship such as testimonies, soloists, choirs, uninspired hymns and choruses and pianos and organs. When the young people in these Churches seek to introduce different innovations they are condemned, not on the basis of Scripture, but on tradition. Therefore, adherence to the regulative principle is all that can liberate us from 'self-imposed worship.'

CHAPTER 3:

Objections to the Regulative Principle of Worship

Despite the fact that the regulative principle (whatever is not ordained by God in His word is forbidden) is one of the doctrines most clearly taught in the word of God, many professing Christians still object to it. This chapter (relying heavily on some secondary sources) shall hopefully answer any objections that the reader may be faced with.

All of life is worship?

Some people argue that the Bible makes no distinction between specific activities of worship and life in general; therefore all of life is worship. They regard texts such as Deut. 4:2 as referring to a general rule that our lives should conform to God's revealed will (His word), and since all of life contains many activities that are not precisely regulated in Scripture, there can be no such thing as a regulative principle of worship. However, this is based upon a poor understanding of the verse in question. Brian Schwertley explains that 'Deuteronomy 4:2 teaches that men are not permitted to add or detract from God's commandments. In other words, God is the sole source of ethics for personal, family, institutional and civil life.' (*Sola Scriptura and the Regulative Principle of Worship*, p. 68). In relation to worship, God's ordinances are regulated by Himself, therefore men cannot be permitted to add or diminish from His word. Other areas of life that entail activities that are neither commanded nor forbidden and involve no violation of God's law; such as, the decision to wear a pair of blue jeans or a pair of black ones. In order to demonstrate the foolishness of the notion that Deut. 4:2 doesn't refer to regulation of worship only according to God's word, lets take it to its logical conclusion. Since the Lord has not (allegedly) strictly appointed how He is to be worshipped, could a Church decide to drop the Lord's Supper as a mere matter of indifference? Or could the Church not start inventing its own sacraments (like Roman Catholicism with its seven instead of two)? Why bother with a sermon on the Sabbath morning or evening? Why not just allow the congregation to sit back and watch a video? What's the point of the congregation singing? Why not divide them up into teams and have a five-a-side football tournament? I doubt very much that people who buy this interpretation would go to all of these extremes, but like it or not, that is where their logic is taking them.

Nevertheless the view that all of life is worship does appear to be a pious one. Certainly, those who adopt this position are correct to recognise that everything in life is to be done for the Lord's honour 'whether you eat or drink, or whatever you do, do all to the glory of God' (1 Cor.10:31). However, to conclude from this that there is no difference between our worship and the rest of our lives - is stretching the point to an unwarranted extreme. Needless to say the Bible teaches no such thing; a clear distinction is made between acts of worship and the other activities in life. Let's look at a few texts to establish this:

Psalm 22:22: **'I will tell of your name to my brothers; in the midst of the congregation I will praise you.'** Here David states that he engages in worship 'in the midst of the congregation (or 'church' Septuagint LXX)' as a separate event from other things in life.

Psalm 27:4 **'One thing have I asked of the LORD, that I will seek after: that I may dwell in the house of the LORD all the days of my life, to gaze upon the beauty of the LORD and to enquire in his temple.'** Why would David be so desirous to attend upon the worship of God 'in the house of the LORD' if in fact all of his life was worship? If we do not distinguish between worship and other activities the verse becomes meaningless.

Psalm 84:1-2: **'How lovely is your dwelling place, O LORD of hosts! My soul longs, yes, faints for the courts of the LORD; my heart and**

flesh sing for joy to the living God.' The Psalmists longing to be in the 'courts of the LORD' and attend upon His ordinances was a little pointless if all of life is worship.

Psalm 87:2: **'the LORD loves the gates of Zion more than all the dwelling places of Jacob.'** The Puritan writer David Clarkson noted that here the Lord states His preference for public worship over private:

> The Lord may be said to love the gates of Zion before all the dwellings of Jacob, because he prefers public worship before private...Public worship is to be preferred before private. So it is by the Lord, so it should be by his people.(Cited in Ibid, p. 74).

So if God prefers His public worship before that done in private, then it seems reasonable to assume that since He distinguishes between different types of worship, then the Lord must also differentiate between worship and other activities in life.

Ecclesiastes 5:1-2: **'Walk prudently when you go to the house of God; and draw near to hear rather than to give the sacrifice of fools, for they do not know that they do evil. Do not be rash with your mouth, and let not your heart utter anything before God. For God is in heaven, and you on earth; therefore let your words be few'** (NKJV). Here the Lord very clearly distinguishes between His public worship and other events in human life. Brian Schwertley writes 'there is to be a solemn recognition of the special presence of God in public worship and thus great care must be taken to be sincere, reverent, composed, deliberate and attentive.' (Ibid. p. 75). Solomon is saying here that when we attend public worship we should be ultra-careful about what we say; he encourages people to listen rather than to speak because of the special presence of God in such worship. Therefore, if we are to be more careful about what comes out of our mouths in public worship, then in the rest of our lives, a distinction must surely exist between the rest of life and worship.

Leviticus 23:3: **'For six days shall work be done, but the seventh day is a Sabbath of solemn rest, a holy convocation. You shall do no work. It is a Sabbath of the LORD in all your dwelling places.'** In this verse, God tells Moses that the weekly Sabbath is a day of 'solemn rest' for worship. No ordinary work, which was lawful on other days, was to be performed on this day of worship. Consequently, if the Lord has set apart one day of the week specifically for worship, then worship must be distinct from other legitimate things in life. Brian Schwertley further writes;

> After Israel was settled in the land, this requirement of weekly public worship could only be put into practice if there were many congregations meeting throughout the land of Israel. These decentralised congregational worship services would of course not contain the ceremonial elements of tabernacle or

temple worship (such as animal sacrifices). (Ibid, p. 76).

These local congregations would appear to have been the forerunner of the Jewish Synagogue and the New Testament local Assembly. Keep in mind, that just as they wouldn't have had sacrifices in their worship, nor would they have had musical instruments, as both these things were part of the ceremonial law.

Hebrews 10:24-25: **'And let us consider how to stir up one another to love and good works, not neglecting to meet together [or 'not forsaking the assembling of ourselves together' NKJV], as is the habit of some, but encouraging one another, and all the more as you see the Day drawing near.'** The inspired writer to the Hebrews rebukes those who forsake the meetings of the Church, which are a means of grace to encourage 'one another to love and good works.' Doubtless those who neglected the means of grace would have heartily agreed with those who claim that all of life is worship; after all if that is the case why should Christians bother meeting together? John Brown, on the other hand, points out the value of Christians meeting for worship:

It is by means of the public assemblies or churches of the saints that the visible profession of Christ's name is kept up in the world; and the exercises in which Christians there engage – reading, preaching the word, prayer, the Lord's Supper – are all well calculated to strengthen their faith and hope. (J. Brown, *Hebrews*, pp 465-6).

Therefore if worship is a means by which believers are built up in the faith, which they are not to neglect, then it must differ from the rest of life. A fair-minded analysis of the Biblical data leads one to the conclusion that all of life is not worship.

To further expose the absurdity of such a notion, let's see where this type of reasoning would lead us. If all of life was worship then how could the elders call a congregation to worship? Why would there be one day a week set apart for worship if God is to be worshipped equally everyday? If all of life is worship then unbelievers should be allowed to come to the Lord's Supper, since it would be no different from eating an ordinary meal! The fact that non-Christians are forbidden from coming to the Lord's Table (1 Cor. 11:27) shows us that it is a part of something distinct from ordinary life. According to this logic, Baptism would be no different from washing your forehead, preaching from making a speech, reading the Bible would be the same as reading a novel, congregational singing would be indistinct from singing nursery rhymes, and prayer would be no more sacred than chatting to your mate on the telephone. In the light of such nonsensical reasoning, we can only deduce that the worship of God is separate from other aspects of our lives.

John Frame's re-definition of the Regulative Principle

Though he is an able defender of Calvinistic theology and apologetics, Dr. John Frame has in recent years, popularised a strange re-definition of the regulative principle through his book *Worship in Spirit and in Truth*. Despite claiming to adhere to the Scriptural law of worship Dr. Frame would permit, among other things, dance and drama in God's worship. He argues that the regulative principle was established to keep the Church from bringing anything into worship that was offensive to God (which of course is true), and that worship is, in this sense, no different from any other part of the Christian life. So what he has done, is simply explain away the regulative principle by adopting the foolish notion that all of life is worship. He argues:

> The regulative principle for worship is no different from the principles by which God regulates all of our life. That is to be expected, because worship is, in an important sense, all of life. In both cases, "whatever is not commanded is forbidden" – everything we do must be done in obedience to God's commands. (*Worship in Spirit and in Truth*, p. 42).

However, as someone who truly believes in the proper Reformed understanding of the regulative principle, Prof. David McKay rebuffs Dr. Frame's reasoning. He says:

> The difference between worship and the rest of life, however, is that God does not command many thing Christians may legitimately do, for example to join a golf club or holiday in Barbados, whereas he does lay down specific rules to guide the worship of the whole Church. For individual decisions about holidays or leisure pursuits, Christians must apply the general principles of the Bible, for example regarding stewardship of money, but the regulative principle of worship, as traditionally understood, removes the need for individual decisions regarding the elements of worship. Frame, however, makes application the key procedure in worship too, and all of worship…must be determined in this way. The end result of Frame's method is in fact a version of the principle "what is not forbidden is allowed", characteristic of Lutheranism, Anglicanism and most Evangelicalism. (*The Bond of Love*, p. 231).

What John Frame has done is simply explain away the regulative principle so as to turn it into the normative principle that whatever is not forbidden is permitted. However, as has been demonstrated previously, this is not a conclusion that an examination of the Bible's teaching will sustain. Dr. Frame's re-definition of the regulative principle should be refuted in the same way that one would argue against the normative principle.

Jesus accepted Human Traditions

Some enemies of the regulative principle argue that the Lord Jesus Christ participated in human traditions in worship; so He must not have believed in the regulative principle. Now this is a serious allegation. If it can be proved from the rest of Scripture that to break the regulative principle is a sin, then we would have to conclude that Christ sinned in violating this principle. However, this is not a conclusion that the Bible will allow us to come to; it says that our Lord 'knew no sin' (2 Cor. 5:21). Therefore, if breaking the regulative principle is a sin, and Jesus never committed sin, then Jesus did not break the regulative principle. Also, it would have been somewhat hypocritical of the Lord to have condemned the scribes and Pharisees for observing human traditions in worship (Matt. 15:1-9) while He Himself observed them. So to argue that because Christ was present at Jerusalem when the (apparently unauthorized) Feast of Dedication was taking place (John 10:22-23), that He gave His approval to human traditions is an irresponsible way to handle Scripture. The fact that He elsewhere condemns man-made inventions tells us he doesn't approve of them. Keep in mind the advice of the *Westminster Confession* 'when there is a question about the true and full sense of any Scripture (which is not manifold, but one) it must be seconded and known by other places that speak more clearly'

(Chapter 1: Section 9). Since John 10:22-23 doesn't tell us whether or not Christ approved of human traditions we must go to other passages in order to know the mind of the Lord more clearly. To use a (fictional) historical example, if you read a biography of John Knox and the author said 'Mr Knox was in Edinburgh while Mary Queen of Scots was listening to Mass being said' would you jump to the conclusion that John Knox approved of the Romish Mass. I should hope not! So when you come to a text like John 10:22-23 why assume that Christ approves of human inventions in worship when elsewhere he condemns them.

Misrepresentation of the Regulative Principle

We may face the objection from Baptists and Seventh Day Adventists that Reformed Presbyterians are inconsistent in claiming to hold to the regulative principle because we practice things like infant baptism and first day Sabbath keeping, things that are not explicitly commanded in the New Testament. Oftentimes this is used to get-around the regulative principle rather than remain faithful to it. However, they misrepresent the regulative principle as teaching that it only refers to explicit commands in Scripture. This is to define the regulative principle in a manner that is not Scriptural or rationally defensible. On this logic we would have to reject the doctrine of the Trinity, because there is not one verse in the whole Bible that explicitly says that the Father, Son and Holy Spirit are co-equal and co-eternal. However, by analysing what the word of God says about each person of the God-head, we can by logical inference deduce from Scripture that the Father, Son, and Holy Spirit are all divine persons who are of one essence. That is why the *Westminster Confession* says:

> The whole counsel of God concerning all things necessary for His own glory, man's salvation, faith, and life, is either set down in Scripture, or by good and necessary consequence may be deduced from Scripture. (Chapter 1: Section 6)

While there is no command to baptise the infants of believers in the New Testament; such a command is not needed because God made it perfectly clear in the Old Testament that the children of believers were included in the Covenant of Grace and are part of the visible Church (Gen. 17:1-14). The sign of the covenant and Church membership was circumcision in the Old Testament, this has been changed to baptism in the New Testament (Matt. 28:18-20; Acts 2:38; Gal.3:27-29; Col. 2:11-12). God has only told us that the sign has changed, since he has not told us that infants are not to receive the sign anymore (and Gal. 3:14-17 teaches that the covenant with Abraham is still in force) nor has He told us that the children of believers have been excommunicated from His visible Church (texts such as Acts 2:38; Acts 16:15; Acts 16:31-34; 1 Cor. 1:16; 1 Cor 7:14; Eph 6:1; Col 3:20 indicate that they are part of the Church) then it is only logical to conclude that they must still receive the sign of the covenant, which is now Baptism. This method of Scriptural interpretation was used by the Lord Jesus Christ to refute the Sadducees who denied the doctrine of the resurrection. In Matthew 22:31-32 Christ said to the Sadducees:

And as for the resurrection of the dead, have you not read what was said to you by God: I am the God of Abraham, and the God of Isaac, and the God of Jacob? He is not the God of the dead but of the living.

What the Lord is telling the Sadducees is that if God could tell Moses (Ex. 3:6) that He was the God of the living, not of the dead, yet quotes the names of Abraham, Isaac and Jacob who had long since died, then the only logical conclusion is that there must be a bodily resurrection. Because how else could God be the God of the living if the dead did not rise again?

Another legitimate hermeneutical principle is that of using historical examples in the Bible to prove that a worship practice is acceptable. For example, although it is not explicitly recorded in Scripture that God ever commanded a Synagogue, it can be proved to have been a lawful practice by the fact that Christ and the Apostles attended worship in the Synagogues. An explicit command may have been given by a prophet that was not recorded in Scripture; nevertheless the approval given to the Synagogue by Jesus is enough to teach us that it was in accordance with the regulative principle. Also, the fact that the early Christians met on the first day of the week (Acts 20:7;

1 Cor 16:2) in light of Christ's resurrection (Luke 24:1-3) for worship indicates that the Sabbath, and remember that Jesus said 'the Son of man is Lord of the Sabbath' (Mark 2:28) and that it was a creation ordinance 'made for man' (Mark 2:27) not just for the Jews, has now changed from Saturday to Sunday. If it had been otherwise then surely God would have told the Church that they no longer needed to obey the fourth commandment.

The Regulative Principle only applies to Public Worship

Some Reformed Christians are happy enough to admit that the regulative principle applies in public worship, but think that it doesn't in private or family worship. However, the second commandment (Ex. 20:4-6) knows of no such distinction. If we say the regulative principle doesn't apply in private fellowship, family or secret worship; would it be alright then to bow down to idols or burn incense? Of course not! This is not to pretend however, that the regulative principle doesn't apply differently in private informal fellowship meetings or family worship. For example, the prohibition on ladies participating in speaking and praying only applies to public assemblies (1 Cor. 14:34; 1 Tim 2:8; 1 Tim 2:11-15) yet this doesn't apply to private meetings for mutual edification (Acts 16:13; Acts 18:26) such as the United Society meetings of the Covenanters. Nor do we administer the sacraments or preach the Word in family worship; yet the regulative principle, as far as it applies to differing circumstances, remains in force. So to argue that while you can only sing Psalms in public worship, yet sing uninspired hymns in family worship, is not logical; as the rules for the material to be sung in praise do not alter.

CHAPTER 4:

The Circumstances of Worship

The *Westminster Confession of Faith* teaches us that:

> There are some circumstances concerning the worship of God, and government of the Church, common to human actions and societies, which are to be ordered by the light of nature and Christian prudence, according to the general rules of the Word, which are always to be observed. (Chapter 1: Section 6).

In the following pages I will seek to explain what the Confession means when it refers to circumstances of worship; and show that these are distinct from what we refer to as regulative principles of worship.

Circumstances necessary but not essential to worship

When we talk about indifferent circumstances of worship, we refer to things that are not essential as to whether or not the worship of God takes place, but they are necessary in order that public worship may be conducted in an orderly way. These circumstances differ from what Gordon H. Clark calls 'prescriptions, such as singing, prayer, and preaching, the Lord's Supper and Baptism, cannot be omitted from the regular church program. Nor may a chess game or a genuflection be added.'(*What Do Presbyterians Believe*, p. 27). Although the Bible exhorts us not to be 'forsaking the assembling of ourselves together' (Heb. 10:25 NKJV) it does not specifically lay down the precise time at which a local congregation should meet for worship on the Sabbath day. This is left to the discretion of the elders of each congregation to arrange a time that would be suitable in order to allow the members of the congregation to attend. Obviously, if the morning service was at 4.00 am few people would be up in time; so it is customary to meet at a more reasonable time (such as 11.30 am or 12.00 noon). Nor would it be a wise move to have the evening service at 11.00 pm, a time when parents want their children to be in bed, so a more sensible time of 7.00 pm is chosen. Likewise, the Bible doesn't tell us whether or not we should hold our services of worship in a meeting house, or in someone's home, or in the open air, yet we usually worship in a meeting house, not because there is anything sacred about certain buildings as Romanists and Episcopalians believe (the term 'house of the Lord' should never be applied to a meeting house), but in order to accommodate everybody and so that the worship will be uninterrupted by the weather. Nor is it ordained in Scripture precisely what clothes we should wear when attending Church. However, the Bible contains a 'general rule' that we should dress modestly and decently and in a way that is not viewed as rebellious in our culture (for example dressing like Gothic's). To this end we read in 1 Tim. 2:9-10 that when attending public worship: 'women should adorn themselves in respectable apparel, with modesty and self-control, not with braided hair and gold pearls or costly attire, but with that which is proper for women who profess godliness with good works.' Obviously a woman wearing a mini-skirt or exposing a bare mid-drift in Church is not wearing 'respectable apparel, with modesty and self-control'; nor is a lady, wearing a hat which cost £100, obeying the instruction not to wear inordinately 'costly attire' because as Geoffrey Wilson said 'ostentation and extravagance in dress hardly point to a mind set on heavenly things.' (*New Testament Commentaries*, vol. 2, p. 228). Moreover, he wisely comments 'obviously, the practical application of the principle have set forth will always be expressed in a manner that is considered appropriate to the cultural and social climate of the time. What is important is to remember the principle: "Let all things be done decently and in order" (1 Cor. 14:40 ASV).' (Ibid. p. 229). So what Paul is here saying is that, not that there are any sacred clothes for worship, but that when Christians meet together they are not to dress in a fashion that is regarded as immoral or extravagant in their society (this is something we will return to later).

This truth serves as a corrective to some Fundamentalists who teach, for example, that all Christian men should wear an expensive suit, along with a shirt and tie and brightly polished shoes, when they attend public worship. As this is not taught anywhere in the Bible we can, and should, reject such teaching as mere human tradition that is not founded on the word of God. If one is going to argue that men should wear suits on the basis that they are all that is decent and modest in worship, then they should be made to wear them all the time in public; because in the New Testament there are no holy clothes. However, as wearing, for example, a pair of blue jeans and a sweatshirt isn't regarded as immodest in our culture; then it is acceptable to wear such clothing in worship. Therefore one must come to the conclusion that men are under no obligation to wear suits at Church meetings; nor should they feel any compulsion to submit to such bondage: 'Stand fast therefore in the liberty by which Christ has made us free, and do not be entangled again with a yoke of bondage' (Gal. 5:1 NKJV). One extra-Biblical argument which some Fundamentalists use (and I have even heard this from the pulpit) is that 'if you were going to visit the Queen you would wear a suit; but when you come to worship the King of kings you think that you can just dress casually.' Such reasoning is seriously flawed; the Queen is a civil magistrate therefore she can determine how people dress in her presence (Rom. 13:1-7). However, in the Church, we have only one King and Head, Jesus Christ (Matt. 28:18-20); as He has not prescribed particular forms of dress for worship we have no right to enforce such a practice. Moreover, the apostle James condemned the idea of paying respect to individuals due to their rich clothing. He says in James 2:2-9:

> My brothers, show no partiality as you hold the faith in our Lord Jesus Christ. For if a man wearing a gold ring and fine clothing comes into your assembly, and a poor man in shabby clothing also comes in, and if you pay attention to the one who wears fine clothing and say, "You sit here in a good place", while you say to the poor man, "You stand over there", or, "Sit down at my feet", have you not then made distinctions among yourselves and become judges with evil thoughts? Listen, my beloved brothers, has not God chosen those who are poor in the world to be rich in faith and heirs of the kingdom, which he has promised to those who love him? But you have dishonoured the poor man. Are not the rich the ones who oppress you, and the ones who drag you into court? Are they not the ones who blaspheme the honourable name by which you were called? If you really fulfil the royal law according to the Scripture, "You shall love your neighbour as yourself", you are doing well. But if you show partiality you

are committing sin and are convicted by the law as transgressors.

I dread to think what James would have thought of modern Fundamentalists, who not only display such partiality, but would even question a fellow Christian's profession of faith on the basis that they don't wear a suit to Church. As Matthew Henry wisely said 'there is many a humble, heavenly, good Christian, who is clothed meanly; but neither should he nor his Christianity be thought the worse of on this account.' (*Commentary on the Whole Bible*, vol. 6, p. 787). Yet, like the Pharisees, many Fundamentalists reject the regulative principle of worship and introduce human innovations such as soloists, testimonies, joking preachers, musical instruments, altar calls, and other gimmicks into divine worship. Thus they 'leave the commandment of God and hold to the traditions of men' (Mark 7:8).

On a similar basis we must also reject the enforcement on ministers having to wear ecclesiastical vestments when conducting divine worship. One cannot argue that ministers should wear vestments because the Old Testament Priests wore them, due to the fact that the sacrificial priesthood has been abolished (Heb. 9:9-10). John Owen comments that priestly dress and such things were imposed on the Jewish Church 'until the time of reformation' (when Christ abolished the ceremonial law by his death) so that 'they might feel their weight, and groan under the burden of it…They were never designed to continue for-ever.' (*An Exposition of the Epistle to the Hebrews*, vol. 6, p. 256). Therefore, such forms of dress have been abolished, and to impose their wearing upon New Testament ministers, who aren't sacrificing priests, is to return to the bondage of the Old Covenant. As this is the practice adopted by the Church of Rome with its sacrificing priesthood, many of the Puritans refused to submit to the wearing of such garments, not only on the basis that they infringed their Christian liberty, but that they were also inconsistent with the reformation from Popery. Thus Horton Davies, in his book *The Worship of the English Puritans* explains their position:

> The radical Puritans stated their case for the abolition of vestments on the following grounds. First and foremost, they were regarded as an infringement of their Christian liberty; the Church which had been freed by Christ from the bondage of the |ceremonial| law was now attempting to infringe the crown rights of the Redeemer by introducing new burdens on the consciences of believers. Moreover, these vestments were disliked because of their association with Romish superstition; they were "badges of Anti-Christ" upholding the priesthood of the clergy and, by their implication, denying the priesthood of all believers; they were, further, sacrificial vestments that had been associated in recent memory with the sacrifice of the Mass. Furthermore, they were symbols of pomp and grandeur, ill-befitting the humility

with which all men should approach God, and contrary to the simplicity of the first disciples and apostles of Christ. Besides, these garments had a Jewish origin belonging to the Aaronic priesthood, not to the Christian ministry. And, the radical Puritans pleaded, even if they were indifferent matters, as their opponents held, it was inexpedient to retain them, for the sake of the weaker brethren who associated them with the old superstitious religion. (pp 59-60).

As there is no command for the imposition of clerical vestments in New Testament worship, the Puritans were correct to flee from this Jewish, Romish and Prelatic bondage out of faithfulness to Christ our Great High Priest. Because if you are going to have priestly dress, then you are going to have to have priests, and if you are going to have priests (whose function is to sacrifice) then you are going to have to have sacrifices; which is an insult to Christ's finished sacrificial work on the cross for His people's sins.

Natural Circumstances of Worship - The Issue of Female Preachers

When the *Westminster Confession* states that certain things pertaining to the worship of God are determined 'by the light of nature' (Chapter 1: Section 6) it may well have in mind the divine prohibition on females teaching and speaking in public worship. Writing to his fellow minister Timothy, the apostle Paul said:

Let a woman learn quietly with all submissiveness. I do not permit a woman to teach or to exercise authority over a man; rather, she is to remain quiet. For Adam was formed first, then Eve; and Adam was not deceived, but the woman deceived and became a transgressor. (1 Tim. 2:11-14)

Here Paul teaches that women, in conformity to the created order, are not to be found teaching in public worship. As this is a duty which belongs to a minister (or men who are aspiring to the ministry) the woman would be exercising authority over the male members of the congregation and therefore would not be in submission. Geoffrey Wilson explains:

Although Paul elsewhere shows that woman have equal standing with men in Christ [Gal. 3:28], he also insists that fellowship in Christ does not remove the natural distinction between the sexes, which was established by the priority given to man in creation. Paul will not permit a woman to assume the place of leadership in the church as an authoritative teacher of doctrine, because that would set aside the order of nature and put her in a position of exercising authority over the men in the congregation. (*New Testament Commentaries*, vol. 2, p. 229).

Unlike matters relating to forms of dress (1 Tim 2:9; 1 Cor 11:2-16) this cannot vary according to culture, because it is dealing with the functions of these exercising an office in the Church which doesn't vary from one society to another. Moreover, what Paul says here is not out of line with the previous teaching of Scripture. As the famous Southern Presbyterian Robert Lewis Dabney explained:

> The Old Testament, which contained, in germ, all the principles of the New, allowed no regular church office to any woman. When a few of that sex were employed as mouthpieces of God, it was an office purely extraordinary, and in which they could adduce a supernatural attestation of their commission. No woman ever ministered at the altar, as either priest or Levite. No female elder was ever seen in a Hebrew congregation. (*Discussions*, vol. 2, p. 102)

Dabney further explains that:

> Presbyterians at least believe that the church order of the Old Testament Church was imported into the New, with less modification than any other part of the old religion... the primeval presbyterial order continued unchanged. The Christianized synagogue became the Christian congregation, with its eldership, teachers, and deacons, and its

women invariably keeping silence in the assembly. (Ibid.).

Some might object that because there were female prophets then it must follow that women should be allowed to teach. While they are correct in asserting that women under the inspiration of the Spirit, did prophesy (Acts 2:18); this must only have taken place in general situations, and not in public worship, because Paul reminds the Corinthians that women are forbidden to prophesy in Church; 'the women should keep silent in the churches. For they are not permitted to speak, but should be in submission, as the law also says' (1 Cor 14:34). Moreover, in the New Testament, the call to be a public teacher of God's word goes together with that to be a ruling elder; thus Paul said 'Let the elders who rule well be considered worthy of double honour, especially those who labour in preaching and teaching' (1 Tim 5:17); as Dabney comments 'there were ruling elders who were not preachers, but never was the regular preacher heard of who was not *ex officio* a ruling elder.'(Ibid. pp 102-3). Considering that an elder or overseer (not 'bishop' AV/NKJV) must be 'the husband of one wife' (1 Tim 2:2; Titus 1:6), and throughout Titus chapter 1 Paul refers to the elder as a 'He', then it would be reasonable to assume that the preacher or minister (teaching elder) should only be a man. However, as this only applies to public worship it does not prohibit women from teaching other women (Titus 2:3-4), instructing their own children their own children or a Sabbath school class

(2 Tim 1:5; 3:14-15) or to exhort men in fellowship meetings for mutual edification (Acts 18:26).

Circumstances Common to Different Human Societies

When the *Westminster Confession* asserts that some circumstances relating to the public worship of God are 'common to human actions and societies' which are to be observed 'according to the general rules of the Word' (Chapter 1: Section 6) it takes account of the cultural diversity which exists in the world. The most famous example we have of this in Scripture is Paul's treatment of the issue of women's head covering in 1 Cor. 11:2-16. However, not everyone agrees with this interpretation and some faithful Christians have concluded that Paul is laying down a regulative principle of worship. While commending such people for taking the word of God seriously; it shall be shown that this position cannot be sustained by an analysis of 'the whole counsel of God' (Acts 20:27). I will also seek to prove that the cultural interpretation is the Reformed understanding of the passage.

Head coverings – Not a Regulative Principle of worship

There are serious problems with the position that 1 Cor. 11:2-16 refers to a universal command by Paul for all women to have their heads covered with some form of head gear (usually a hat or beret in Fundamentalist circles, though Paul was probably talking about a veil or headscarf) in all circumstances when the gathered Church meets for public worship. Firstly, if Paul is referring to a regulative principle to be maintained in congregational worship, then it can only refer to those who 'pray or prophesy' (v.4-5); as he has nothing to say about how those who remain silent should adorn themselves. Since woman are forbidden to speak in public worship (1 Cor. 14:34), Paul's instruction cannot only relate to how women dress in church. Some would claim that the words 'praying' and 'prophesying' are general terms referring to public worship; however, the context of 1 Corinthians forbids such an interpretation. Remember that while the Bible was written for us it was not written to us; therefore those who read this in first century Corinth would have understood praying and prophesying as referring to prayer and prophesy. It would appear more likely that Paul is saying that when women exercise spiritual gifts in general situations they are not to cast of their cultural sign of submission to male authority (v.6-7) as the Christian faith does not free us from existing social order. Moreover, the context in which this instruction has been written, favours the interpretation that the apostle is not specifically referring to the Church's worship. After he deals with head coverings Paul goes on to rebuke the Corinthians for their abuses of the Lord's Supper. Here he condemns them specifically for what takes place in their public meetings: 'In the following directives I have no praise for you, for your meetings do more harm than good. In the first place, I hear that when you come together as a church, there are divisions among you, and to some extent I believe it' (v.17-18 NIV). Now notice here Paul refers to their conduct when they 'come together as a church' (v.18) which can only lead one to the conclusion that previously in verses 2-16 he was not making reference only to what went on when they met together for public worship. This leads one to believe that when Paul was discussing head coverings he was referring to a practice distinct to their society, whereas at verse 17 he begins to deal with matters relevant to the church in all ages and places. Therefore, if you believe that verses 2-16 is a universal command, then women must have their heads covered in all public situations (not just in Church) and men are never allowed to have their heads covered in all public situations (not just in Church) because, if a man does, he 'dishonours his head' (v.4). This would mean that even on a freezing cold day a man would be forbidden from wearing a hat; a most unreasonable conclusion. The argument that Paul's use of the word 'traditions' (in verse 2) signifies that he is talking about something that specifically takes place in worship services cannot be sustained. Firstly, head covering isn't actually included as one of the 'traditions' because in verse 3 Paul moves on to discuss matters that are different to the traditions that he had previously 'delivered' (v.2) to the Corinthians. Thus explaining why he commends them in verse 2 and then reproves them in verse 3. Moreover, when Paul speaks of 'the tradition you have received from us' in 2 Thess. 3:6, he is not referring to an ordinance of public worship but to the apostolic injunction for Christians to abstain from idleness and earn their own living by working hard in lawful employment (2 Thess. 3:7-12). So the use of the word 'tradition' no more verifies that head covering is a regulative principle of worship than it proves that earning a living by honest work is.

We might face the objection that head covering cannot be cultural because Paul bases his argument on the order of creation: 'For man was not made from woman, but woman from man' (v. 8). However, what Paul is saying is that, by virtue of the created order, men have authority over women, and in the cultural context of first century Greece the outward sign of a woman's submission to her husband's authority was that of wearing a veil symbolising the modesty and propriety suitable for a submissive female. If we conclude that head covering is a regulative principle of worship, established at creation, we run into serious difficulties when examining the rest of the Bible. Firstly, if head covering is a creation ordinance then how come Eve was uncovered in worship and in the very presence of God in the garden of Eden (remember that prior to the fall they did not wear any clothes Gen. 2:25; Gen. 3:21)? Did Eve sin by not wearing a head covering before the fall? The answer is obviously no because God created her without a head covering; therefore, head covering is not a creation ordinance. It would appear that Paul is only referring to the created order to highlight how women are to submit to men and applying it to a particular cultural circumstance. Indeed, there is strong Biblical evidence to suggest that the significance of female head coverings varied in different social, historical and cultural contexts. For example, when Judah's daughter-in-law Tamar wore a veil it was a sign that she was a prostitute (Gen. 38:15-19). Likewise, in Solomon's time the description of one as 'a veiled woman' (Song of Songs 1:7 NIV) indicated that the individual in question was engaged in prostitution. So in these historical and cultural settings head dress was a sign of immorality; whereas in first century Corinth the wearing of a female head covering was a symbol of modesty and decency (1 Cor. 11:5-6). Moreover, when ladies wore head dresses in Isaiah's day, God looked upon it as a sign of extravagance and humbled them by removing these items of head gear from them (Isa. 3:18-19; 47:2). However, in Corinth, the laying aside of head coverings by females displayed a spirit of pride and rebellion (1 Cor. 11:8-9).

So the moral principle of 1 Cor. 11:2-16 is that women should submit to male authority by not casting aside modest dress; the wearing of a head covering was merely a circumstance common to that society. Furthermore, if Paul's command is a part of regulated worship Greg Price asks:

> How then was the Church of the Old Testament not commanded to do that in worship which was an ALLEGED creation ordinance based upon such universal principles of headship, submission, proper order, decorum, and distinction between men and

women? If Paul's command is a part of regulated worship, it should have bound not only the New Testament saints, but Old Testament saints as well. But such is not apparently the case. Since there is no other command found in Scripture which requires men to be universally uncovered in worship and for women to be universally covered in worship, and since there are places in Scripture where men and women did not keep this command in worship, how can we interpret Paul's command in 1 Corinthians 11 to be applied universally in all ecclesiastical circumstances ALONE? (*A Brief Introduction to Headcoverings*, p. 2)

Indeed when one takes the time to study the worship of the Old Testament, one finds that God positively commanded men to wear head coverings in worship (Ex. 28:4, 40; Zech. 3:5). This means that if head covering is an unchanging moral principle, based on the order of creation, then God actually commanded something in His worship that was positively sinful. Such a conclusion is unthinkable, especially when one considers that Aaron's turban had the words 'HOLINESS TO THE LORD' (Ex. 28:36 NKJV) engraved on it. This means we can only conclude that the head covering mentioned in 1 Cor. 11:2-16 was a cultural sign of female submission; although it doesn't say that in 1 Corinthians it is nevertheless a valid logical deduction from other Biblical passages.

Moreover, there is also evidence in the New Testament itself that women did not universally cover their heads with a material covering. In 1 Tim 2:9 Paul calls for women to have respectable hairstyles when they attend the public worship of God. However, if 1 Cor. 11:2-16 was a regulative principle of worship, applicable in all ages and places, then it would have been impossible for Timothy to have known whether or not the ladies he preached to were drawing attention to themselves with extravagant hairstyles as their hair would have been covered, thus rendering Paul's instruction completely irrelevant. As Timothy was working outside Corinth when Paul wrote this instruction, it gives us further reason to believe that the apostle Paul was dealing with an issue unique to one particular cultural setting when he wrote about head covering in 1 Cor. 11:2-16.

If someone is still convinced that head covering is a regulative principle of worship, while I respect their position, I have this challenge to put to them: hats will not suffice. In order for a garment to be a head covering it must cover the entire head, while a hat (or beret) does not cover the entire head and is thus a decoration and not a covering. So ladies wearing hats to Church are not covering their heads. Interestingly, because many Fundamentalists assume that head covering refers to western hats, it is worth keeping in mind that this sort of garment was actually a part of the priestly dress in the Old Testament (Ex. 39:28 NKJV), therefore a hat cannot be a distinctly female form of attire in every culture. For modern Churches to enforce the wearing of such garments, would appear to be a return to the bondage of the ceremonial law, which the New Testament tells us to flee from (Gal. 5:1). Moreover, hats act as a distraction in public worship, often ones view of the pulpit is obscured by an inordinately large item of headgear. And if hats are a regulative principle, applicable to all parts of worship, then the question must be raised how can a woman be Baptised in a hat? Surely, according to this logic, if she removes her hat to receive the sacrament, she would be dishonouring her head. How strange is it that some Fundamentalist Churches will forbid a woman from attending the Lord's Table for not wearing a hat (thus persecuting other Christians) while admitting them to Baptism supposedly un-covered. Such inconsistency beggars belief. Furthermore, hats are not a symbol of submission to male authority or of modesty in our culture in the same way that a veil or headscarf was in the ancient world; of anything they are a sign of flamboyance i.e. Ascot Races.

It is worth remembering that the only reason we cover our bodies at all is because, since the fall, we are required to wear clothes, as uncovering our nakedness would be immodest and would arouse lust in the opposite sex. Thus Paul explains to the Corinthians why we cover specific parts of the human body because 'our un-presentable parts are treated with greater modesty' (1 Cor. 12:23). Notice that he says this just after explaining why women should cover their heads, therefore he must have been calling upon them to cover their heads on the basis that it was immodest for a lady to be dressed otherwise in this cultural context (remember what constitutes 'modest apparel' 1 Tim 2:9 NKJV varies from one society to the next). This would probably explain why Paul compares an uncovered woman with one that has her hair 'shaved' (v.5) or 'shorn' (v.6 NKJV), because all of these things were signs of indecency and the subversion of proper social order. However, in our culture it is not viewed as immodest for a woman to be seen in public without a hat.

In light of the above mentioned considerations we should conclude that our Reformed forefathers at the Westminster Assembly were correct not to list head covering as a regulative principle of worship in the *Westminster Confession of Faith*.

The Historic Reformed View of Head covering

I shall now seek to prove, beyond all reasonable doubt, that the position that 1 Cor. 11:2-16 is not referring to a regulative principle of worship is the historic Reformed interpretation of the passage by quoting from some of the leading lights of the Reformed faith.

John Calvin

Although it was the practice of women during Calvin's time at Geneva to wear a fabric head covering in public, this does not mean that it was considered to be a regulative principle of worship. On reading Calvin's commentary on 1 Cor. 11:2-16 may have thought that he believed head coverings were a permanent ordinance; however, a careful reading of his *Institutes of the Christian Religion* proves that this was not the case. Speaking of proper decorum in the Church, Calvin says that: 'there are examples of the first sort in Paul: that profane drinking bouts should not be mingled with the sacred supper of the Lord (1 Cor. 11:21-22), and that women should not go out in public with uncovered heads (1 Cor. 11:5).' (*The Practice of Headcoverings in Public Worship*, p. 7). Notice that he regarded women's head covering as referring to general situations in public, and not just worship, so he couldn't have believed it to have been a regulative principle. Furthermore he went on to state that matters of this nature were to be determined by the cultural standards of society:

But because he [God] did not will in outward discipline and ceremonies what we ought to do (because he foresaw that this depended upon the state of the times, and he did not deem one form suitable for all ages), here we must take refuge in those general rules which he has given, that whatever the necessity if the church will require for order and decorum should be tested against these…lastly, because he [God] has taught nothing specifically, and because these things are not necessary to salvation, and abrogate traditional practices and to establish new ones. (Ibid., p. 8)

So if Calvin believed that female head covering was an unchanging moral commandment, in every age and place, why did he say it should be 'accommodated to the customs of each nation and age'? The only answer is that he viewed the head covering in 1 Cor. 11:2-16 as a cultural sign; which would explain he wore a hat when he preached in public.

The Geneva Bible

In the notes of the famous *Geneva Bible*, which was highly esteemed by both the English Puritans and Scottish Covenanters, Theodore Beza (Calvin's successor) comments upon 1 Cor. 11:4 'Every man who prays or prophesies with his head covered dishonours his head':

> By this he [Paul] gathers that if men do either pray or preach in public assemblies having their heads covered (which was a sign of subjection), they robbed themselves of their dignity, against God's ordinance...It appears, that this was a political law serving only for the circumstances of the time that Paul lived in, by this reason, because in these our days for a man to speak bareheaded in an assembly is a sign of subjection. (Ibid.).

If the other Reformed theologians at Geneva didn't accept this cultural interpretation - why was there never an uproar about these comments being printed in the Bible version which most of the Genevan Reformed people used? To this question there is only one satisfactory answer; this interpretation was the one accepted by the Reformed Church in the 16th century. Helping to explain why a man like John Knox, who studied at Geneva, carried on the work of Reformation in Scotland while preaching in a hat.

Francis Turretin

Turretin was a Reformed teacher of theology at Geneva in the 17th century. Unsurprisingly he agrees with his predecessors that women's head covering was not a permanent ordinance. In his *Institutes of Elenctic Theology* he says:

> Certain ordinances of the Apostles (which referred to the rites and circumstances of divine worship) were variable and instituted only for a time (as the sanction of not eating blood and of such things strangled Acts 15:20); concerning the woman's head being covered and the man's being uncovered when they prophesy (1 Cor. 11:4-5) because there was a special cause and reason for them and (this ceasing) the institution itself ought to cease also. (Ibid. p. 9).

Therefore it is clear that while women in Geneva wore head coverings in both ordinary society and public worship, the Reformed theologians there did not understand 1 Cor. 11:2-16 to be referring to an unchangeable regulative principle of worship.

Samuel Rutherford

In his work *The Divine Right of Church Government* this noted scholar of the Covenanted Church of Scotland interprets the head covering in 1 Cor. 11:2-16 as being only a cultural symbol:

> Uncovering the head, seems to be little older than Paul's Epistles to the Corinthians. The learned Salmasius thinks it but a National sign of honour, no ways universally received...The Jews to this day, as of old, used not uncovering the head as a sign of honour: But by the contrary, covering was a sign of honour. If therefore the Jews being made a visible Church, shall receive the Lord's Supper, and pray and Prophesy with covered head, not out of disrespect to the ordinances of God; though Paul, having regard to National custom in Corinth, did so esteem it. (Ibid., p. 4).

Did Rutherford's fellow Covenanter ministers regard him as some sort of liberalising feminist for teaching that head covering was but a national sign? Certainly not! In fact, he was considered by many to be the brightest light of the Second Scottish Reformation alongside the learned George Gillespie.

George Gillespie

Despite his youth, Gillespie (along with Rutherford) was instrumental in the framing of the

Westminster Standards, as both of them served as commissioners of the Church of Scotland in the Westminster Assembly. In his book *English Popish Ceremonies* Gillespie also regarded head coverings as being cultural:

> Customable Signs; and so the uncovering of the head, which of old was a sign of pre-eminence, has through custom, become a sign of subjection...Secondly, customary signs have likewise place in divine service; for so a man coming into one of our churches in the time of public worship, if he sees the hearers covered, he knows by this customary sign that the sermon has begun. (Ibid. p. 3).

Since this issue was never a controversy among the Covenanters it appears reasonable to assume that they agreed that 1 Cor. 11:2-16 referred to a cultural practice.

The Westminster Assembly

Because the Westminster Divines did not name women's head covering as a regulative principle of worship in Chapter 21 ('Of Religious worship and the Sabbath Day') of the Confession of Faith or in the Shorter and Larger Catechisms, then it appears reasonable to assume that they considered it to be a circumstance of worship 'common to human actions and societies' (Chapter 1: Section 6). If this were not the case you would expect some reference to it in *The*

Directory for the Public Worship of God which they produced. However, the issue is never even mentioned. Therefore, if the Westminster Divines believed that head coverings were a regulative principle of worship their failure to include it in the Westminster Standards was a serious mistake. The only conclusion left to us is that they did not consider the issue of head coverings to be a principle of worship, but instead a mere circumstance. For this reason the present *Testimony of the Reformed Presbyterian Church of Ireland* affirms nothing contrary to the opinions of her fore-fathers by not listing head covering as a regulative principle of worship.

Chapter 5:

Worship is to be given to God Alone

In his famous book *Roman Catholicism* Loraine Boettner wrote:

> Nothing is more clearly revealed in Scripture than that divine worship is to be given to God alone "You shall worship the Lord your God and him only shall you serve" (Matt. 4:10). Nothing is more severely rebuked than idolatry of every kind and form. (p. 197).

For this reason the *Westminster Confession* says 'Religious worship is to be given to God, the Father, Son, and the Holy Ghost; and to him alone' (Chapter 21: Section 2). All three persons of the Godhead are to be worshipped because, as the Confession elsewhere states, 'In the unity of the Godhead there be three persons, of one substance, power and eternity; God the Father, God the Son, and God the Holy Ghost' (Chapter 2: Section 3). One of the clearest Biblical proofs that all three persons of the Trinity are to be worshipped is seen in the apostolic benediction recorded in 2 Cor. 13:14 'The grace of the Lord Jesus Christ and the love of God and the fellowship of the Holy Spirit be with you all.' This is evidently a prayer, and as prayer is a part of worship, which is to be given to God alone (Deut. 6:13), then each of the persons to whom this prayer is addressed must be God. So by this method of logical deduction we prove that worship is to be given to the triune God. The same holds true of the formula for Baptism, which also being a part of worship, is to be performed in 'the name of the Father and of the Son and of the Holy Spirit' (Matt. 28:19). If all three persons were not fully divine then it would be an act of idolatry to carry out this act of worship in any name other than that of one who was God. Obviously God does not sanction idolatry, so when the Bible tells us to carry out an act of worship in the name of the Father, the Son and the Holy Spirit, then we can only assume that all three of them are divine persons.

In asserting that God alone is to be the object of Christian worship our Confession continues by saying that such worship is not to be given 'to angels saints, or any other creature' (Chapter 21: Section 3). God has never authorised the worship of anything or anyone other than Himself, to do this would be to rob the Lord of the glory of that which belongs to Him alone 'Worthy are you, our Lord and God, to receive glory and honour and power, for you created all things and by your will they existed and were created' (Rev. 4:11). The worshipping of angels is expressly condemned in Scripture; Paul warned the Colossians 'Let no one disqualify you, insisting on asceticism and worship of angels' (Col. 2:18). Moreover, the apostle John was rebuked for almost lapsing into angel worship while on the island of Patmos. He wrote:

I, John, am the one who heard and saw these things. And when I heard and saw them, I fell down to worship at the feet of the angel who showed them to me, but he said to me, "You must not do that! I am your fellow servant with you and your brothers the prophets, and with those who keep the words of this book. Worship God." (Rev. 22:8-9).

Despite the clarity of the Bible's teaching that God alone is to be worshipped, the Roman Catholic 'Church' authorises the worship of the Virgin Mary and the saints. Using the simplest form of logic, the syllogism, we can explain to Roman Catholics why the worship of Mary (or any other creature) is wrong:

- The Bible tells us only to worship God
- Mary (or any other saint) is not God
- Therefore the Bible forbids us to worship Mary

However, as A.A. Hodge explains, Rome has a clever way of wriggling out of the charge that they are committing idolatry by worshipping the saints and Mary:

> To avoid the charge of idolatry made upon them for these practices, they distinguish between (a.) *Latria*, or the highest religious worship, which is due to God alone, and (b.) *Doulia*, or that inferior religious worship which is due in various degrees to saints and angels, according to their rank. Some also make a middle degree of worship, which is due to the Virgin Mary alone, by the term *Hyperdoulia*. (*The Confession of Faith*, p. 273).

The major problem with this distinction is that it has absolutely no support in the word of God. If we adhere to the Scriptural law of worship (that whatever God has not authorized is forbidden) then we will demand Biblical warrant for any lesser form of 'worship' to be ascribed to the saints. As Boettner pointed out 'nowhere in the Bible is there the slightest suggestion that prayer should be offered to Mary. If God had intended that we should pray to her, surely He would have said so.' (*Roman Catholicism*, p. 187). Not to mention the fact that praying to Mary is completely contrary to reason. How can Mary hear the prayers of 100 million Roman Catholics world-wide, listening to thousands of petitions made simultaneously in hundreds of different languages? In order for Mary to be able to do this she would have to posses the powers of deity; Mary would need to be omnipresent and omniscient. Rome cannot have her cake and eat it; if Mary is to be worshipped they must admit that she is God, if she is not God then she must not be worshipped. Notice also that when the wise men came to visit the Lord Jesus in His child-hood we are told that 'they saw the child with Mary his mother, and they fell down and worshiped him' (Matt. 2:11). If they had been Romanists they would have worshipped Mary; but they only worshipped Christ because He is God (Col. 2:9), Mary, on the other hand, was not to be worshipped because she is not God.

The idea that lower forms of worship should be ascribed to Mary and other saints is blatantly un-Scriptural; infallible apostles like Peter and Paul, even though they had seen the risen Christ, refused to receive worship from other men. When Peter went to the house of Cornelius we read that 'when Peter entered, Cornelius met him and fell down at his feet and worshipped him. But Peter lifted him up, saying "Stand up; I too am a man"' (Acts 10:25-26). Moreover, when Paul had healed a lame man at Lystra, the multitude made an attempt to worship him and Barnabas. However, we are told 'But when the apostles Barnabas and Paul heard of it, they tore their garments and rushed out into the crowd, crying out, "Men, why are you doing these things? We also are men, of like nature with you"' (Acts 14:14-15). Considering that the Biblical definition of a saint is one who is 'in Christ Jesus' (Phil. 1:12) then, according to Rome's logic, Christians would be justified in praying to one another. However, such a practice would be, to put it frankly, absolutely ridiculous as mere human beings can't answer prayer because they are not Almighty God. Loraine Boettner further explains how any form of saint worship violates the Scriptural law of worship:

> In Old Testament times the Jews prayed to God, but never to Abraham, or Jacob, or David, or to any of the prophets. There is never the slightest suggestion that prayers should be offered to anyone other than God. Nor did the apostles ever ask the early Christians to worship, or venerate, or pray to Mary or to any other human being. (*Roman Catholicism*, p. 187).

Yet if we accept the normative principle, that whatever God has not explicitly forbidden in worship is permitted, then we can justify saint worship on the basis that God has never told us not to pay a lower form of worship to them. Therefore, to accept such a broad principle is highly dangerous. Only the regulative principle can shut the door on such abominations entering the house of the Lord. Whatever God has not commanded is idolatry, saint worship is not commanded, therefore, saint worship is idolatry. As A.A. Hodge said 'If the Romanists be not idolaters, the sins forbidden in the First and Second Commandments have never been committed.' (*The Confession of Faith*, p. 274).

Worship through the Mediation of Christ Alone

In affirming that religious worship is to be given to God alone the *Westminster Confession* also maintains that 'since the fall' men cannot worship God 'without a Mediator; nor in the mediation of any other but Christ alone' (Chapter 21: Section 2). Prior to Adam's fall into sin, man had access to God at all times; but ever since we have only been able to worship God acceptably through the mediation of Jesus Christ. That is why He said 'I am the way, and the truth, and the life. No one comes to the Father except through me' (John 14:6). Consequently, the apostle Paul strongly affirmed 'there is one God, and there is one mediator between God and man, the man Christ Jesus' (1 Tim. 2:5). Geoffrey Wilson explained that Jesus 'is the one mediator who could bridge the infinite gulf which separated the holy God from sinful men. This unique function belongs to Christ in virtue of the fact that He alone is both God and man.' (*New Testament Commentaries*, vol. 2, pp 226-7). Because nobody else is fully human and fully divine, no-one else can mediate between God and man, so our worship can only be acceptable to God if it is offered through the mediation of Christ 'For through him we both have access in one Spirit to the Father' (Eph. 2:18). The supposed 'worship' of unbelievers cannot please the Lord because they have not been reconciled to God through Christ's work as mediator. Whereas, for believers, Christ has carried out every necessary function as mediator, both on earth and in heaven, so that we can have access to God through

Him alone. By His sacrificial death on the cross, Christ has purchased our redemption from sin so that we can worship God:

He entered once for all into the holy places, not by means of the blood of goats and calves but by means of his own blood, thus securing an eternal redemption. For if the sprinkling of defiled persons with the blood of goats and bulls and with the ashes of a heifer sanctifies for the purification of the flesh, how much more will the blood of Christ, who through the eternal Spirit offered himself without blemish to God, purify our conscience from dead works to serve the living God. (Heb. 9:12-14)

John Calvin rightly believed that we must be justified on account of Christ's merits (His blood) before our worship can be acceptable to the God of holiness:

Nothing can proceed from us that can be pleasing to God until we are purified by the blood of Christ; for as we are all enemies to God before our reconciliation, so he regards as abominable all our works; hence the beginning of acceptable service is reconciliation. And then, as no work is so pure and so free from stain, that it can of itself please God, it is necessary that the purgation through the blood of Christ should intervene, which can alone efface all stains. (*Commentary on Hebrews*, p. 205).

In heaven the Lord Jesus continues to intercede for His people by virtue of the atoning sacrifice that He has made for their sins. So the author of Hebrews tells us:

He holds his priesthood permanently, because he continues for ever. Consequently, he is able to save to the uttermost those who draw near to God through him, since he always lives to make intercession for them. (Heb. 7:24-25).

As John Owen comments 'It must be granted, that the virtue, efficacy, and prevalency of the inter-cession of the Lord Christ, depends upon and flows from his oblation and sacrifice.' (*An Exposition of the Epistle to the Hebrews*, vol. 5, p. 540). However, as part of her rebellion against the Head of the Church, Roman Catholicism teaches that angels, saints and especially the Virgin Mary are also mediators and intercessors between God and man. They claim that while Christ Jesus is the only mediator of redemption; angels and saints join him as being mediators of intercession. However, this notion has no Biblical support; Heb. 7:24-25 makes it obvious that Christ intercedes for His people on the basis of his accomplished work of redemption for them. Robert Shaw refutes this Popish blasphemy, saying that 'the Scripture...gives no warrant for these distinctions. It represents the intercession of Christ as founded upon the invaluable merit of his atoning sacrifice. He who is our Advocate with the Father is also the propitiation for our sins (1 John 2:1-2).' (*An Exposition of the Westminster Confession of Faith*, pp 266-7). Indeed, the suggestion that there could be other mediators and intercessors would seem to indicate that Christ's atoning work is somehow deficient and that we need the meritorious works of the saints to supply what is lacking in Christ's work. Such reasoning is nothing less than an insult to the Lord Jesus Christ; is He not a sufficient Saviour? Rome forgets that the saints who are in heaven are only there because the free grace of God, in Christ, so they have no merit to earn God's favour for themselves let alone to apply to others. In light of such blasphemous teaching the importance of the regulative principle is brought to the fore. Only this can offer resistance to the foolish man-made teachings and practices that are crippling the Church of Christ. If it is abandoned what will stop the Protestant Churches from following Rome to apostasy?

CHAPTER 6:

Image Worship: The Antithesis of the Regulative Principle

The clear teaching of the Bible, in both Old and New Testaments, is that the Lord detests all 'worshipping of God by images, or any other way not appointed in his Word' (*Westminster Shorter Catechism*, answer to question 51), this is summarised by the second commandment 'You shall not make for yourself a carved image, or any likeness of anything that is in heaven above, or that is in the earth beneath, or that is in the water under the earth' (Ex. 20:4). The *Westminster Confession* declares that God is 'not to be worshipped...under any visible representation' (Chapter 21: Section 1) because the word of God condemns the making of images for religious devotion as an extreme breach of the regulative principle of worship. In Jeremiah 10:14-15 the Lord condemns the making of idols in the strongest terms: 'Every man is stupid and without knowledge; every goldsmith is put to shame by his idols, for his images are false, and there is no breath in them. They are worthless, a work of delusion.' In reality, images are just man's idea of what he wants God to be like; they are a total misrepresentation of God as He is revealed in Scripture. For this reason Paul condemned the heathen, who did not possess the word of God, because they 'exchanged the glory of the immortal God for images resembling mortal man and birds and animals and reptiles' (Rom. 1:23). Thus the making of images breaks down the fundamental distinction between the creature and the Creator (Rom. 1:25); as no image can give a true representation of the invisible God who is Spirit (John 4:24). Thus J.G. Vos explains 'because God is a pure Spirit, without bodily form...any picture or representation which man can make can only give a false idea of the nature of God.' (*The Westminster Larger Catechism: A Commentary*, p. 291). Like all religious worship which he has not authorised, images only serve to give a false impression of God because they are the inventions of men's minds. For this reason Paul instructed the Athenian Philosophers 'we ought not to think that the divine being [God] is like gold or silver or stone, an image formed by the art and imagination of man' (Acts 17:29). Moreover, God tells us that images cannot truly represent Him because they are no greater than the people who made them 'To whom then will you liken God, or what likeness compare with him? An idol! A craftsman casts it, and a goldsmith overlays it with gold and casts for it silver chains.' (Isa. 40:18-

19). The Lord is incomparable with any image that man can make – so if we use images in worship, we don't worship God, rather we worship the works of men's hands. Thus we read in Psalm 115:4-8:

Their idols are silver and gold, the work of human hands, they have months, but do not speak; eyes, but do not see. They have ears, but do not hear; noses, but do not smell. They have hands, but do not feel; feet, but do not walk; and they do not make a sound in their throat. Those who make them become like them; so do all who trust in them.

Since images give us a false and un-Biblical impression of God it is not surprising that Paul exhorted the Corinthians to 'flee from idolatry' (1 Cor. 10:14). There can be no 'Christianising' of religious images in order to make them acceptable to God; as the early Covenanter minister James Durham explains 'images are only mentioned as made use of by heathens in all their worship (Lev. 26:1). The Lord will not have his people doing so to him (Deut. 12:3-5).' (*A Practical Exposition of the Ten Commandments*, p. 93).

Amazingly, in extreme rebellion against and apostasy from God's word, the Roman Catholic 'Church' justifies the use of religious images in worship. The infamous Council of Trent decreed that images of Christ, Mary and the saints 'are to be had and to be kept, especially in Churches, and due honour and veneration are to be given to them' (Session 25). In order to get around the charge of idolatry Rome tells us that they don't actually worship the images but they worship through the means of these icons. However, while this might seem like a clever answer (and to some extent it is) it is the same answer as that given by the Israelites when they worshipped the golden calf in the wilderness. When it was proclaimed - 'These are your gods, O Israel, who brought you up out of the land of Egypt!' (Ex. 32:4) it did not mean that they had thrown off the worship of the true God completely; because in the next verse we read 'When Aaron saw this, he built an altar before it. And Aaron made proclamation and said, "Tomorrow shall be a feast to the LORD" (v.5). So it would appear that the Israelites thought they were worshipping the true God by means of this image. The same also is true when Jeroboam placed the golden calves at Dan and Bethel (1 Kings 12:28-30). Due to the fact that he quotes Ex. 32:4 Jeroboam probably thought that Israel could worship God with the assistance of these calves rather than in God's appointed way. However, the second commandment makes no such distinction and therefore all religious images are idolatrous. The fact that images are not commanded would alone render them illegitimate, because the regulative principle does not allow us to use religious ceremonies that have never been appointed by God, how much more when they have been explicitly forbidden time after time again in Scripture.

Pictures of Christ

Sadly many modern Protestants have followed Roman Catholicism into thinking that it is legitimate to have pictures of the Lord Jesus Christ in Church or to use them in books for religious instruction. This is not however in line with the historic Reformed view of the subject. *The Westminster Larger Catechism* asks in question 109 'What are the sins forbidden in the second commandment?' to which the answer is given:

> The sins forbidden in the second commandment are...the making any representation of God, of all or of any of the three persons, either inwardly in our mind, or outwardly in any kind of image or likeness of any creature whatsoever.

Since the Lord Jesus Christ is the second person in the Holy Trinity (God the Son) the Catechism obviously condemns any pictures that men may presume to make of Him. At this point it might be argued that since Jesus was (and is) a man then it is alright to have pictures of Him as long as they are only of His human nature. However, those who use this type of argument forget that while Christ became a man, he never for one moment ceased to be 'the eternally blessed God' (Rom. 9:5; see also Phil. 2:6-8). Therefore since He is 'our great God and Savour Jesus Christ' (Titus 2:13), and it is wrong to make pictures and carved images of God, then it must be a sin to make a picture of Jesus Christ who is God the Son. Moreover, if pictures of Christ can be justified then we must also allow for images of God the Father because Jesus said 'whoever sees me sees him who sent me' (John 12:45), so if we are permitted to make pictures of Christ on the basis that He was seen in the flesh, then why not the other persons of the Trinity since they are all of one essence? The fact that the Lord once walked the earth as a man can provide no justification for the use of pictures of Him. Remember that Paul said 'Even though we once regarded Christ according to the flesh, we regard him thus no longer;' (2 Cor. 5:16) what the apostle is saying here is, that while they once knew Christ in person while He was in His humiliation, we are no longer to think of him as being in a state of humiliation (which pictures of Christ inevitably do) but as being exalted at God's right hand (Heb. 1:3-4). Moreover, when Paul told the Galatians 'It was before your eyes that Jesus Christ was publicly portrayed as crucified' (Gal. 3:1) was he saying to them that he presented them with a crucifix or some other picture of Christ while he was being crucified? Certainly not, what he means is that Christ was preached to them as crucified through the proclamation of the gospel (1 Cor. 1:18-24). It is interesting that even the apostles, who knew exactly what Christ looked like, did not leave us with any pictures of the Master or ever sanctioned any to be used. Obviously they realised that, as God, the Lord Jesus could not be worshipped with images. So if the apostles, who knew about Christ's physical appearance, didn't make any pictures of him; how much less ought we, who don't even know what He looked like, to make or devise pictures of Christ. As no picture was taken of the Lord during His earthly ministry it is simply untrue to point to a drawing and claim that this is a genuine picture of what the Lord Jesus looked like. Furthermore, if it was, you would be perfectly justified in worshipping it because Christ received worship while on earth (Matt. 2:2). However, since you can't, with any certainty, know that it is a true picture of the Son of God, then to worship it would be idolatry. So if you can't worship it in case it's not a true portrayal of Christ how then can you claim that a picture of Jesus is a true representation of Him. Moreover, the falsehood of such pictures is further exposed by the fact that they reflect the theological bias of the artist. Pictures drawn by liberals, mystics and feminists are hardly going to give us a true impression of the Biblical Christ. For example, the reason liberals want us to focus on Christ's humanity is because they deny His deity. Furthermore, it should be remembered that the Bible has little to say about Christ's physical appearance; all we are told is that 'he had no form or majesty that we should look at him, and no beauty that we should desire him?' (Isa. 53:2) What right then has any artist to go beyond this?

Some Evangelicals would argue that they don't use pictures of the Lord for worship but as a useful means of instruction especially for children. However, such a distinction is erroneous because if they are true pictures of Jesus they should be worshipped. Moreover, God has told us to abstain from such idolatry because if we don't he will visit 'the iniquity of the fathers on the children to the third and the fourth generation of those who hate me' (Ex. 20:5). As G.I. Williamson insightfully remarks:

> It is to be noted that God mentions children as one of the important reasons for not using such pictures. The reason for this is evident: we all tend to accept as true and right whatever we learn from our parents and teachers…Pictures of Jesus first came in through the pages of the Sunday school materials. Little by little the children became accustomed to them. They grew up feeling that these pictures of Jesus were good. Now, these same people – in adult life – are bringing these pictures into worship services. (*The Westminster Shorter Catechism: For Study Classes*, pp 213-4).

Inevitably, one thing leads to another; pictures of Christ are first used in Sabbath School, that generation grows up and introduces them into public worship. Also, to say that we 'need' pictures of the Lord for the purposes of instruction is to deny the sufficiency of Scripture. Paul said 'All Scripture is breathed out by God and profitable for teaching' (2 Tim. 3:16) therefore the Bible should be able to tell us all we need to know about the Lord Jesus Christ. Keep in mind that Paul reminds Timothy 'that from child-hood you have known the Holy Scriptures, which are able to make you wise for salvation through faith which is in Christ Jesus' (2 Tim. 3:15 NKJV). If the

Scriptures were enough to make Timothy wise unto God's salvation, and remember that he only had the Old Testament writings, then how much more should a complete Bible suffice for today's youngsters? If we want to know more about Christ then we should do as Jesus said 'search the Scriptures...it is they that bear witness about me' (John 5:39). Also, when we make pictures of our Saviour we dishonour the Holy Spirit who enables us to understand the word of God (John 15:26; 16:14). Pictures of Christ cannot help us grow in our faith or love to Christ because they are lies; whereas the Lord prayed that the Father would 'Sanctify them [His people] in the truth; your word is truth' (John 17:17) and, like all human inventions which breach the regulative principle, they have 'an appearance of wisdom in promoting self-made religion...but they are of no value in stopping the indulgence of the flesh' (Col. 2:23).

CHAPTER 7:

Biblical Prayer

Though some professing Christians, both of an Arminian and Hyper-Calvinist persuasion, would question why we, as Reformed believers, emphasise the necessity of prayer, since we believe that God is the Sovereign Lord 'who works all things according to the counsel of his will' (Eph. 1:11). They would claim that if God has predestined whatever comes to pass, then what need is there for Christians to pray? However, this is to misrepresent Calvinistic doctrine as some form of fatalism more in line with the Islamic religion than Biblical Christianity. As true Calvinists we believe that God is 100% Sovereign while man is 100% responsible; prayer is the divinely appointed means by which we, as creatures, acknowledge that we are dependent on God and through which we express to Him our wants and desires. This is what the Lord taught about prayer in the Sermon on the Mount, when He said:

**Ask, and it will be given to you; seek, and
you will find; knock, and it will be opened
to you. For everyone who asks receives,
and the one who seeks finds, and to the one
who knocks it will be opened. Which one
of you, if his son asks him for bread, will
give him a serpent? If you then, who are
evil, know how to give good gifts to your
children, how much more will your Father
who is in heaven give good things to those
who ask him!** (Matt. 7:7-11).

We pray because the Lord has told us in His word
that we are to do it, regardless of what objections
Arminian and Hyper-Calvinist logic might present
in opposition to the Biblical command. Remember
that Scripture alone is our guide in matters of faith
and worship, not fallen man's reason which cannot
reconcile the doctrines of divine sovereignty and
human responsibility. Such people, to paraphrase
C.H. Spurgeon, need to realise that because these
two teachings are clearly taught in God's word there
is no need to reconcile such good friends.

Prayer as a part of worship

The *Westminster Confession* recognises prayer as
an element of God's worship:

Prayer, with thanksgiving, being one special
part of religious worship, is by God required
of all men: and that it may be accepted, it is to

> be made in the name of the Son, by the help of His Spirit, according to His will, with understanding, reverence, humility, fervenancy, faith, love and perseverance, and, if vocal, in a known tongue (Chapter 21: Section 3)
>
> Prayer is to be made for all things lawful, and for all sorts of men living, or that shall live hereafter: but not for the dead, nor for those of whom it may be known that they have sinned the sin unto death. (Chapter 21: Section 4).

Prayer is to be made in the public worship of God's people (1 Tim. 2:1-2), fellowship meetings (Acts 16:13), family worship (Jer. 10:25 NKJV) and in our secret devotions (Matt. 6:6). Our prayers may include adoration of God (Acts 4:24), confession of sin (1 John 1:9), supplication, intercession and thanksgiving for God's mercies (Phil. 4:6). The last point is especially important because if prayer is the means by which we ask God for His blessing upon us (James 1:5; 4:3) then it is right and proper that we return thanks to God when we receive these blessings. So when the lord instructed us to ask God for our daily bread (Matt. 6:11) it is noteworthy that he also intended us to give thanks for it when we receive it (Mark 6:41).

As no man is independent of God ('in him we live and move and have our being' Acts 17:28), and prayer is recognition of our dependence upon God, then it must follow that prayer is required of all men. The fact that the unregenerate are unable to pray rightly does not excuse them from this duty; surely part of the guilt of the ungodly is that they do not acknowledge God's goodness to them in common grace (Matt. 5:45). Some though, would argue that unbelievers aren't to pray because they cannot pray acceptably. While it is true that only the prayer of faith will be accepted by the Lord, Robert Shaw proves that this can't release unbelievers from this duty:

(1) Prayer is a duty required by the mere light of nature, and, must therefore, be incumbent on all men (Jonah 1:5, 6, 14).

(2) Prayer is a duty enjoined upon men indiscriminately, and universally in the Word of God (Psalm 65:2; Phil. 4:6; 1 Thess. 5:17).

(3) If unbelievers, or unregenerate men ought not to pray, then their omission of prayer is always represented in Scripture as highly criminal (Psalm 10:4; Jer. 10:25).

(4) The Apostle Peter required Simon Magus to pray unto God, though he was then "in the gall of bitterness, and in the bond of iniquity" (Acts 8:22-23 AV).

(5) Prayer is an appointed means of grace which all men ought to improve. Though it is not for our praying, yet it is in the way of prayer, as God's instituted order, that we may expect any blessing (Matt.

7:7). Everyone that needs and desires any good thing from God is, therefore, bound ask it by prayer.

(6) Though the prayer as well as the ploughing of the wicked be sinful, because not done by them in a right manner, yet the matter of it being lawful and good in itself, their neglect of it is a greater abomination (Prov. 15:8; 21:4). For these reasons we must maintain, agreeably to our Confession that "prayer is by God required of all men." (*An Exposition of the Westminster Confession of Faith*, p. 269).

Nonetheless the prayers of the wicked are still rejected because they are not made 'in the name of the Son.' When the Confession says that we are to pray in the name of Christ, it does not mean that we have to end every prayer with the words 'in Jesus' name, Amen', as this would not be beyond the ability of an unregenerate person. However, what it does mean is, that when we come to God the Father, we are to come before Him in absolute dependence upon the work of Jesus Christ. G.I. Williamson explained 'It means that we come to Him consciously on the basis of what Christ has done for us.' (*The Westminster Shorter Catechism: For Study Classes*, p. 313). That is why Jesus said 'Whatever you ask in my name, this I will do, that the Father may be glorified in the Son. If you ask me for anything in my name, I will do it' (John 14:13-14). As William Hendriksen commented 'His name is his self-revelation in his works; here particularly, his self-revelation in the sphere of redemption.' (*An Exposition of the Gospel According to John*, p. 274). Because Christ has accomplished His work of redemption we can 'draw near to the throne of grace, that we may receive mercy and find grace to help in time of need' (Heb. 4:16). This is why we cannot join in ecumenical prayer or multi-faith services, because in such gatherings, prayer is not made in dependence on Christ's mediation; hence these prayers are an abomination in God's sight.

When we come to the Lord in prayer, God is not interested in hearing eloquent words or an endless list of theological terms, but He is interested in hearing the lawful desires of our hearts. That is why Jesus told us 'when you pray, do not heap up empty phrases as the Gentiles do, for they think that they will be heard for their many words' (Matt. 6:7). As every experienced Christian knows, prayer is not easy, it takes hard concentrated effort and many believers feel discouraged because the words don't flow out of their mouths. When we want to pour out our hearts to God, we find ourselves stuttering along barely able to string two words together. However, this is exactly how the Bible itself represents prayer and explains to us why we need the help of God's Spirit 'the Spirit helps us in our weakness. For we do not know what to pray for as we ought, but the Spirit himself intercedes for us with groanings too deep for words' (Rom. 8:26). Though in the Garden of Eden prayer was easy for Adam because talking with God was the desire of his sinless heart, but this has not been the case since the fall, even for sinners who have been born again. Due to the effects of the fall and indwelling sin, which is at war with their desires for spiritual things, a Christian's 'spirit indeed is willing, but the flesh is weak' (Matt. 26:41). Therefore, the words of a popular uninspired hymn, must be rejected as contrary to the Scriptural teaching on the nature of prayer and the experience of every prudent Christian:

> Sweet hour of prayer, sweet hour of prayer,
> The joys I feel, the bliss I share
> Of those whose anxious spirits burn,
> With strong desires for thy return
> With such I hasten to the place,
> Where God my saviour, shows his face,
> And gladly, take my station there,
> And wait for thee, sweet how of prayer

Doubtless many Christians have sung this and wondered why their experience has not been the same. However, the New Testament provides us with a much more realistic assessment of the believer's experience in prayer. For example, Christ's disciples were unable to stay awake and pray with their Master for an hour (Matt. 26:36-46). Clearly they didn't have a 'sweet hour of prayer' in Gethsemane. This illustrates the danger of uninspired hymns giving sincere Christians a completely false view of the Christian life; many believers wouldn't have such unrealistic expectations if they were to sing the Psalms in worship. Hence we see that human compositions, like all man-made inventions in worship, are 'of no value in stopping the indulgence of the flesh' (Col. 2:23). They can't help us to grow in grace because they are not the means of truth through which we are sanctified (John 17:17).

If we are to pray according to God's will ('this is the confidence that we have towards him, that if we ask anything according to his will he hears us' 1 John 5:14) then our desires in prayer must not be for anything contrary to God's word, that would be to ask God for something sinful, which is an abomination in the sight of Him who is 'of purer eyes than to behold evil, and cannot look on wickedness' (Hab. 1:13). So it is only for things lawful that we are to 'let your requests be made known to God' (Phil. 4:6). However, even when praying for things that are lawful, but not promised to us in the word, we must be prepared to submit to God's providence (as it is His Sovereign choice as to whether or not He grants our desires) in waiting to see if our requests will be granted to us. In such circumstances we must follow our Lord's example and say 'not my will, but yours, be done' (Luke 22:42). Moreover, if our prayer is according to God's will, then it should put the glory of the Lord and the advance of His Kingdom at the top of its priorities. This is why the Lord's Prayer begins with God's interests and not our needs 'hallowed be your name. Your kingdom come, your will be done, on earth as it is in heaven' (Matt. 6:9-10). Our prayers, on the other hand, can tend to be a selfish list of demands, with little concern for the glory of God, His Church's welfare or the advance of

His Kingdom. Serving to further highlight the difficulty of true prayer; it is just so contrary to sinful human nature.

Furthermore if our prayers are to be offered to God in a correct manner there are certain things that they are to be made with (understanding, reverence, humility, fervency, faith, love, and perseverance). Robert Shaw helpfully explains these in greater detail:

(1) With understanding (Psalm 47:7); with some knowledge of God, the above object of prayer; of wants, the subject-matter of prayer; of the person and work of Christ, the alone medium of acceptable prayer; and of the promises, which we are our encouragement in prayer.

(2) With reverence (Heb. 12:28), arising from a deep sense of the infinite majesty and unspotted holiness of God.

(3) With humility (Gen. 18:27), arising from a deep impression of our own unworthiness and sinfulness.

(4) With fervency (James 5:16), arising from a lively apprehension of our own wants, and of the invaluable nature of the blessings which we ask of God.

(5) With faith (James 1:6), believing that we shall receive what we ask according to the will of God.

(6) With love (1 Tim. 2:8), cherishing an ardent desire after God's presence with us, and an affectionate regard to all those for whom we ought to pray.

(7) With importunity and perseverance (Matt. 15:22-28; Eph. 6:18), pressing our suit [case], and renewing our petition again and again until a gracious answer, is obtained.

(8) Hopefully, looking upon God, with submission to His will, and looking for an answer to our supplications (Psalm 5:3; Micah 7:7). (*An Exposition of the Westminster Confession of Faith*, p. pp 270-1).

The Confession teaches when prayer is vocal (when two or more persons are present) it is to be said in a 'known tongue'. This condemns the Romish practice of saying prayers in Latin or that of modern Charismatics of ecstatically uttering unintelligible words in prayer. The reason for this is obvious; if someone prays in French, while everyone else can only speak English, then how can that person's prayer profit the listeners when they can't understand it? As Paul told the Corinthians 'you may be giving thanks well enough, but the other person is not being built up' (1 Cor. 14:17). The apostle had no time for show-offs; he said that he 'would rather speak five words with my mind in order to instruct others, then ten thousand words in a tongue' (1 Cor. 14:19). Someone praying in an unknown language would only cause confusion (1 Cor. 14:33), and if any unbelievers were present Paul warns us that they would think 'you are out of your minds' (1 Cor. 14:23).

When praying for others, in prayers of intercession, we are permitted to pray for all types, races and social classes that exist among mankind, and especially for civil magistrates (1 Tim. 2:1-2). We may even pray for generations to come as to the Lord did in His High Priestly Prayer (John 17:20-21). However, we may not pray for the dead as this has no basis in Scripture. The Church of Rome encourages such practices because of its doctrine of purgatory, the place where most of its adherents supposedly go after death until they are fit for heaven. Rome believes that the dead in purgatory can be helped by 'Christians' on earth praying on their behalf. However, the Bible teaches that there are only two states beyond death – heaven and hell (Luke 16:25-26) with no mention of anywhere in between. As A.A. Hodge pointed out 'if there is no purgatory…there can be no prayers for the dead, since those in heaven need no intercession, and for those in hell none can avail.' (*The Confession of Faith*, p. 278). We are also forbidden from praying for those who have 'sinned the sin unto death.' This is because the apostle John said 'There is a sin that leads to death; I do not say that one should pray for that' (1 John 5:16). This probably refers to the type of person who professes to be a Christian but then apostatises and becomes an open enemy of the gospel; for believers to pray for such people is pointless 'since they crucify again for themselves the Son of God and put *Him* to an open shame' (Heb. 6:6 NKJV). If someone falls away to such an extent it is impossible 'to renew them again to repentance' (Heb. 6:6 NKJV). They can't be saved, so don't waste your prayers on them.

Biblical Prayer: Section II

The *Westminster Confession* tells us that 'Prayer, with thanksgiving' is 'one special part of religious worship' (Chapter 21: Section 3). It will be useful, at this stage, to determine whether or not the Church should be required to use a liturgical prayer book (such as the *Book of Common Prayer*) and nothing else in public worship, as is the practice in Episcopalian (Anglican) Churches.

Liturgies: Are they Biblical?

Even though they reject the regulative principle of worship, Episcopalians would argue that the Bible gives warrant to the Church to impose a book of set prayers upon its ministers. This means that their ministers are only allowed to read the prayers in the prayer book, and all extemporary (made up) prayers are forbidden in public worship. Anglicans claim that because Christ gave the Church the Lord's Prayer (Matt. 6:9-13) therefore, the Church must only use set forms of prayer and these are to be uniformly imposed on the ministers without variation. However, there are serious problems with such an argument. Although orthodox Presbyterians believe that it is permissible to say the Lord's Prayer (some radical Puritans like the Separatists did not) they believe that it provides no warrant for the imposition of a man-made liturgy. Firstly, Jesus did not restrict his followers to only use the words of the Lord's Prayer, because He said 'Pray then like this' (Matt. 6:9) meaning that, if anything, the Lord's Prayer was primarily intended to be a pattern to direct us in prayer. Moreover, the account of the Lord's Prayer in Luke 11:2-4 differs slightly from that in Matthew's gospel, so it would appear that Christ was not confining us to using only a precise form of words. Also, it is somewhat presumptuous to argue that because the Lord Jesus Christ gave us the Lord's Prayer that this somehow justifies Episcopalian Bishops imposing a prayer book which we can never diverge from. There is a fundamental difference between something like the Lord's Prayer and a humanly devised prayer book; namely, the fact that the prayers recorded in Scripture were divinely inspired (2 Tim. 3:16; 2 Pet. 1:21) the same cannot be said of a prayer-book produced by an Anglican hierarchy. If you are going to say that because there are set prayers recorded in the Bible, that this automatically excludes all extemporary prayers, then you should only use the prayers of Scripture without any human additions. As we will later see such a position is untenable.

The Biblical passage which is most fatal to the Episcopalian position is 1 Tim. 2:1-2:

First of all, then, I urge that supplications, prayers, intercessions, and thanksgivings be made for all people, for kings and all who are in high positions, that we may lead a peaceful and quiet life, godly and dignified in every way.

Here Paul gives Timothy directions about what he should be praying for in public worship. When one considers that this was written around AD64, and that the New Testament Church had been established more than 30 years previous, why would the apostle be giving Timothy (a minister) advice about what to pray for if the Church was using a uniform liturgy? Such directions would be irrelevant as Timothy would be reading from a prayer book. The only conclusion one can draw is that no book of common prayer had been imposed by the apostles on the Church. Therefore, the Episcopalian practice is un-Biblical; since, in order for something to be a regulative principle, it must have either a specific command, or be logically deduced from Scripture, or have a valid historical Biblical example. As John Owen argued the imposition of set forms of prayers 'is not warranted by the Scripture, nor is it of apostolic example.' (Cited in H. Davies, *The Worship of the English Puritans*, p. 102). In his work *A Discourse Concerning Liturgies and their Imposition*, Dr. Owen further goes on to condemn the practice of imposing set forms of prayer as a violation of the regulative principle:

Neither did the apostles of our Lord Jesus Christ use any liturgies…nor did they prescribe or command any such to the churches, or their officers that were planted in them…truly they must have a great confidence in their own wisdom and sufficiency, who will undertake to appoint, and impose on others, the observation of things in the worship of God which neither our Lord Jesus nor his apostles did appoint or impose. (Works: 15, p. 17).

However, this passage also serves to correct the excesses of the Separatist and some Independent Puritans who argued that all written prayers were automatically wrong. If Paul is writing to instruct Timothy as to what to pray for in Public worship, then it is obvious that public prayer requires forethought; therefore it cannot be wrong for a minister to write out what he is going to pray for beforehand. This explains why John Calvin and John Knox were happy enough to use written prayers as a guide to help them in public prayer, and why the *Directory for the Public Worship of God* (produced by the Westminster Divines) contains written out prayers that ministers could use to assist them in leading their congregations in prayer. These, however, were not exhaustive, as the minister was free to make up his own prayers as he wished, but were useful guides in orderly worship (1 Cor. 14:40). As the proponents of orthodox Presbyterian and Reformed worship we do not condemn written prayer per se, but only the imposition of a common prayer book which the minister can never diverge from. Furthermore, if prayer in public worship is to be orderly and thought out as Ecclesiastes 5:2 also teaches 'be not rash with your mouth, nor let your heart be hasty to utter a word before God, for God is in heaven and you are on earth. Therefore let your words be few'; then only a preacher should lead a congregation in prayer. The practice which is common in the Scottish Highlands, of calling on a male member of the congregation at random to lead in prayer after the singing of a psalm or a sermon does not give him sufficient time to prepare. Often at this type of meeting it is not uncommon to hear perhaps four men pray, and yet not actually ask for anything in their prayers. Such a practice is most unedifying, as men who do not have the gifts or the wisdom to speak in public should not be forced to lead a congregation in prayer, and certainly not without any time to consider what they are going to say. This is one reason why it is wise to arrange private fellowship meetings for prayer and mutual edification, so that male and female members can pray for and with each other. It is much better in congregational public worship that the minister leads in prayer so that proper order can be upheld (and remember that Paul's directive in 1 Tim 2:1-2 was only given to ministers). As Matthew Henry said:

> It is requisite to the decent performance of the duty that some proper method be observed, not only that which is said be good, but that it be said in its proper place and time; and that we offer not any thing to the Glorious

Majesty of Heaven and Earth, which is confused, impertinent, and indigested. (Cited in H. Davies, *The Worship of the English Puritans*, p. 114).

Furthermore, in public worship, the posture for prayer should always be that of standing (Mark 11:25) except at the Lord's Table (Mark 14:17).

Another argument against the imposition of a liturgy is that if the minister is rigidly tied to the words of a prayer book then there is no room for the work of the Holy Spirit to intercede in prayer. Paul said:

The Spirit helps us in our weakness. For we do not know what to pray for as we ought, but the Spirit himself intercedes for us with groanings too deep for words. And he who searches hearts knows what is the mind of the Spirit, because the Spirit intercedes for the saints according to the will of God. (Romans 8:26-27)

While this provides no justification for the unintelligent or ill-thought out prayer common among Charismatics, nevertheless, Paul recognises that mere sinners need the Spirit's assistance to pray properly. Yet how can there be any place for the Spirit's intercession if we can only ever use the exact words of a liturgical prayer book? Charles Hodge explains that the Holy Spirit does 'what it was the special duty of the advocate to perform, i.e. to dictate to his clients what they ought to say, how they should present their case.' (*A Commentary on Romans*, pp 278-9). But if we are tied strictly to the words of a prescribed liturgy the Spirit's work of intercession is deemed redundant, as the liturgy should give us all the help we need. However, such a conclusion is clearly inconsistent with Paul's teaching.

Moreover, the idea of restricting ministers to use the words of a set prayer book fails to take into account the varying needs of believers in different congregations and in different circumstances. Isaac Watts accurately recognised the severe limitations of the *Book of Common Prayer* when he wrote:

> For it is not possible that forms of prayer should be composed, that one perfectly suited to all our occasions in the things of this life and the life to come. Our circumstances are always altering in this frail and unstable state. We have new sins to be confessed, new temptations and sorrows to be represented, new wants to be supplied. Every change of providence in the affairs of a nation, a family, or a person, requires suitable petitions and acknowledgements. And all these can never be well provided for in any prescribed compo-sition. (Cited in H. Davies, *The Worship of the English Puritans*, p. 105).

The apostle Paul teaches us that, in our various circumstances, we are 'by prayer and supplication with thanksgiving let your requests be made known to God' (Phil. 4:6); as John Owen remarks 'how this duty can be attended unto in the observance of a prescribed form of liturgy, from whence it is not lawful to digress, is beyond my understanding to apprehend.' (*A Discourse Concerning Liturgies and their Imposition*, Works: 15, p. 54). In theory, liturgical prayer does not demand that the minister be acquainted with the members of the congregation to know their spiritual and temporal needs. Because, if he is only allowed to recite prayers from a book, then he can't pray for a particular individual's concerns which are not mentioned in the liturgy. This could attract idle and ungodly men to the ministry because they would be aware of the fact that they wouldn't have to work at getting to know the people so as to pray for them in an intelligent and thought out way. Also the divisions that an imposed common prayer book led to in the English Church of the 17th century should warn us that, like all human inventions, liturgies are a source of strife, and that the allowance of extemporary prayer, which ministers themselves compose, is the best way to safeguard the unity of the Church as this is in full conformity with the regulative principle of worship. 'Let us therefore, follow after the things which make for peace' (Rom. 14:19).

CHAPTER 8:

Reading, Preaching and Hearing the Word

Reading the Word of God

   Christians in the Reformed faith ought to have a high view of Scripture; as Robert Reymond says, we believe that 'the Bible in its entirety is the inspired, inerrant Word of living God, made the possession of the Church through divinely governed revelatory and inspirational processes, and thus it is the sole propositional expression of the will of God for his church.' (*A New Systematic Theology of the Christian Faith*, p. 915). We believe that the sixty-six books which make up our Bible are God's special revelation and revealed will which, by the power of the Holy Spirit, is able to make sinners 'wise for salvation through faith in Christ Jesus' (2 Tim. 3:15) and is to believers 'the pure milk of the word' to be digested so that they 'may grow thereby' (1 Pet.

2:2 NKJV). So it is hardly surprising to find that the *Westminster Confession* regards 'the reading of the Scriptures with godly fear' (Chapter 21: Section 6) as a part of religious worship.

The reading of the Word of God should be considered an important part of public worship (Neh. 8:8; Luke 4:16) and should also be central to family worship (Deut. 6:6-9; Psalm 78:5) as well as part of our secret devotions (Psalm 1). Sadly the reading of Scripture is not viewed by many as an important part of our worship, especially that which takes place in the public assembly. This was not the attitude of the apostle Paul wrote to Timothy and exhorted him 'devote yourself to the public reading of Scripture, to exhortation, to teaching' (1 Tim. 4:13) a practice which carried over from the worship of the synagogue (Acts 15:21; 2 Cor. 3:14), into the New Testament congregation. It was common in the synagogue for the preacher to expound the passage that he had previously read; for example, Jesus did this at the synagogue in Nazareth after he read Isa. 61:1-2 (see Luke 4:16-22). However, I think Paul had more than this in mind. He tells us in Col. 4:16 that his epistles were read in the churches, presumably as part of their public worship, 'And when this letter has been read among you, have it also read in the church of the Laodiceans; and see that you also read the letter from Laodicea.' It would be a good practice for ministers to begin systematically reading through books of the Bible in worship services. For example on a Sabbath morning he could read a chapter of Ephesians each week, and in the evenings read a chapter of Hosea. This would encourage the congregation to take the public reading of God's word more seriously and perhaps provoke them read consecutively through books of the Bible in their own private and family devotions. Too many Christians just read their favourite portions of the Bible repeatedly, while missing out on the blessing of becoming acquainted with 'the whole counsel of God' (Acts 20:27) which is 'the word of his grace, which is able to build you up and to give you the inheritance among all those who are sanctified' (Acts 20:32).

As Paul was writing to Timothy, a fellow minister, when he was encouraging the public reading of the word; it would seem to be a reasonable deduction that only the minister is to read in a public assembly. The *Westminster Larger Catechism* asks:

Q.156 Is the word of God to be read by all? Although all are not to be permitted to read the word publicly to the congregation, yet all sorts of people are bound to read it apart by themselves, and with their families: to which end the Holy Scriptures are to be translated out of the original into vulgar languages.

For the sake of good order only a minister may read in the public assembly. The practice in some churches of the entire congregation reading aloud in a service seems to be devoid of Scriptural warrant. Moreover, since it is unlikely that everyone in a congregation would use the same translation; public readings of this nature would sound confused and very unedifying.

As the Scriptures are God's revealed will telling us what we are to believe about the Lord and what duties He requires of us; it is the duty of all people, both Christian and non-Christian, to read the Bible every day (John 5:39; Acts 17:11). Unconverted people should read the Bible as a means of grace, showing them the way of eternal life through Jesus Christ; 'The law of the LORD is perfect, converting the soul; the testimony of the LORD is sure, making wise the simple' (Psalm 19:7 NKJV). Believers should search the Scriptures with a desire to know more about their Saviour (Luke 24:44) and to instruct them about how to live their lives to God's glory 'How can a young man keep his way pure? By guarding it according to your word' (Psalm 119:9). For this reason, the Bible is to be translated out of the original Hebrew and Greek into the 'vulgar [common] language' of the people in every nation in the earth. Although translations are not inspired, they are warranted in Scripture by the fact that the apostles used the Greek Septuagint [LXX] translation which was far from perfect, yet as far as it reflected the original autographs of the Old Testament, it was still the word of God. Presbyterians, who adhere to the Westminster Standards, are bound to use modern translation (such as the ESV, NKJV, NASB and NIV) in their worship services, as these have been written in up-to-date English, which is the ordinary language of the people in our society. Whatever the advantages of older translations (such as the AV, RV, and ASV) their archaic English means that they are unsuitable for public worship, and to continue to use them serves to erect an unnecessary barrier to the gospel being received in our culture (1 Cor. 9:22-23). Moreover, if we were to adopt the position of some Roman Catholics, that the Bible should be kept in some sort of 'holy' language (such as Latin), would make it impossible for the Church to fulfil the Great Commission of teaching all nations the word of God (Matt. 28:18-20). For these reasons the *Westminster Confession* is right to insist upon translations in 'the vulgar language of every nation unto which they come' (Chapter 1: Section 8).

Having established that the reading of God's word is a part of religious worship, it may be useful at this stage to consider in what manner we are to read 'the oracles of God' (Rom. 3:2). The *Westminster Larger Catechism* asks:

> Q.157 How is the word of God to be read?
> The Holy Scriptures are to be read with a high and reverent esteem of them; with a firm persuasion that they are the very word of God, and that he only can enable us to understand them; with desire to know believe, and obey the will of God revealed in them; with diligence, and attention to the matter and scope of them; with mediation, application, self-denial and prayer.

To have a high esteem of Scripture means, that we regard it as infallible and inerrant, as a result of it being 'breathed out by God' (2 Tim. 3:16). As the Bible is the only book which can claim to be God's inspired word we, in consequence, should value it more highly than the writings of mere men and should judge what all other books say in the light of Scripture (Acts 17:11). The psalmist David esteemed the words of the Lord so highly that he said 'More to be desired are they than gold, even much fine gold' (Psalm 19:10). Could we say the same? Or are we more interested in making money than in setting aside a sufficient amount of time to know and understand the word of the Lord?

God tells us that the one who 'is humble and contrite in spirit' is the person who 'trembles at my word' (Isa. 66:2). A Christian should take the word of the Lord extremely seriously as it reveals the mind of God to him. This means that if we treat the Scriptures with reverence we will not use it as a spiritual joke book; the practice, so common among professing Christians, of referring to things in the Bible in a light and frivolous manner is certainly not trembling at God's word. Moreover, to read the word of God with reverence surely means that we give it our full attention when we read it, and don't allow our minds to wander off unto other subjects.

Being firmly persuaded that the Holy Scriptures are 'the very words of God' (Rom. 3:2 NIV), we should also recognise that only the Lord, who gave us the word, can enable us to understand its teachings. Paul tells us that 'the natural person does not accept the things of the Spirit of God, for they are folly to him, and he is not able to understand them because they are spiritually discerned' (1 Cor. 2:14). So men cannot understand the teaching of the Bible, which the Holy Spirit wrote (2 Pet. 1:21), unless the Spirit illuminates their minds to receive the truth (John 16:13). As J.G. Vos wrote in his commentary on the *Westminster Larger Catechism*:

> Only by the regenerating and illuminating work of the Holy Spirit can this natural sinful darkness of the human mind be taken away, so that a person becomes spiritually discerning and receptive of the truth. While regeneration is an act which is complete in an instant of time, the Spirit's work of illuminating the mind's of God's people is a gradual process which must always seek the illumination of the Holy Spirit to understand the Scriptures. (pp 442-4).

When studying the Bible for ourselves, our motives for doing so should primarily be practical. We should have a desire to know, believe, and obey the will of God revealed in them.' A Christian should read the Bible so that he 'may learn to fear the LORD his God by keeping all the words of the law and these statutes, and doing them, that his heart may not be lifted up above his brothers, and that he may not turn aside from the commandment, either to the right hand or to the left' (Deut. 17:19-20). Some people profanely read the Scriptures as if they were merely a piece of literature like Shakespeare, others just to fill their heads with historical facts. Even worse, others study the word of God to satisfy their curiosity or to fuel their desire for theological controversy and so that they can argue better for their doctrinal hobby-horses. This is not what God gave us His word for; the Bible exists so that the way of salvation through the Lord Jesus Christ (John 5:39) and how they may live their lives to the glory of God (1 Cor. 10:31).

When the Catechism instructs us to read the Bible 'with diligence' it reminds us that the study of the word of God is by no means an easy task. Reading the Bible for five minutes a day will clearly not suffice. Too often Christians quickly skim over a number of chapters to appease their conscience then shut the Bible having completely forgotten what they have read about. With such an inadequate amount of time and effort spent on the word, is it any wonder most of us grow so little in grace and holiness? The Bereans, on the other hand, were commended because 'they received the word with all eagerness, examining the Scriptures daily' (Acts 17:11) if the same cannot be said of us there is something seriously wrong. Would you expect to receive a good degree in any subject without putting in any conscious effort? No of course you wouldn't! Yet many Christians think they can grow spiritually without putting in any serious intellectual effort into the study of God's word. For this reason they remain spiritual babies when they 'ought to be teachers'; consequently, they 'need milk, not solid food' (Heb. 5:12). The writer of Hebrews recognises the source of their spiritual immaturity 'everyone who lives on milk is unskilled in the word of righteousness, since he is a child'

(Heb. 5:13). John Owen says this verse describes the sort of person 'who, having some general knowledge of it [the Scriptures], is not able wisely to manage and improve it unto its proper end.' (*An Exposition of the Epistle to the Hebrews*, vol. 4, p. 586). Too many of us have only a very general knowledge of the Bible; and due to our lack of effort we are unable to increase that knowledge and to apply it wisely to our own lives. Rather than moaning because we find Scriptural truth 'too deep' for us we should cry to the Lord 'Open my eyes, that I may behold wondrous things out of your law' (Psalm 119:18). Moreover, with so many good commentaries, Bible Dictionaries and other resources available, we have plenty of tools at our disposal to help us study every portion of the Scriptures in its proper context and setting. We have absolutely no excuse for our ignorance; in this day and age every mature Christian should be an accomplished Biblical theologian.

Indispensable to the reading of God's word is proper meditation upon its contents. To meditate on the word of God means that we seriously think about what it is teaching and how it applies to our lives as individuals. Merely skimming over the surface of a passage of the Bible will not suffice. David described the 'Blessed' man as one whose 'delight is in the law of the LORD, and on his law he meditates day and night' (Psalm 1:2). Notice that he does not say 'blessed is the man who reads three chapters a day'; mere reading is not enough, diligent, vigorous, hard and prolonged thinking upon the Scripture is what is required. As J.G. Vos put it 'the Bible is not a modern supermarket with its names all packaged and arranged on shelves ready to be checked out with the least possible effort; the Bible is a gold mine that has to be methodically and patiently worked if we are to gain possession of its treasures.' (*The Westminster Larger Catechism: A Commentary*, pp 445-6). Furthermore, to read the Bible with 'self-denial' means that we 'do not lean on your own understanding' (Prov. 3:5) but trust in what God has said and accept His word as final even when it contradicts our prejudices and preconceived ideas. Once we are convinced that some opinion is contrary to the word of God we must be prepared to forsake it and submit to what the Lord has written. In order to assist us in such difficult tasks, we should acknowledge our dependence upon God and pray that the Holy Spirit would bless our studies and guide us into the truth of God's word (John 16:13).

Preaching the Word of God

To any serious reader of the New Testament it will be obvious that 'the sound preaching...of the Word' (*Westminster Confession* Chapter 21: Section 5) is a central part of congregational worship. An example of this is seen in Luke 4:20-21 where the Lord Jesus Christ preached on Isaiah 61:1-2 in the synagogue service at His home town of Nazareth. This practice was carried over into worship of the New Covenant Assemblies which can be seen by the various examples of the apostles in preaching the gospel throughout the New Testament, and Paul's instruction to Timothy to 'preach the word' (2 Tim. 4:2) in public worship. Moreover, preaching is the primary means of grace instrumental in the conversion of sinners to Christ. This is why Paul asked 'how are they to believe in him of whom they have never heard? And how are they to hear without someone preaching?' (Rom. 10:14). So if preaching were to be omitted from worship we should not be surprised if few people are converted to Christ. To this end, Stuart Olyott remarked:

> If someone spent a week reading through the Bible, and then a further week getting to grips with the main events of church history, what would they notice? They would notice that God's work in the world and preaching are intimately linked. Wherever God is at work, preaching flourishes. Whenever preaching is devalued or absent, the cause of God goes through a thin time. The kingdom of God and preaching are like conjoined twins who cannot be separated; they stand or fall together. (*Preaching – Pure and Simple*, p. 11).

It is essential therefore, in order to advance Christ's Kingdom, that the word of God is faithfully preached. However, if we fail to adhere to the regulative principle of worship it should not surprise us if preaching is either pushed to one side or totally ignored. To allow that to happen is to show a lack of love for souls, as preaching is the chief means through which God brings sinners to Himself (1 Cor.

1:21). Sadly, in many modern Evangelical Churches the preaching of the word is sidelined in worship, as human innovations are introduced in the hope that their use will lead to more conversions. For example, a minister may shorten his sermon considerably in order to make way for a soloist who 'ministers in song' by 'singing the gospel'. However, this is a violation of the regulative principle because the Bible tells us that the gospel is to be preached, not sung by anyone who feels like it. Likewise, instead of a sermon being preached it is common for an individual to narrate how they were converted by giving the congregation their testimony. Yet it cannot be shown from Scripture that a testimony is a part of worship; while it may have some place in personal witnessing (John 4:29) a testimony may not be used in congregational worship as there is no command for people to relate their conversion experience, nor can it proved to be Biblical from valid logical inference or that the apostles ever used testimonies in worship. Other gimmicks, such as drama, comedy and musical performances have seen the preaching of God's word relegated to a mere epilogue at the end of a service. With the means of grace being so tragically neglected should we be surprised if we see few sinners come to Christ? If we truly love souls we will realise that the means God has appointed are sufficient for building up His Kingdom, to resort to gimmicks simply reveals a lack of faith in the Lord's provision for His Church. We should be faithful in using the means God has given us (in this case preaching) and look to Him to give us growth (1 Cor. 3:7-8) by bringing sinners to Christ Jesus.

In saying that preaching is the principal means through which sinners are converted, I am not suggesting that there are two different types of preaching – one for the saved and another for the unsaved. A study of the words used in the New Testament to describe preaching will demonstrate that this distinction, so common among Fundamentalists and Evangelicals, of having preaching which is purely aimed at believers in the morning service, and preaching which is entirely designed for the unconverted in the evening, is not one which can be sustained by Scripture.

Kerusso

Words from the *Kerusso* family are used in the New Testament to describe the preaching of Jonah (Matt. 12:41), of John the Baptist (Matt. 3:1), of the Lord Jesus Christ (Luke 4:18-19), and of the apostles (1 Tim. 2:7; 2 Tim. 1:11). Stuart Olyott explains that *Kerusso* means to declare a message as a herald does. He says:

It refers to the message of a king. When a sovereign has a message for his subjects, he gives it to heralds. These heralds announce it to the people without altering or amending it in any way. They simply pass on the message that has been given to them. Their hearers know that they are receiving an official proc-lamation. (Ibid. p. 12).

This would explain why Paul described the gospel ministers as 'ambassadors for Christ, God making his appeal through us' (2 Cor. 5:20); as Christ's repre-sentatives, ministers can appeal to sinners 'on behalf of Christ, be reconciled to God' (2 Cor. 5:20b).

euangelizo

This word means 'to announce good news' and where the English verb 'to evangelise' is derived from. However, we should note that heralding (*Kerusso*) and evangelising (*euangelizo*) are not two completely separate things; in Luke 4:18-19 both words are used to describe Christ's ministry, 'to preach the gospel' (*euangelizo*) and 'to preach' (*Kerusso*). So in evangelising the Lord was also heralding. Moreover, evangelising is not something only to be done to non-Christians; as Paul told the Roman believers he was 'eager to preach the gospel to you also who are in Rome' (Rom. 1:15). This is because preaching the gospel means preaching salvation in the fullest sense; it does not simply refer to proclaiming the free offer of the gospel in calling sinners to faith and repentance.

martureo

This verb means 'to bear witness about facts.' In Luke 24:44-48 Christ tells His disciples that they are to herald (*Kerusso*) repentance and forgiveness of sins which should 'be proclaimed in his name to all nations' (v.47); in doing this they are also his 'witnesses' (v.48) to the truth of the gospel (here a word from the *martureo* family is used). So in heralding the good news the disciples also had to bear witness about the facts of the gospel.

Didasko

This is a word used to describe teaching (Matt. 28:20). The way this word is employed in Acts 5:42 where we read that the apostles 'did not cease teaching and preaching Jesus as the Christ' proves that teaching (*didasko*) and preaching the gospel (*euangelizo*) cannot be separated.

True preaching, regardless of the audience, will include all four things that have been mentioned. There is not one type for non-Christians and another for believers. Evidence of this is seen 2 Tim. 4:2-5 where Paul writes to Timothy:

> **Preach the word! Be ready in season and out of season. Convince, rebuke, exhort, with all longsuffering and teaching. For the time will come when they will not endure sound doctrine, but according to their own devices, because they have itching ears, they will heap up for themselves teachers; and they will turn *their* ears away from the truth, and be turned aside to fables. But you be watchful in all things, do the**

work of an evangelist, fulfil your ministry. (NKJV)

Stuart Olyott explains:

> In these verses Paul is writing his final words to a younger man who is already an important Christian leader. He solemnly instructs him to "Preach the word!" At that point he uses the verb *Kerusso*. But why is Timothy to do this? It is because the time is coming when people will not endure sound 'doctrine' (a word from the *didasko* family) and will heap up for themselves 'teachers' (another word from the *didasko* family). Paul is obviously telling Timothy that to preach (*Kerusso*) is the way to teach (*didasko*) the Church and to protect it from error. But that is not all. Paul also tells Timothy to do the work of an 'evangelist' (a word from the *euangelizo* family). He means, of course, that as Timothy preaches (*Kerusso*), and therefore teaches (*didasko*), he is to make sure that the true gospel (*euangelizo*) is kept to the forefront. And so we see in a single paragraph that three of our four words are used to describe Timothy's task. If he is a true preacher he will not be doing just one of these things, but all of them. Wherever true preaching is found, several things are happening at the same time.' (Ibid. p. 17).

This means the notion that ministers shouldn't preach any doctrine is one which is completely foreign to Scripture; the idea of a non-doctrinal preaching is a contradiction in terms. Preaching devoid of doctrinal content is not true preaching at all.

In order for the word to be preached faithfully the minister must give a sound exegesis (explanation) of the text of Scripture that he is preaching on, properly bringing out the meaning of the passage in question. Preachers are not to pick texts at random and use them as a springboard for speaking on some political or social issue which is not taught in the passage. This is an irreverent abuse of Holy Scripture and those who do this are a disgrace to the office of the gospel ministry. As Stuart Olyott put it 'a herald is a traitor if he does not convey exactly what the King says.' (Ibid. p. 29). In order for preaching to be exegetically accurate it must take into account the grammatical meaning of the words of a text, the literary style in which these words are found, the immediate and wider context that a passage has been written in, the historical setting, and interpret the passage in light of what is written in other places of Scripture. If any of these are neglected don't be surprised if preaching is unbalanced, confused and highly misleading.

Also, the *Westminster Larger Catechism* gives some useful directions about how the word of God is to be preached:

Q. 159 How is the word of God to be preached by those that are called thereunto?

A. They that are called to labour in the ministry of the word, are to preach sound doctrine, diligently, in season and out of season; plainly, not in enticing words of man's wisdom, but in demonstration of the Spirit, and of power; faithfully, making known the whole counsel of God; wisely, applying themselves to the necessities and capacities of the hearers; zealously, with fervent love to God and the souls of his people; sincerely, aiming at his glory, and their conversion, edification, and salvation.

When Paul wrote to Titus he told him to 'teach what accords with sound doctrine' (Titus 2:1). In order to edify his hearers Titus was told that his teaching must be in accordance with the truth as it is revealed in Scripture. As Geoffrey Wilson commented 'In contrast to the disease of heresy, Titus must continue to speak what befits sound doctrine, for wholesome teaching promotes the spiritual health which is manifested in obedient walk.' (*New Testament Commentaries*, vol. 2, p. 297). The practice of ministers not preaching on doctrine in case it harms or offends their hearers is blatantly un-Biblical as proper doctrinal teaching is a means to promoting godliness among the hearers (see Titus 2:2-10). This must be done with diligence as preaching is one of God's appointed means of saving souls (Rom. 10:14), sanctifying His people (John 17:17) and extending His Kingdom (Matt. 28:19-20). A minister who has a true burden for the conversion of sinners and the building up of believers in the faith will be diligent to 'preach the word...in season and out of season' (2 Tim.4:2). A minister must be zealous in proclaiming God's truth from the pulpit on every given opportunity.

Although a minister ought not to withhold the truth out of fear of offending the hearers, this does not mean that he is to give a philosophical lecture to his congregation every week, using as many fancy terms and difficult words as possible. Paul told the Corinthians that 'my speech and my message were not in plausible words of wisdom, but in demonstration of the Spirit and of power that your faith might not rest in the wisdom of men but in the power of God.' (1 Cor. 2:4-5). Paul did not want to impress his listeners with a tremendous philosophical lecture, in case people attributed the conversion of the Corinthians to the power of Paul's message. A good minister, as J.G. Vos said, 'is not to place his trust in his own ability as an orator or public speaker, nor to depend on the psychological influence of his own manner of presenting the message but to depend on the Holy Spirit blessing the message and applying it to the hearts of the hearers.' (*The Westminster Larger Catechism: A Commentary*, p. 452). Instead he used plain and ordinary speech which the common man could understand, so as not to make it unnecessarily difficult. Nevertheless this cannot excuse ministers who smooth over doctrines that are offensive to the natural man or who refuse to instruct their congregations on proper Christian conduct and duty. To neglect to do this means that a minister is not making known 'the whole counsel of God' (Acts 20:28) to his congregation. The best way to do this is for the books of the Bible to be systematically preached through in an expository fashion, so that no profitable Scriptural truth is neglected. Obviously his message will have to be adapted 'to the necessities and capacities of the hearers' for example, by using different illustrations to help them understand the word more clearly, so not to obscure the truth. The minister who is zealous for God's glory, the salvation of sinners and in the sanctification of believers will earnestly strive to teach his congregation what God has revealed, regardless of personal popularity or popular applause.

Of course if we are to be faithful to the regulative principle, we must also remember that preaching is not a duty to be performed by everyone. The *Larger Catechism* asks:

Q. 158. By whom is the word of God to be preached?

The word of God is to be preached only by such as are sufficiently gifted, and also duly approved and called to that office.

One of the gifts that the ascended Christ has given to His Church is that of teachers of the word (Eph. 4:11). A minister is an elder 'who labour[s] in preaching and teaching' (1 Tim. 5:17). Whereas the other elders rule, the minister publicly teaches the congregation in addition to ruling. Some sects have adopted the view that every Christian man should publicly teach the congregation, in protest to what they see as 'one man ministry'. Consequently, anyone who feels like it is allowed to get up and teach regardless as to whether or not he has got the gifts necessary for the task. If this was Biblically correct why then did James say 'Not many of you should become teachers, my brothers, for you know that we who teach will be judged with greater strictness' (James 3:1)? Seems like a pretty pointless thing to write if all the men in a congregation are allowed to teach. Moreover, why did Paul ask the Corinthians 'Are all teachers?' (1 Cor. 12:29). Obviously the answer to his question is that all are not teachers, so if all are not teachers, then obviously only some people are teachers i.e. those sufficiently gifted and called to the work of the ministry. Therefore, only those men who are in the ministry, or aspiring to that office, should take it upon themselves to teach in the public assembly of God's people.

Hearing the Word of God

Besides the reading and preaching of Holy Scripture, the *Westminster Confession* recognises that the 'conscionable hearing of the Word' (Chapter 21: Section 5) is also one of the ordinary parts of religious worship. This is not something which needs to be debated at any length; obviously if preaching is an act of worship then those that listen to that preaching must also be engaging in worshipping the Lord. Moreover, the *Westminster Larger Catechism* gives us some useful instructions as to how we are to hear the word of God preached:

Q. 160. What is required of those that hear
the word of God preached?

A. It is required of those that hear the word
preached, that they attend upon it with diligence, preparation, and prayer; examine what
they hear by the Scriptures; receive the truth
with faith, love, meekness, and readiness
of mind, as the word of God: meditate, and
confer of it; hide it in their hearts, and bring
forth the fruit of it in their lives.

Hearing the preaching of the word of God is
not something to be taken lightly. Far too many
of us are either sloppy in our attendance upon the
preaching, or else if we do bother to turn up, we sit
day-dreaming about everything under the sun rather
than paying attention to the minister's message. This
sort of behaviour is a violation of Christ's command
to 'take care then how you hear' (Luke 8:18). We
ought to be diligent not only upon attending, but also
in listening to the word preached, as it is the spiritual milk which is the means of helping us grow in
the Christian life (1 Pet. 2:1-3) and 'the sword of the
Spirit' (Eph. 6:17) which enables us to fight in the
midst of a spiritual warfare. Don't be fooled if we
are careless in our attendance upon this ordinance,
Satan, on the other hand, most certainly is not. As
the Puritan George Swinnock put it 'the devil is very
diligent at duties; he is every Lord's Day the first at
church. His great design is to render this engine of
the word fruitless, whereby the strongholds of his
kingdom have been battered and broken down.' (*The*

Christian Man's Calling, Works: 1, p. 157). However, if we treat this ordinance frivolously should we be surprised if 'the evil one comes and snatches away what has been sown in |our| heart' (Matt. 13:18)? In order to attend the preaching of the word, not in a cold, formal or heartless manner, we need to take sufficient time to prepare our hearts for the reception of God's word. This means that we should take care of all worldly business on a Saturday and abstain from all unnecessary works and lawful recreations on the Sabbath (Isaiah 58:13-14). Therefore sports, secular music, newspapers, non-religious television programs etc. are to be set aside on the Lord's Day, so that are minds are free to hear the word without distraction. Prayer of course, is indispensable to such preparation, each of us should ask that the Lord would 'Open my eyes, that I may behold wondrous things out of your law' (Psalm 119:18). Moreover, J.G. Vos tells us that:

> We should pray that the Holy Spirit will bestow spiritual gifts upon the minister, so that he may expound the Scriptures truly and effectively. We should also pray that we and others may be given the grace of the Spirit to receive the Word, that the Holy Spirit will accompany and follow the preaching with his gracious working, so that sinners will be converted to Christ and the saints built up in their Christian faith and experi-

ence. (*The Westminster Larger Catechism: A Commentary*, p. 457).

If we neglect such prayer and preparation our attendance upon the word will be just a cold and lifeless ritual in which we simply go through the motions to keep up religious appearances. Richard Baxter (another Puritan) warned believers against such conduct in his magisterial work *A Christian Directory*:

> Take heed of a customary, formal, senseless heart that tolerates itself from day to day, to do holy things in a common manner, and with a common, dull, and careless mind: for that is to profane them. Call in your thoughts when you feel them dull. Remember what you are about, and with whom it is that you have to do, and that you tread on the dust of them who had such opportunities before you which are now all gone, and so will yours. You hear and pray for more than your lives; therefore do it not as in jest or as asleep. (p. 617).

Attentive listening to the word does not, however, mean that we are bound to believe everything that the minister tells us. Certainly not! We are to imitate the Bereans, who upon hearing Paul and Silas 'received the word with all eagerness, examining the Scriptures daily to see if these things were so' (Acts 17:11). Blind following is not an option; every Christian should only accept what the minister is saying if he is convinced that his doctrine is in accordance with the word of God. However, we should not go to the other extreme of rejecting everything that the preacher says because of some mistakes in his message. The censorious spirit evident among some people, who go to hear sermons in order to criticise everything the minister says, is to be severely condemned. Richard Baxter has some good advice for such individuals:

> When you meet with a word in a sermon or prayer, which you do not like, let it not stop you, and hinder your fervent and peaceable proceeding in the rest; as if you must not join in that which is good, if there be any faulty mixture in it. But go on in that which you approve, and thank God that He pardons the infirmities of others as well as your own. (Ibid.).

Rather than adopt a censorious spirit, the Catechism tells us to receive the word 'with faith, love, meekness, and readiness of mind, as the mind of God.' We are not to be like those in Moses' day, who did not benefit from the word that was preached to them 'because they were not united by faith with those who listened' (Heb. 4:2). When unbelievers hear the word of God proclaimed to them, and go on rejecting it, far from profiting them it further adds to their guilt before God (Rom. 2:5). Christians on the other hand are those who 'love the truth' (2 Thess. 2:10) of Scripture, and love to hear that truth faithfully proclaimed. Furthermore, we should 'receive with meekness the implanted word' (James 1:21); this is necessary because there is much in the Scripture that is offensive to our sinful nature. Therefore, regardless of what offence it may cause us, when the Scripture corrects our beliefs or conduct, we must meekly bring our lives into conformity with it. George Swinnock, in *The Christian Man's Calling*, left us with this advice:

> When the word of God comes like a mighty rushing wind, rooting up the tall trees of your sins, bringing down high thoughts, overturning all before it; when as fire it burns within you, consuming your lusts, and turning you into its own likeness, making you holy, spiritual, and heavenly, this is hearing to purpose!...when the word comes with power the soul hears it, as Peter heard the cock; he goes out and weeps bitterly, when he hears of the boundless mercy which he has deserted, and the matchless misery which he has deserved, and the infinite love which he has abused, and the righteous law which he has transgressed; he is cut to the heart; he goes out and weeps bitterly. (p. 160).

Rather than rising up in rebellion when the word of God rebukes us, we should be like Josiah, who when he 'heard the words of the law, he tore his clothes' (2 Chron. 34:19) as a sign of personal repentance for his failure to conform to God's law. This is because we should receive the teachings of Scripture 'not as the word of men but as what it really is, the word of God' (1 Thess. 2:13).

In order for the word to bear fruit in the lives of Christians (Matt 13:23) it is most necessary that they carefully meditate on the teaching they have received. Jesus tells us that we are to 'let these words sink into your ears' (Luke 9:44); we will only do this if we imitate Mary who 'treasured up all these things in her heart' (Luke 2:51). Meditation upon the word preached will help us to remember how we are to live in a manner that is pleasing to God so that we will be able to say with the Psalmist 'I have hidden your word in my heart that I might not sin against you' (Psalm 119:11 NIV). It is also profitable for Christians to discuss the word with each other in fellowship meetings for Christian conference. The disciples on the road to Emmaus talked 'with each other about all these things that had happened' (Luke 24:14); and should we not be like those in Malachi's day, who as a result of fearing the Lord, 'speak to one another, and the LORD listened and heard them; so a book of remembrance was written before Him for those who fear the LORD and who meditate on His name' (Mal. 3:16 NKJV). Because the Lord listens when his people speak to one another, meditating 'on His name' (His name refers to all by which He makes Himself known, and this is primarily through His word Psalm 138:2) then it must be a duty for believers to converse with one another on what they have heard preached. If these means are prayerfully used then believers should expect to see real spiritual growth in their lives.

In conclusion, Thomas Watson (yet another Puritan) gives us some more reasons to highly esteem the public preaching of God's word as a part of congregational worship:

It may be the last time that God will ever speak to us in His Word; it may be the last sermon that we shall ever hear; we may go from the place of hearing to the place of judging. If people would think this when they come into the house of God, "Perhaps this will be the last time that God will counsel us about our souls, the last time that ever we shall see our minister's face", with what devotion would they come! How would their affections be all on fire in hearing! We give great attention to the last speeches of friends. A parent's dying words are received as oracles. Oh, let all this provoke us to diligence in hearing! Let us think, "this may be the last time that Aaron's bell shall sound in our ears, and before another day is past we may be in another world." (*Heaven Taken By Storm*, pp 17-8).

CHAPTER 9:

Exclusive Psalmody

Do the Westminster Standards teach Exclusive Psalmody?

The *Westminster Confession of Faith* affirms that the 'singing of psalms with grace in the heart' (Chapter 21: Section 5) is another element of religious worship. At this point the question is often raised as to whether the Confession is referring to the Book of Psalms or to religious songs and hymns in general? Before examining the Biblical case for total psalmody I shall first of all seek to prove, beyond all reasonable doubt, that the Westminster Standards only authorise the singing of the divinely inspired book of Psalms in Christian praise.

Many conservative and Bible believing Christians in denominations bearing the name 'Presbyterian' (and who profess to adhere to the *Westminster Confession*) claim that because the word 'psalm' is not capitalised in the *Westminster Confession*, it merely is a vague directive to sing praise. Whereas, if the Confession had said 'the singing of the book of Psalms' then it would have been teaching exclusive psalmody, but due to the fact that the Confession doesn't do this it must leave room for uninspired hymns to be used in praise. There are some very serious objections to this view. Firstly, these Presbyterian opponents of exclusive psalmody have failed to notice 'that the authors of the Westminster Standards only capitalised the word Psalms when it was used as a title of the whole book.' (B.M. Schwertley, *Sola Scriptura and the Regulative Principle of Worship*, p. 183). Evidence of this can be seen by referring to *The Directory for the Public Worship of God* which was also published by the Westminster Assembly. In the section of the Directory entitled 'Of Public Reading of the Holy Scripture' it says:

> We commend also the more frequent reading
> of such scriptures as he that reads shall think
> best for edification of his hearers, as the book
> of Psalms, and such like.

Notice that the word 'Psalms' is capitalised, in this context, because it is referring to the title of the canonical book. In the next section entitled 'Of Public Prayer before the Sermon' it says 'After the reading of the word, (and singing of the psalm,)'; here 'psalm' is not capitalised because it is only referring to an individual psalm and not to the title of the book. So when the Confession says 'the singing of psalms with grace in the heart' it must be referring to the singing of individual psalms. Moreover, the section called 'Of Singing of Psalms' we see that the word 'psalm' is never capitalised when it does not refer to the book of Psalms:

> It is the duty of Christians to praise God publicly, by singing of psalms [individual psalms] together in the congregation, and also privately in the family. In singing of psalms [individual psalms], the voice is to be tune-ably and gravely ordered; but the chief care must be to sing with understanding, and with grace in the heart, making melody unto the Lord. That the whole congregation may join herein, every one that can read is to have a psalm book [if it had been referring to the title it would have said "the book of Psalms"]; and all others, not disabled by age or other-wise, are to be exhorted to learn to read. But for the present, where many in the congre-gation cannot read, it is convenient that the minister, or some other fit person appointed by him and the other ruling officers, do read the psalm [individual psalm], line by line, before the singing thereof.

It is clearly evident that when the Westminster Divines referred to the title of the book of Psalms they used capitalisation. However, when they referred to an individual psalm or to a psalter (psalm book) they did not use capitalisation. So the fact that the word 'psalm' is not spelt with a capital in the *Westminster Confession* does not prove that it referred to any other songs outside the book of Psalms. Therefore, the Confession must teach that only the exclusive singing of the psalms 'breathed out by God' (2 Tim. 3:16) is what the regulative principle of worship permits in the singing of praise to the Lord.

Further proof of the Westminster Assembly's commitment to total psalmody is shown by the fact that it actually sponsored the production of a metrical psalm book for singing. This was later called *The Scottish Metrical Version* which only contains translations of the 150 inspired psalms. If the Westminster Divines believed that uninspired hymns were consistent with the regulative principle of worship then why didn't they include them in the manual of praise which they sponsored? To omit something from worship which one believes actually a regulative principle is most certainly a serious error. Should we accuse the Westminster Assembly of being guilty of this? No there isn't any need to because, as is evident from the Confession and the Directory, they did not believe that the Scriptural law of worship required the singing of uninspired hymns. In fact the debate at the Westminster Assembly concerning the subject of what was to be sung in praise, was not whether the Church should only sing psalms or to permit the use of uninspired hymns. The issue debated was which Psalter should the church sing from? Uninspired hymns never got a look in. In the end the assembly only authorised the singing of Francis Rouses' translation of the Psalms (which later became the *Scottish Metrical Version*). So judging by the evidence, the notion that the 'singing of psalms' in the confession was only a vague term for religious song, is clearly a fallacy. If denominations bearing the name 'Presbyterian' are going to be faithful to the doctrinal standards which it professes to hold to, then they must cease from singing uninspired songs and return to the exclusive use of the Psalter in praise or else clearly state that the believe the *Westminster Confession* to be in error.

Why then have so many conservative Presbyterians abandoned total psalmody, which is the position of their Confession of Faith? Some of them believe that there are good Biblical reasons for using uninspired hymns in worship and would argue against exclusive psalmody from a theological perspective. Others have been influenced by 19th century revivalism and Wesleyan Arminianism, and have adopted hymns for the pragmatic reason that the Church should 'sing the gospel' through evangelistic songs, so that more people will be saved. Such people are more influenced were by sentiment and tradition than by Scripture; as they often have little understanding of the regulative principle it is very difficult to reason with them from a Reformed perspective. However, Brian Schwertley points out that various Presbyterian churches abandoned exclusive psalmody as a result of watering down the regulative principle. He tells us that they:

> Lost the Biblical understanding of the regulative principle of worship and thus applied it to the public worship service. "Private"

gatherings, family and private worship were considered areas of life outside the strict parameter of divine warrant. Virtually all the innovations of the eighteenth and nineteenth centuries came into the churches through practices that were arbitrarily placed outside of "Sola Scriptura". (*Sola Scriptura and the Regulative Principle of Worship*, p. 188).

By thinking that the regulative principle didn't apply to fellowship meetings, family worship, Sabbath Schools, children's meetings etc, many Presbyterians taught that it was fine to sing hymns in these contexts. However, if the second commandment (the regulative principle) doesn't apply beyond public worship what is to stop us from having a Mass in family worship? As this distinction is completely untenable it wasn't long before uninspired hymns made their way into the public worship of most Presbyterian churches. Be warned; the only way to safeguard exclusive psalmody is to confine our praise to the book of Psalms in all of our worship, whether private, family or public.

The Singing of Divinely Inspired Psalms is a Regulative Principle of Worship

The singing of praise unto the Lord, from His own 'God-breathed' (2 Tim. 3:16 NIV) manual of praise, the book of Psalms, is a part of sacred religious worship. We know this to be true not only by the specific commands in Scripture, but also from valid historical examples of Psalm-singing in the Bible, and from logical deductions that we can make from the word of God. First of all, the book of Psalms itself contains numerous commands to praise the Lord in singing, Psalm 105:2 (NKJV) reads 'Sing to Him, sing psalms to Him' (see also Psalm 81:2; 95:1-2; 98:4-6; 100:2). This, at the very least, must refer to the singing of the book of Psalms because the title of the Psalter in Hebrew (*Sepher Tehillim*) is "Book of Praises" which would seem to infer that its contents are to be sung. Moreover, the musical terminology found throughout the titles of the Psalms and in the Psalms themselves indicates that they were made to be sung; along with the fact that many Psalms are called songs, psalms (melodious songs), and hymns. One point, which is often overlooked, is the fact that God has put a large book of 150 worship songs in the middle of His Bible. Why would He do this if these songs were not to be used as our praise songs in worship? The only reasonable explanation is that the Lord intends for us to sing these songs in His praise. This is also confirmed by the fact that there are many examples in Scripture of the Psalms being employed in God's worship (1 Chron. 16:2; 2 Chron. 5:13; 20:21; 29:30; Ezra 3:11; Matt. 26:30; Acts 16:25). So when we sing the Psalms in God's worship we know beyond a shadow of a doubt that we are doing something that the Lord has authorised in Scripture. The question that remains then is whether or not we should use uninspired songs, along with the Psalms, in our praise?

Even in most conservative Presbyterian denominations today Psalm-singing is a minority pursuit; uninspired hymns are chiefly used in praise, and at best, only one Psalm is sung in a service (and that is usually in the morning). Worse still, in many Evangelical Churches, the Psalms are totally neglected in favour of a constantly changing supply of uninspired hymn-books. The question which we, as Reformed Christians who adhere to the regulative principle, must ask is 'can this practice be warranted from Scripture?' As song is part of God's worship we have no other option but to lay aside long-standing prejudices and pre-suppositions, and be guided solely by what the Bible says on this subject. To be guided by anything but Scripture alone, would be, as Prof. Edward Donnelly once pointed out, to pretend 'as if God had little or nothing to say about that which most intimately concerns his glory.' (Cited in J. Price, *Old Light on New Worship*, p. 6). This, of course, is not an option open to those of us who wish to take the Bible seriously.

Although many of our respected brethren in the Reformed faith (such as Dr. Martyn Lloyd-Jones and Rev. Iain Murray among others) have defended the use of uninspired songs in worship; I honestly, though to some extent unwillingly, believe that despite their good intentions and high regard for God's word and worship, they are mistaken on this point. However, I want to make it clear that I am not saying that exclusive Psalm singers are any better or smarter than anyone else, and I do recognise that others have looked into this subject and come to a different conclusion. As none of us are blessed with infallibility, let us not proudly frown upon other Reformed Christians and Reformed Churches who differ with us on this issue. Let us all remember Paul's instruction that 'the Lord's servant must not be quarrelsome but kind to everyone, able to teach, patiently enduring evil, correcting his opponents with gentleness' (2 Tim. 2:24-25). If you are reading this and remain unconvinced of the case for total psalmody, I would request that you keep an open mind and be like the Bereans who 'received the word with all eagerness, examining the Scriptures daily to see if these things were so' (Acts 17:11) before coming to any firm conclusion on this issue.

My first reason for rejecting the idea that uninspired songs are an acceptable part of religious worship, is that in the Bible, prophetic inspiration, being 'carried along by the Holy Spirit' (2 Pet. 1:21), was an absolute requirement in order to compose worship songs that were acceptable in God's sight. This fact has been largely ignored by nearly all modern Evangelicals, even among those who subscribe to the regulative principle. Yet the Scriptural evidence for this assertion is overwhelming. Some examples include the song of Moses (Ex. 15:1-18), the song of Miriam the prophetess (Ex. 15:20, 21), the inspired song of Deborah the prophetess (Judges 5:1-31), and the songs of the prophets Isaiah, and Habakkuk (Isa. 5:1; 12:1-6; Hab. 3:1-19). Furthermore, the writers of the Psalter (the permanent hymn-book of the Church) wrote every word of their songs under the inspiration of the Holy Spirit. David 'the sweet psalmist of Israel'

(2 Sam. 23:1) was the mouthpiece of the Holy Spirit when he wrote his psalms; that is why the apostle Peter said 'the Holy Spirit spoke beforehand by the mouth of David' (Acts 1:16) and David himself said 'the Spirit of the LORD speaks by me; his word is on my tongue' (2 Sam. 23:2). In fact, as Brian Schwertley noticed 'the writing of worship songs in the Old Testament was so intimately connected with prophetic inspiration that 2 Kings 23:2 and 2 Chron. 34:30 use the term "Levite" and "prophet" interchangeably.' (*Sola Scriptura and the Regulative Principle of Worship*, p. 218). Therefore, in order to write a song acceptable in God's worship you had to be inspired by the Holy Spirit. Since nobody can claim to posses such inspiration nowadays all songs that they produce are uninspired and therefore not acceptable in God's sight.

The notion, so prevalent among many in the Reformed faith, that theological accuracy is all that is required to compose worship songs falls short of the Biblical requirement for divine inspiration. One should hardly be surprised that the inspiration of the Holy Spirit was necessary for writing praise songs for the Lord, after all, as Rev. Malcolm Watts pointed out 'God is infinitely exalted above all the conceptions of finite minds (Job 11:7; Psalm 145:3). Since praise is the extolling of his glories and excellencies, God himself must supply the matter for praise.' (*God's Hymnbook for the Christian Church*, p. 9).

Since we have so clearly seen that in order for the song we use in worship to be acceptable to the Lord they must be 'breathed out by God' (2 Tim. 3:16);

then we (regretfully) have to come to the logical conclusion that the only way one could argue for the use of uninspired hymns in worship is to deny the regulative principle. Thankfully, many people who argue for uninspired hymns do not go this far, but it is difficult to understand how they can justify this inconsistency. Before we examine the development of inspired Psalmody in Scripture let us hear some general reasons from Rev. W.I. Wishart why the book of Psalms is superior to all human compositions in worship:

1. The superiority of the Word of God over all words of men will be admitted, and the Psalms of inspiration are certainly more fit to be used in the offering of praise than the best compositions of human genius.

2. The Psalms have a strength in their conception of God which is peculiar to themselves, and which makes them especially helpful as a medium of devotion.

3. The Psalms express more fully than any other book the religious experience of believers.

4. No system or collection of merely human hymns has ever proved satisfactory to the Church at large. They all lack at important points.

5. The Psalter is the only absolutely safe hymn-book. It contains no error. It teaches no false-

hood. It needs no amendment or expurgation. It is the Word of God.

6. The Psalter is the true union hymn-book. This statement follows on naturally from the one last made. There is much talk of a union of the Churches...it would seem that the matter of praise might be adjusted very easily by adopting the one hymn-book in which all Churches believe, the God-given Songs of Zion. (Cited in J. McNaughter (ed), *The Psalms in Worship*, p. 58).

The Development of Psalmody in the Old Testament

Strange as it may seem the singing of praise was not always a part of the Church's worship. In fact the earliest record of religious song among God's people is the song of Moses and the song of Miriam recorded in Exodus 15. Indeed, it was another two hundred years before we find another song recorded in Scripture, that being the song of Deborah and Barak which is found in Judges 5. However, as these were songs of civil celebration they were sung by Israel, not as a Church, but as a nation. Although Psalm 90 is ascribed to Moses, there is no evidence that this was used in the Church's worship until David's day, when the Psalter was beginning to be gathered together. So praise songs did not constitute a regular part of the Church's worship until the time of David 'the sweet psalmist of Israel' (2 Sam.

23:1); prior to this there was no service of song in the worship of the Tabernacle. David's reign as King of Israel (1010-970 BC) marked a new period in redemptive history, his kingdom was a type of the future kingdom of Christ. Noting the significance of this, Rowland Ward writes:

> This new epoch was accompanied by much new revelation. A considerable number of religious songs of unique character were written, many of them showing by the inscription 'for the choir director' that they were specifically intended for use in the centralised worship at Jerusalem. (*The Psalms in Christian Worship*, p. 8).

Therefore, we see that, in David's day, the singing of inspired songs of praise became part of the ordinary worship of the Church of God. Moreover, when the Temple was built in Solomon's time 'the service of song in the house of the Lord' (1 Chron. 6:31) was divinely established (cf. 1 Chron. 6:31-48). Sadly, because of the Church's corruption this pure form of worship often fell into decay. However, it is highly significant that when the Church's worship was reformed, the singing of Psalms by the Levites was restored according to the appointment of David. This can be seen in Jehoiada's reforms of 835 BC (2 Chron. 23:18), in the Covenanted Reformations of Hezekiah in 715 BC (2 Chron. 29:30) and Josiah in 622 BC (2 Chron. 35:15), at the laying of the foundation of the second Temple around 537 BC (Ezra

3:10) and in the dedication of the wall of Jerusalem in 434 BC (Neh. 12:45-46).

Obviously if the Levites were to sing praise unto the Lord, it would be necessary for them to have a manual of praise which they could sing from for more permanent usage. The existence of such a manual is implied from the time of David (who alone wrote 73 psalms) and is explicitly asserted in 2 Chron. 29:30 which says 'And Hezekiah the king and the officials commanded the Levites to sing praises to the LORD with the words of David and Asaph.' From this it is evident that the Psalms were being brought together into a single book which would eventually become the Church's exclusive manual of praise. This collection of Psalms passed into its final form in the time of Ezra when the Jews returned from their exile in Babylon; keep in mind that the last psalms (Psalm 126 and 137) were written during and after the captivity, the exiles return gave them the perfect opportunity (under God's guidance) to finally complete the Psalter, a staggering 1000 years after the first psalm (Psalm 90) was written. Our information on how this final editing was carried out is limited to say the least; no-one can say for definite why certain earlier inspired songs were omitted or why very similar psalms were included (e.g. Psalms 14 and 53; and Psalms 40 and 70). However, as Rowland Ward quite rightly says 'If the reasons for such matters are hidden, at least we can be sure that in the present Psalter we possess all God intended for the abiding use of his Church in the service of song.' (Ibid., p. 9).

Moreover, the completion of the Psalter coincides with the completion of the Canon of the Old Testament (Malachi's prophecy was also written in the time of Ezra and Nehemiah). Michael Bushell highlighted the significance of this:

> This fact is often overlooked because it is so obvious. The existence of a definite inspired Psalm book in the Old Testament canon, the termination of additions to that book after the close of the canon, and the exclusive use of this manual of praise in the Temple thereafter, all provide conclusive proof, we believe, that in the Old Testament Church at least, praise in song was considered to be a matter of divine prerogative, requiring inspired songwriters for the production of acceptable worship song. (*The Songs of Zion*, p. 64).

If uninspired hymns are acceptable in worship why did God take 1000 years to gather together an inspired manual of praise and put it in the middle of our Bibles? Seems a bit pointless if merely human songs were adequate? And why after the completion of the Psalter did the Jews not begin to write their own hymns for worship? The only rational answer that can be given to these questions is that the 150 Psalms of Psalter became Israel's permanent hymn-book once it was completed, thus making the need for uninspired hymns or even other in-scripturated (written down) inspired songs redundant. If uninspired songs were permitted the Jews would surely have sung them in the period between the Old and New Testaments. However, the evidence suggests that from the time of Ezra to the coming of Christ they used the Psalms exclusively in worship.

Often one hears people refer to the Psalter as the 'hymn-book of the Old Testament Church' as if to imply that the Psalms were better suited to the Church in the former dispensation. However, this is a very misleading and inaccurate statement. When one considers that the Psalter was only completed very late in the Old Testament era the idea that it was primarily designed for the Church of the Old Covenant falls to the ground. If this had been the case then the Psalms would surely have been brought together far sooner. The fact that the collection was not finished until so very late in Old Testament times shows us that the Psalms are in fact chiefly meant for the usage of the New Testament Church. Whereas most people who lived under the Old Covenant only had some of the Psalms, we in the New Testament age have the whole collection plus the actual writings of the New Testament to enable us to understand them much better than the saints in the Old Testament did. Why then would we want to replace this perfect manual of inspired praise with the inventions of men? Rather let us heartily use what God has graciously provided for us.

The Existence of Songs outside the Psalter

At this point some of you may be thinking 'hold on a minute, surely there are other songs in the Bible outside the book of Psalms. How then can we restrict our praise to the singing of Psalms only?' This is indeed a very good and well thought out question which must be answered respectfully. I openly admit that the existence of inspired songs outside the Psalter is by far and away the best, and most rational, objection to the doctrine of exclusive Psalmody. However, it is important to remember that the songs which we find in our Bibles, outside of the book of Psalms, were 'given by inspiration of God' (2 Tim. 3:16 NKJV) and so cannot provide us with any warrant at all for uninspired hymns. To appeal to the existence of these songs in order to justify singing human compositions in worship is a bit like appealing to the fact that Paul wrote epistles which were not preserved in the canon of the New Testament (1 Cor. 5:9; Col. 4:16) for the right to preach from uninspired books. To reach such a conclusion would appear to be stretching things to an unwarranted extreme; yet it is exactly the sort of logic many people will employ in order to legitimise the singing of uninspired hymns. If those who reject exclusive Psalmody on the basis that there are other inspired songs in Scripture should at least sing them in worship and not use them as a reason to sing from man-made hymn books. The fact that virtually none of the opponents of total Psalmody do this indicates that they are merely using the existence of inspired songs outside the Psalter as an excuse to ignore the implications of the regulative principle on their praise.

However, the existence of other inspired songs outside of the book of Psalms does not present us with any problem when defending exclusive

Psalmody. This is because prior to the completion of the Psalter at the close of the Old Testament canon (during the time of Ezra and Nehemiah) the question of the exclusive use of a book of songs was out of place, because such a book of praise had not finally been completed. As Michael Bushell explained 'some songs were sung in Old Testament worship which were not finally included in the Psalter, just as we grant that Paul wrote some letters that functioned authoritatively in the Church but which were not finally included in the canon of Scripture as we now have it.' (Ibid., p. 58). If the other songs in Scripture were meant to be continually used in worship then we must ask - why were they not included in the 'book of Praises' (the Hebrew title for the book of Psalms)? The only reasonable answer is that these songs were only for temporary use and were never meant to be sung repeatedly. After all, is there any example in the Bible of anyone singing any of these songs once the Psalter was completed? Due to the fact that no evidence exists to say that anybody did we cannot just assume that this was the case.

Further evidence that the Psalter is the Church's permanent manual of praise is seen by the fact that some of the songs recorded elsewhere in Scripture were included in the book of Psalms (2 Sam. 22; 1 Chron. 16:7-36) while others were deliberately excluded (Ex. 15:1-19; Hab. 3:1-19). One can only conclude that the reason why some of them have been excluded is because they were not meant to be used perpetually by the Church in its praise. If this was not the case, then why were they not put into the

Psalter, which is the 'book of Praises'? The fact that a collection of praise songs forms a place in the canon of Scripture has to be of major significance. Malcolm Watts said: 'there must be some reason why this collection called "the book of Psalms" (Luke 20:42; Acts 1:20) – occupies a distinct and separate portion in the canon. It can only be that this book was intended for standing and exclusive use in the Church.' (*God's Hymnbook for the Christian Church*, p. 17). No doubt his reasoning at this point is sound. The only reason why the Lord would have gathered together a manual of praise over a 1000 year period, and included some previous material while excluding other songs, is because He intended the book of Psalms to be the final and exclusive manual of praise for the Church on earth. If the other songs in the Bible were meant to be sung continually why did the Lord gather together a book of inspired songs? Why didn't He just scatter them throughout the Scriptures? The only answer is that the Psalms are the permanent book of praise, while the others were only used before the Psalter was completed, after that it was no longer necessary to employ them in praise. So why then were these other songs recorded in Scripture. D.A. McClenahen comes up with a most rational explanation:

> Moses…Habakkuk…and others wrote songs, which for historical reasons were retained in their historical place in the canon, but which were omitted from the permanent praise book of the Church for reasons which seemed good

to the divine mind. (Cited in J. McNaughter
(ed), *The Psalms in Worship*, p. 87).

While these songs are still of benefit to the
Church in order to understand the history of the Old
Testament, their exclusion from the inspired manual
of praise gives us a strong indication that they were not
meant to be continually sung in worship. Moreover,
when one considers that the Psalms (under God's
guidance) were gathered into little hymnals, then
these hymnals were combined into five Psalm books
and eventually these five books were combined into
one Psalter, then one has to conclude that surely the
other songs in Scripture would have made it if they
were meant to be permanently used. When the editors
of the Psalter were collecting the songs of praise the
only possible reason why they would have excluded
these other inspired songs is because the Lord no
longer intended them to be used in praise.

Some may object that if the Psalter is the final
hymn-book for the Church then how come there are
songs recorded in the New Testament such as the song
of Mary (Luke 1:46-55)? However, a closer inspec-
tion of the text of Scripture will show us that many of
these alleged songs cannot actually be proved to be
songs at all. For example Luke 1:46 reads 'Mary said'
it does not say 'Mary sang', so we cannot just assume
that it is a song. The same is also true of Zechariah's
'song' (Luke 1:68-79); here before Zechariah speaks
it says 'Zechariah was filled with the Holy Spirit and
prophesied, saying' (Luke 1:67), again no mention
is made of him singing anything. While the song of

the angels (Luke 2:13-14) may have been a song, it has no relevance to what we sing because if was never sung by a human being on earth, and again the evidence for it even being a song is ambiguous as the text reads that they were 'praising God and saying' (v.13); no clear mention is made of them singing. Moreover, the allegation that parts of Paul's epistles contain fragments of early hymns (such as Phil. 2:6-11; and 1 Tim. 3:16) is nothing more than pure speculation, without any evidence in the text. Also the 'new song' in Revelation 5:9-10, (which the proponents of uninspired hymnody make so much of) was only sung by angelic beings in heaven; the apostle John himself did not sing it, which explains why he wrote 'they sang' (Rev. 5:9) and not 'we sang'. The only songs outside the Psalter, which were sung in the New Testament Church, were the charismatic psalms in 1 Cor. 14:26; these however, were inspired prophecies sung by one individual and not by the whole congregation ('if any one of you has a psalm' NKJV). The fact that these were never written down proves that they were only a temporary gift and were not intended for continual usage. This absence of inscripturated (written down) songs after the completion of the Psalter indicates most strongly that the book of Psalms constitutes the one permanent hymn-book for the Christian Church.

For those who are still not convinced by the logic of this argument, and still wish to sing the other songs recorded in the Old Testament, I have a number of questions. Firstly, as with the alleged songs of the New Testament, it is doubtful whether or nor many of the supposed songs in the Old Testament were actually sung at all. The 'song of Hannah' (1 Sam. 2:1-10) cannot be proved to be a song because the passage reads 'Hannah prayed and said' (v.1), so it can't be conclusively shown that this was a song. The 'psalm of Jonah' (Jonah 2:2-9) is actually a prayer 'Jonah prayed to the LORD his God from the belly of the fish saying' (Jonah 2:1). And the 'song of Hezekiah' (Isa. 38:10-20) is just described as 'A writing of Hezekiah King of Judah' (Isa. 38:9) not as a song. So already the number of these alleged songs, which you can sing with any certainty, has been greatly reduced. Moreover, of those which actually were songs how many of them were ever used in the Church's public worship? The songs of Moses (Ex. 15:1-18), Miriam (Ex. 15:21) and Deborah and Barak (Judges 5:1-31) were civil, and not ecclesiastical (Church) songs, so we have no certainty that the Church is meant to use them today. Also, the songs of Isaiah (Isa. 5:1-30; 12:1-6) cannot definitely be shown to have been used by others in public worship (though they may have been). The song of Habakkuk (Hab. 3:1-19) has the strongest claim to have been used in public worship because of the inscription 'to the choirmaster with stringed instruments' (v.19) which is found at the conclusion of the song. But, due to the fact that this is missing in some early translations we can't be 100% certain that it is original. The large amount of doubt which exists as to the suitability of this, or in fact any of the other songs outside the Psalter for public worship (or even private worship) today, should restrain us from singing them. Remember Paul said 'whatever does not proceed from faith is sin' (Rom. 14:23); you cannot sing any of these inspired songs with any assurance that what you are doing has God's approval. Therefore, you should only sing from the book of Psalms, as you know with certainty that the Lord looks favourably on what you are offering to Him in worship. The bottom line is that God commands us to sing praise to Him in song; He has provided us with the Psalter, a 'book of Praises', therefore we should only sing praise to the Lord from this book.

Psalmody in the New Testament

Before dealing with the objections to exclusive psalmody, it will be useful to examine the New Testament usage of the Psalms. Undoubtedly the inspired writers of the New Testament Scriptures held the book of Psalms in the highest esteem; in fact, more than one hundred psalms are alluded to by the New Testament writers and about fifty per cent of their Old Testament quotations were actually taken from the Psalter. Furthermore, nowhere in the New Testament has the ordinance of Psalm singing been revoked, therefore we must assume that it is still obligatory upon the Church today. Furthermore, the New Testament itself contains historical examples of the Psalms being used in worship, as well as exhortations to sing praise to the Lord. Some of these shall be looked at below and others when we come to answer the objections to total psalmody.

Matthew 26:30; (cf. Mark 14:24)

In this text we read 'And when they had sung a hymn, they went out to the Mount of Olives.' It is universally agreed among New Testament scholars (few of whom would be in favour of total psalmody) that the word 'hymn' that is used here refers to the Great Hallel (i.e. Psalms 113-118) which was sung by the Jews after the Passover. Though he goes on to criticise exclusive psalmody, Princeton theologian J.A. Alexander admitted that the word hymn was 'referring no doubt to the series of psalms usually chanted at the Passover and known in later Jewish ritual as the Great Hallel. There is of course no allusion to the modern distinction between psalms and hymns.' (*A Commentary on Mark*, p. 382). So there is no reason to believe that the Lord Jesus Christ and his disciples departed from ordinary Jewish practice of singing from the book of Psalms in worship. If this had been an entirely new practice then surely the inspired writer would have made it plain that what they were doing was a break with Jewish tradition; however, no evidence exists to suggest that they did so we must assume that they only sang from the Psalter. Michael Bushell notes the significance of the employment of psalmody at the beginning of a period of transition from the Old Covenant to the New:

> We do not deny that the institution of the Lord's Supper marks the beginning of a period of transition from the Old Testament rite to the New Testament counterpart, but

we do find it very significant that the Psalms were sung at precisely this point of transition. The singing of appropriate psalms was an integral part of the Passover celebration and hence of the institution of the Lord's Supper. Psalmody and the Lord's Supper are no more separable now than psalmody and the Passover ritual were in Old Testament times. There is no instance of Scripture that shows more clearly than this the abiding significance of the Old Testament Psalms for the New Testament church. And on this passage alone we are quite content to rest our claim that the singing of the inspired Psalms is an obligation as binding on the New Testament church as it is upon the Old. (*The Songs of Zion*, pp 78-9).

As the Lord's Supper is an ordinance of public worship, and Psalms were sung at it institution, then it is only logical to assume that the Psalms are to be used in the public praise of the New Testament Church as their use is clearly sanctioned by the example of Christ and His apostles. This truth has caused Brian Schwertley to ask the rather penetrating questions:

Does your church follow the example of Jesus Christ and the Apostles by singing the Spirit-inspired Psalms of Scripture whenever you partake of the body and blood of our precious Saviour? If the head of the church chose Spirit-inspired Psalms for praise, comfort, and edification, should not His bride do like-wise? Who are we to set aside the ordinance of the Son of God? (*Exclusive Psalmody: A Biblical Defence*, p. 17).

Since Christians are to be imitators of Christ (1 Cor. 11:1), surely we should follow the example of the Lord Jesus and use the book of Psalms as our exclusive manual of praise.

Acts 16:25

This verse reads: 'About midnight Paul and Silas were praying and singing hymns to God.' Considering that Paul and Silas were in a Phillipian jail they could not have had the luxury of bringing modern hymn-books into their cell with them. Moreover, as a devout Jew, it is more than likely that Paul had committed many of the Psalms to memory (if not the entire book), and since there is no positive evidence in the text for uninspired songs, one can only assume that they were singing from the book of Psalms. For if they had contradicted previous practice it surely would have been clearly recorded for our learning. This verse also shows us that there is no reason for us to sing any uninspired material in either private devotions or fellowship meetings; the manual of praise in these contexts is the same as that used in public worship, the divinely inspired book of Psalms.

Romans 15:8-9

In these verses the apostle Paul writes 'For I tell you that Christ became a servant to the circumcised to show God's truthfulness, in order to confirm the promises given to the patriarchs, and in order that the Gentiles might glorify God for his mercy. As it is written, "Therefore I will praise you among the Gentiles and sing to your name".' In verse 9 Paul quotes from the Greek Septuagint translation of Psalm 18:49. This verse refers to Christ praising God among the nations through His Church. Yet, as Brian Schwertley comments, 'when Christ praised Jehovah during his earthly ministry He used the Old Testament Psalms (cf. Matt. 26:30).' (Ibid., p. 25). If Jesus was content only to use the book of Psalms when praising God, why should His people seek to lay aside the Psalter for human compositions that do not have our Saviour's approval?

Hebrews 2:11-12

Here the writer of the letter to the Hebrews quotes from Psalm 22:22 with reference to the Lord Jesus Christ: 'For he who sanctifies and those who are sanctified all have one origin. That is why he is not ashamed to call them brothers, saying, "I will tell your name to my brothers; in the midst of the congregation ['church' AV] I will sing your praise."' This passage teaches us that Christ, through His church 'the congregation' still sings praise to God. This means that when we sing the Psalms, Jesus is spiritually present in our worship services. This can only be true when we sing from the Psalter, the only hymn book that 'the Spirit of Christ' (1 Pet. 1:11) wrote through His prophets. But, as Malcolm Watts says 'we cannot conceive of Him ever using the hymns of fallible and erring men: rather, we believe that he can only identify with the words of the divinely inspired and inerrant Psalms. It follows that, when we sing the Biblical Psalms, we enjoy sweet communion with the Lord Jesus Christ.' (*God's Hymnbook for the Christian Church*, pp 10-11). Isn't it comforting to know that when we sing from the book of Psalms we praise God with the words that the Lord Jesus not only sang Himself, but actually wrote for us to sing about Him? After all, no merely human song could ever tell us more about our Saviour and His suffering than Psalm 22 can.

Hebrews 13:15

When exhorting the Hebrew Christians to persevere in following Jesus (Heb. 12:1,2) the author of the epistle wrote 'Through him then let us continually offer up a sacrifice of praise to God, that is, the fruit of lips that acknowledge his name.' When one remembers that the letter to the Hebrews was written to a Jewish audience, who had been brought up to exclusively sing the Psalms in the synagogue, it is completely inconceivable that the original readers would have understood this as referring to uninspired hymns, so he must have been exhorting them to sing from the Psalter.

James 5:13

This verse in the NKJV reads 'Is anyone among you suffering? Let him pray. Is anyone cheerful? Let him sing psalms ['praise' ESV; 'praises' NASB]'. Again, when one takes into account that James was writing his epistle to a Jewish audience 'the twelve tribes in the Dispersion' (James 1:1) and his own strong Jewish leanings (he was so Jewish that the Judaizers wrongly claimed him as one of their own Gal. 2:12) then it simply unimaginable that James could have been referring to anything outside the book of Psalms which was used exclusively by the synagogues of the Dispersion. In fact the Greek word that James uses here for 'praise' was also used in the title of the book of Psalms in the Greek Septuagint version. As the Septuagint Psalter is what the Jews of the Dispersion would have sung from, James' use of this word indicates that he intended them to sing from the Greek translation of the book of Psalms. Moreover, it is important to keep in mind that James' epistle is the first book of the New Testament, yet, far from telling them to abandon the Psalter, he exhorts them to continue using it. As this verse, in its context, is referring to private acts of devotion, we see that we have no Biblical warrant for singing from material outside the Psalter in our own times of private worship. Even such a stalwart defender of exclusive psalmody as Dr. John Kennedy of Dingwall slipped up at this point. He thought that uninspired hymns were only prohibited in public worship; saying:

Some desire them [hymns] because of an experience of enjoyment in using them, in private or in social Christian conference, to express their feeling of sorrow, hope or gladness. Let these continue to use them; I will yield to name in my desire to have them as a vehicle of any strong spiritual feeling that stirs my heart; but to use them in the worship of God in the sanctuary is quite another thing. (Cited in I.H. Murray, *The Psalter the Only Hymnal*, p. 18).

Although I believe he is greatly mistaken on this issue, Iain Murray was certainly right to point out that Dr. Kennedy, and those who took his view, 'provided no evidence that there is a Scriptural warrant for the distinction they wanted to draw.' (Ibid., p. 19). The evidence would suggest that the Bible makes no distinction between what is to be sung in public and private worship. We must conclude then that the Psalter is adequate for all of our praise.

The Psalter – The Only Hymnal of the New Testament Church

By considering the New Testament texts which we have analysed we can see that the Church in the New Covenant era has no other hymnbook apart from the book of Psalms. This should not surprise us as the Psalms are full of the Lord Jesus Christ. They were composed by men infallibly guided by 'the Spirit of Christ' who was 'in them...when he predicted the sufferings of Christ and the subsequent glories' (1 Pet. 1:11). Indeed, James A. Kennedy claimed:

> Surely our Lord is here as he is in no other Book of Scripture, not excepting the Gospels. They are quoted by the New Testament writers in proof of Christ's divinity more than all the other Old Testament books combined. And He is not pictured as a Saviour to come, not once, but as already come, not as prophetic, but the historic Christ; and for this reason they are better adapted to our use than they were to the use of the ancient [Old Testament] Church. (Cited in J. McNaughter, *The Psalms in Worship*, p. 64).

Although I shall come back to this when dealing with common objections to exclusive psalmody, the idea that the Psalter doesn't tell us enough about Christ (as Iain Murray argues, though without much Scriptural proof) is clearly a non-starter. If anything, the Psalms are much more relevant to the New Testament worship than that of the Old Covenant, as we have greater light to enable us to understand them better (Luke 24:44). If the Psalter was no longer sufficient for the Church, then surely God would have given us a New Testament hymnbook. After all, He replaced circumcision and the Passover with Baptism and the Lord's Supper, as the former ordinances were not adequate for the needs of the Church in the New Testament, yet He has not done this with the Church's manual of praise. Nor has He given any gift of hymn-writing in the New Testament age. As Kennedy further points out: 'when Jesus ascended up on high and gave gifts, there were apostles, prophets, evangelists, pastors, and teachers given [Eph. 4:8-12], but no psalmist. And among the great diversity of gifts given by the Spirit [1 Cor. 12; Rom. 12] the gifts of psalmody is not mentioned.' (Ibid.). The simple fact that God has not promised to give anyone the gift of hymn-writing in the New Testament, is alone enough to prove that uninspired songs have no place in New Covenant worship. No uninspired hymn-writer can ever claim to have had the guidance that David received, 'the man who was raised on high, the anointed of the God of Jacob, the sweet psalmist of Israel' (2 Sam. 23:1). If you find the Psalms difficult to understand when you sing them, then I would encourage you to familiarise yourself with them better. Sing them, study them, meditate upon them, read some fine expositions of them; and you will find them more than adequate for all of your devotional needs. Neither Christ nor His apostles needed any other manual of praise, and nor should we.

Psalms, Hymns and Spiritual Songs – Breathed out by God or Invented by Men?

One of the most common objections to exclusive psalmody, set forth by other Reformed believers who adhere to the regulative principle, is that the apostle Paul, in Eph. 5:19 and Col. 3:16, permits the use of uninspired songs in worship. Let us read the two texts in question:

And do not get drunk with wine, for that is debauchery, but be filled with the Spirit, addressing one another in psalms and hymns and spiritual songs, singing and making melody to the Lord with all your hearts. (Ephesians 5:18-19)
Let the word of Christ dwell in you richly teaching and admonishing one another in all wisdom, singing psalms and hymns and spiritual songs, with thankfulness in your hearts to God. (Colossians 3:16)

In order to interpret these passages of Holy Scripture correctly we cannot determine the meaning of 'psalm', 'hymn' or 'song' by assuming that these terms mean what modern Christians think they mean. Rather, we must seek to find out what the apostle Paul meant when he used these terms, and how his original readers in first century Ephesus and Colossae would have understand these terms. Keep in mind that the Bible was written for us, not to us, so when we seek to interpret a passage of Scripture it is vitally important to consider the historical and cultural context in which it was written. We cannot approach the Bible wearing 21st century spectacles; instead we need to read the text considering how the original readers would have understood it. This principle will be of invaluable assistance in helping us to understand these disputed passages correctly.

There is one important fact which we need to remember when looking at Eph. 5:19 and Col. 3:16, these letters were written to two churches which Paul had founded in Asia Minor (modern day Turkey), in these churches they used a Greek version of the Old Testament called the Septuagint (LXX). It was from this source that the Greek speaking audiences Paul addressed got much of their religious terminology. As the terms 'psalms', 'hymns' and 'songs' cannot, with any real certainty, be determined from the immediate context of either Eph. 5:19 and Col. 3:16, then it is most wise for us to examine how these terms are used in the Septuagint translation of the Old Testament Scriptures.

The Greek word for 'psalms' (*psalmos*) occurs eighty seven times in the Septuagint, seventy eight of these references are in the book of Psalms, and sixty seven of these are in the titles of individual Psalms. Indeed, the word *psalmos* means a 'song of praise'. Prof. John Murray and William Young observed that 'the frequency with which the word *psalmos* occurs in the titles is probably the reason why the book of Psalms is called, in the LXX version, simply *psalmoi*. In the Hebrew it is called *tehillim* [Praises].' (*The Minority Report*). So to the first century reader, Paul's exhortation to sing 'psalms' would seem to have been pointing them in the direction of the book of Psalms which contained 150 such psalms for singing. Furthermore, the Greek word for 'hymn' (*humnos*) appears seventeen times in the Septuagint and thirteen times in the book of Psalms. In about five or six instances *humnos* is used in the titles of individual Psalms as a translation of the Hebrew word *neginoth*. Also, it is very significant to note that in the text of the Psalms *humnos* is used to translate the Hebrew word *tehillah* [praise] which is the word used to designate the book of Psalms in Hebrew [the book of Praise]. Murray and Young state 'this shows that psalms may be called hymns and hymns called psalms. Psalms and hymns are not exclusive of one another. A psalm may be not only a psalm but also a hymn.' (Ibid.). Besides, at the end of the seventy-second psalm it says in the Septuagint 'the hymns of David the son of Jesse are ended' (Psalm 72:20). Moreover, the Greek word for song (*odee*) occurs eighty times in the Septuagint, forty-five times in the Psalter and thirty six times in the Psalms titles. Murray and Young were undoubtedly correct to observe that the word '*odee* occurs so frequently in the titles of the psalms that its meaning would be definitely influenced by that usage.' (Ibid.). It is clearly foolish to presume that Paul is talking about songs outside the Psalter when the word for song which he uses is used with such frequency in the book of Psalms itself.

The evidence would, in fact, suggest that the words 'psalms', 'hymns' and 'songs' are synonymous terms that may be used interchangeably to describe the inspired compositions contained in the book of Psalms. This is borne out by the fact that the title of Psalm 76 (in the Septuagint) contains all three terms: 'For the end, among the hymns, a psalm for Asaph, a song for the Assyrian.' While we don't know what the distinction between psalms, hymns, and songs was in the mind of the average Hebrew; nevertheless, we do know that these terms are used as to describe the compositions which make up the book of Psalms. As Charles Hodge said 'a psalm was a hymn, and a hymn a song.' (Cited in J. McNaughter (ed), *The Psalms in Worship*, p. 155). Moreover, among the headings of some of the individual Psalms in the Septuagint the terms *psalmos* (psalm) and *odee* (song) occur together on twelve occasions. For example, the title of Psalm 4 says 'a song of David among the psalms.' Also, the terms *psalmos* (psalms) and *humnos* (hymn) appear with each other twice as 'a psalm of David among the hymns' (Psalms 6; 67). The Septuagint translation of Psalm 137:3 provides us with a most interesting rendering: 'For there they that had carried us captive asked of us the words of a song and they had carried us away asked a hymn, saying, "sing us one of the songs of Zion".' Even literature outside the Bible supports the idea that the terms Paul uses in Eph. 5:19 and Col. 3:16 are synonymous. The Jewish historian Josephus, who wrote after the time of Paul's epistles, said 'David...composed songs and hymns to God' and 'he also made instruments of music, and taught the Levites to sing hymns to God.' (Ibid., pp 154-5).

In light of the fact that the terms 'psalms', 'hymns' and 'songs' are used in the Greek Bible to describe the uninspired songs of the Psalter; it seems highly unreasonable to assume that in Eph. 5:19 and Col. 3:16 that Paul is referring either completely to uninspired songs or to inspired songs along with uninspired songs. As Murray and Young commented:

> We see then that psalms are inspired. Songs are inspired because they are characterised as "spiritual". What then about hymns? May they

be uninspired? ...it would be strange to the point of absurdity if Paul should be supposed to insist that songs had to be inspired but hymns not. (*The Minority Report*).

Surely it is not wise to assume that the word 'hymns' refers to uninspired compositions, in light of its usage in the Septuagint and the fact that it is placed between 'psalms' and 'spiritual songs' which obviously refers to inspired compositions? However, some might object that the word 'spiritual' used in these two texts (Eph. 5:19; Col. 3:16) merely refers to religious songs and not necessarily to inspired ones. But considering that the word 'spiritual', as it is used in the New Testament, usually means 'of the Holy Spirit' or 'proceeding from the Holy Spirit' the assumption that Paul uses it merely to distinguish between religious and secular songs is not a reasonable deduction. Moreover, Dr. B.B. Warfield explains how the term 'spiritual' is generally employed in the New Testament:

Of the twenty-five instances in which the word occurs in the New Testament, in no single case does it sink even as low in its reference as the human spirit; and in twenty-four of them is derived from *pneuma*, the Holy Spirit. In this sense of belonging to, or determined by, the Holy Spirit, the New Testament usage is uniform with the one single exception of Eph. 6:12, where it seems to refer to the higher though superhuman intelligences.

The appropriate translation for it in each case is spirit given, or spirit led, or spirit-determined. (Cited in M. Bushell, *The Songs of Zion*, pp 90-1).

As no uninspired song can claim to be a production of the Holy Spirit, the only conclusion that we can reach is that Paul is exhorting his readers to sing the inspired songs found in the book of Psalms. Often, at this point, the objection is raised by the opponents of exclusive psalmody that it would have been absurd for Paul to say, 'sing psalms, psalms and psalms.' However, it was a common literary method among Jewish people at this time to use more than one expression to convey an idea (what is known as parallelism). Elsewhere in Scripture the Holy Spirit, through the inspired Jewish writers, used a variety of titles to describe the same thing. Such as God's 'commandments and his statutes and his rules' (Deut. 30:16), and of 'mighty works |miracles NKJV| and wonders and signs' (Acts 2:22); so why assume that 'psalms, hymns and songs' refers to totally different compositions, especially considering that all these terms are used in the book of Psalms to describe inspired Psalms. Furthermore, if one is going to contend that 'hymns' and 'spiritual songs' refers to uninspired compositions then we must ask the question 'what is the difference between a hymn and a spiritual song?' This is a question that no proponent of uninspired hymns has ever been able to answer from Scripture. Certainly many have guessed at what the distinction *might* be; but nobody has ever been able to open the Bible and conclusively prove what the difference actually is. Do you wish to build your worship practice upon such an uncertain foundation? I certainly don't because 'whatever does not proceed from faith is sin' (Rom. 14:23); as you cannot sing an uninspired hymn with any faith that this is what Paul is talking about it would be most unadvisable to proceed with singing them.

Also, there are many logical reasons for concluding that Paul was not instructing his readers to sing uninspired hymns in worship. The context in which these passages appear would seem to excluded uninspired material, as we are commanded to 'be filled with the Spirit' (Eph. 5:18) and to 'Let the word of Christ dwell in you richly' (Col. 3:16). As G. I. Williamson explained 'to be filled with the Spirit requires the indwelling of the word of Christ. One cannot be filled with the one unless he is filled with the other. If the words with which we are filled are not those of the Holy Spirit how can they be the means by which we are filled with the Holy Spirit? And how can the Spirit fill us with anything other than His own words?' (*The Singing of Psalms in the Worship of God*, p. 12). Many hymn-singers would claim that the Psalms cannot be the 'word of Christ' as they are only Old Testament writings. However, the inspired writers of the Psalms were 'carried along by the Holy Spirit' (2 Pet. 1:21) and we are told that 'the Spirit of Christ in them...predicted the sufferings of Christ and the subsequent glories' (1 Pet. 1:11). So if the Spirit of Christ wrote the book of Psalms, it must logically follow that the Psalms are the 'word of

Christ.' Certainly, the expression 'the word of Christ' could not be applied to uninspired hymns; especially considering that it is used in Romans 10:17 to describe inspired Scripture. Would anyone seriously argue that when Paul said 'faith comes from hearing, and hearing through the word of Christ' he was referring to merely human writings? I very much doubt any Reformed Christian would, yet this is exactly what many do when the same expression is used in Colossians 3:16. If we are to 'teach' and 'admonish' one another with 'the word of Christ' in song; how better could we achieve this than by singing from the inspired book of Psalms which Jesus tells us speak clearly about His person and work (Luke 24:44)?

Furthermore, how can these passages possibly provide warrant for uninspired song when the apostle merely commands his readers to sing, not write, songs that presumably already existed? These verses contain no command to compose songs of praise, but only to sing them. And if Paul had instructed these Gentile converts to write new hymns for worship, would this not have stirred up considerable controversy among Jewish brethren? Prof. John McNaughter notes that the Jewish Christians:

> Brought with them from the synagogue the highly cherished Psalms, those Psalms which were associated with their holiest traditions, and which were known to have been meet for the Master's use, and thereby doubly consecrated. Clinging to these with an inherited reverence, they must have resented vigor-

ously an uninspired Gentile hymnody. The fact, therefore, that on the subject of praise there is not the slightest echo of discord or controversy in the Apostolic Church, indicates that there was no intrusion of any alien element. (*The Psalms in Worship*, p. 130).

Would Paul really have instructed his readers to do something which would have caused widespread division in the Church? If he had, no doubt his enemies, the Judaizers, would have had plenty of ammunition to attack him with. Also, when one considers that Paul wrote the letter to the Colossians to refute the Gnostic heresy, that some in that Church had been infected with, what then would have been better for them than to have sung the inspired and inerrant book of Psalms. If the Colossians had written their own hymns, no doubt these would have been tinged with Gnostic error; and Paul, writing under the inspiration of the Spirit, would not have told them to do anything which would have caused them to sin. Plus it is also highly unlikely that any of the Colossians or Ephesians would have had the literary capabilities to compose songs of praise. As McNaughter further states:

It is altogether improbable that hymnists, as measured by even human standards, could be found in the churches of this date. The Gentile members, within whose circle the search is confined, had been but recently rescued from the ignorance and pollution of heathenism,

and they had immature, often faulty understanding of religious doctrine. Their literary
capabilities, too, must have been limited,
for "not many wise after the flesh, not many
mighty, not many noble, were called." Indeed,
the low social status of the early Christians
was the standing reproach of hostile critics.
All this being true, where are we to find the
mellow piety, the spiritual discernment, the
education, and poetic genius and art which
must be taken for granted if uninspired songs
fit to be named alongside the Psalms are
here in mind? Men who deny the genuine-
ness of Ephesians and Colossians allege that
the reference is to just such songs, and then
proceed to conclude that for this very reason,
among others, these Epistles betray themselves as later than the Apostolic era. (Ibid.,
p. 131).

To conclude then that Paul was instructing
them to write uninspired songs seems to be entirely
contrary to reason, and requires one to divorce these
verses from their historical context, which is not a
sound method of Biblical interpretation. The only
rational conclusion which we can reach concerning
these passages is that the apostle Paul wanted these
early Christians to mutually edify one another by
singing from the Church's permanent praise book,
the Psalter.

Common Objections to Exclusive Psalmody

While it would be impossible to answer every single objection that the natural man could put up to exclusive psalmody, nevertheless, I shall endeavour to answer some of the most common arguments set forward against total psalmody.

The Analogy of Prayer

Some people argue that since God allows us to compose our own prayers, then it must follow that he also wants us to use our own words in song. However, this argument forgets that God's requirement for the separate parts of worship is different. For example, in reading the word we only read the words of inspired Scripture; however, in the preaching of the word the minister uses his own words to expound, explain and apply Holy Scripture. So we can't just assume that what is true for one part of worship is also appropriate for an entirely separate element.

Furthermore, the analogy of prayer argument is not a reasonable deduction from Scripture, because, in the Bible, we are given directions about how we are to pray. For example, in the Lord's Prayer, Jesus tells us 'Pray then like this' (Matt. 6:9) and then goes on to provide us with a pattern for prayer. However, nowhere in Scripture, does Christ do this in the matter of song. There is no example where the Lord said to the disciples 'Sing then like this' and provided them with a model song which they could base all their own songs on. If He had done this then the analogy of prayer would be a logical deduction from Scripture, and it would be absolutely right to compose uninspired hymns. But due to the fact that the Lord Jesus has never done any such thing the analogy of prayer cannot be considered to be a reasonable inference from the Bible's teaching.

Moreover, God has promised believers the assistance of the Holy Spirit when we engage in prayer. So we read in Romans 8:26-27 'Likewise the Spirit helps us in our weakness. For we do not know what to pray for as we ought, but the Spirit himself intercedes for us with groanings too deep for words. And he who searches hearts knows what is the mind of the Spirit, because the Spirit intercedes for the saints according to the will of God.' We clearly see that the Lord has provided us the Spirit's help in uttering prayers to God. Yet, where in the Bible do we read about the Holy Spirit assisting us in composing our own worship songs? Because the Church does not have a set prayer-book, Paul observes that 'we do not know what we should pray for as we ought'; however, we do know what we should sing due to the fact that God has provided us with a divinely inspired manual of praise. The Lord's provision for these elements of worship is entirely different. After all, our songs of praise would be very unedifying if it was necessary for the Holy Spirit to intercede for us 'with groanings too deep for words.'

G.I. Williamson has explained, perhaps better than anyone else, why the argument from the analogy of prayer as a justification for uninspired hymns in worship is fallacious and confuses the elements of worship:

(a) In public prayer one speaks for all and so no prayer book is needed, since the Holy Spirit is promised to enable prayer to be made according to God's will. But in public praise all must sing together, and an inspired book of praise has been given so that we may all sing these words of God which are according to His will.

(b) In prayer we speak of our varying needs. But in praise we exalt the unchanging God. Each prayer must be different, but the appropriate songs of praise are the same from age to age. Our needs change, but God who is to be praised changes not.

(c) If prayer and praise were really analogous, it would be as reasonable to argue that only the prayers of the Bible should be used (because only the psalms of the Bible should be sung), as to argue from the reverse side of the matter. But the argument from analogy is not justified. And to avoid such confusion God has plainly commanded that which is proper for each element of worship. And for each element of worship the same principle applies: what God has not commanded is therefore forbidden. (*The Singing of Psalms in the Worship of God*, pp 21-2).

The Psalms do not include the name of Jesus

Many sincere Christians worry that if we restrict our praise to the book of Psalms we will not be able to sing the name of Jesus and consequently dishonour our Saviour. It is wise for us to recognise that this presents many godly believers, who desire to honour the Lord Jesus Christ, with a problem. Therefore, we should seek to instruct them on this point in a gentle and mild manner, commending them for being so interested in the honour and glory of Jesus Christ our Lord. Although disagreeing with their scruples, let us be humble, and learn to love Christ with as much sincerity as those who raise this objection.

However, this objection (though often a sincere one) is based on something of a misunderstanding of what Scripture means when it says 'at the name of Jesus every knee should bow' (Phil. 2:10). Paul was not telling us that we are to worship and serve the word "Jesus"; instead we exalt and glorify the person whom the name represents. Indeed, in the verse in question Paul uses the 'name of Jesus' to refer to recognition of the power, authority and majesty of Jesus at the last day. Commenting on this passage John Calvin wrote:

> Paul speaks of Christ's whole dignity, to restrict his meaning to two syllables, as if any one were to examine attentively the letters of the word *Alexander*, in order to find in them the greatness of the name that Alexander acquired for himself...But worse than ridicu-

lous is the conduct of the Sorbonnic Sophists, who infer from the passage before us that we ought to bow the knee whenever the name of Jesus is pronounced, as though it were a magic word which had all virtue included in the sound of it. Paul, on the other hand, speaks of the honour that is to be rendered to the Son of God – not to mere syllables. (Cited in B.M. Schwertley, *Exclusive Psalmody: A Biblical Defence*, p. 58).

Furthermore, the Reformed Baptist theologian Dr. John Gill makes this extremely important observation that Paul's reference to bowing at the name of Jesus:

Is to be understood, not of the outward act of bowing the knee upon hearing the name, and the syllables of the mere name Jesus pronounced; for in the bare name there can be nothing which can command such peculiar respect; it was a name common with the Jews: Joshua is so called in Heb. 4:8 [Check this out in the AV were it reads 'Jesus'] and the name of Elymas the sorcerer was Bar-Jesus; that is, the son of Jesus, Acts 13:6. Now, how monstrously ridiculous and stupid would it be, for a man, upon hearing these passages, and upon the pronouncing of this word, to bow the knee? Moreover, the words ought not to be rendered at, but in the name of Jesus; that is, in and by reason of the power, authority, and dignity of Jesus, as exalted at God's right hand, every creature is to be subject to him. (Cited in Ibid.).

Since the Greek word for 'Jesus' is the equivalent of the Hebrew word for 'Joshua', which is used in the Old Testament as the name for mere men, we can see that 'there is nothing *intrinsically* sacred, mystical or holy regarding the word "Jesus".' (ibid. p. 57). Due to the fact that the word 'Jesus' in our English Bibles is a translation of a Greek word, and the book of Psalms was translated from Hebrew (an entirely different language from Greek), it is unreasonable to expect the book of Psalms to contain the actual word 'Jesus'. Therefore, though Christians who exclusively sing from the Psalter are not using the actual word 'Jesus', they are not losing out on anything because the Psalms adequately recognise, beyond the capability of any uninspired hymn, the person, work, power, authority, majesty, and glory of the Lord Jesus Christ. When we use the Psalms in worship we exalt the name of Jesus because the Psalms exalt the person of our Saviour. Hence, it is not necessary for us to invent and sing human compositions to properly honour the name of the Lord Jesus. We know this because the name Jesus means 'Jehovah is salvation'; (that is why our Lord was called Jesus because 'he will save his people from their sins' Matt. 1:21), and the book of Psalms teaches us about Christ's role as His people's Saviour (Ps. 2:7-12; 8:5; 16:9-11; 22; 24:17-20; 35:11; 40:7-9; 41:9; 45:6; 47:5; 50:3-4; 68:18; 69; 72; 110). So when Christians sing from the book of Psalms, which alone are authorised by

God in His praise, they can do so with full assurance that they are honouring and worshipping the name of the Lord Jesus Christ.

The Imprecatory Psalms

One of the more sinister objections to exclusive psalmody is that certain passages of the Psalter are considered to be unfit for New Testament worship, because the writer calls down imprecations and curses upon God's enemies. David even goes so far as to cry out 'let them be blotted out of the book of the living' (Psalm 69:28); and the author of Psalm 137 pronounced woe upon the Babylonians for leading Judah into captivity:

O daughter of Babylon, doomed to be destroyed, blessed shall he be who repays you with what you have done to us! Blessed shall he be who takes your little ones and dashes them against the rock. (vv. 8-9)

Much as these verses might disturb the natural man (and don't get me wrong they are truly awesome statements), they are, nevertheless, part of Holy Scripture. The authors of the imprecatory psalms did not simply record their own feelings against people they disliked, for 'no prophecy of Scripture...was ever produced by the will of man' (2 Pet. 1:20-21), but instead what they wrote was inspired by God's Spirit 'men spoke from God as they were carried along by the Holy Spirit' (2 Pet. 1:21). As Michael

221

Bushell has rightly pointed out 'the Psalms are all inspired compositions, and any accusations levelled at them are directed ultimately at the Holy Spirit who wrote them.' (*The Songs in Zion*, p. 33). Therefore, for any Christian to regard the content of the imprecatory psalms as somehow false and erroneous is to call into question the inerrancy and infallibility of Scripture.

Perhaps the reason why so many of us have a difficulty singing the Psalms which call down God's judgement is because so few uninspired hymns ever speak of God's justice; it has almost became a forgotten attribute in modern evangelical praise. Such a perspective is foreign both to the Old and New Testament Scriptures. Paul tells us that we are to 'consider the goodness and severity of God' (Rom. 11:22 NKJV); while many are happy enough to think about God's goodness (His grace, love and mercy) few people consider that He is 'a just God' (Isa. 45:21 NKJV) who is 'of purer eyes than to behold evil, and cannot look on wickedness' (Hab. 1:13 NKJV). This means that He must punish sin and He will 'by no means clear the guilty' (Ex. 34:7). Interestingly, imprecatory psalms are actually quoted in the New Testament. For example, in Acts 1:20 the apostle Peter cites Psalm 69:25 in reference to Judas Iscariot 'May his camp become desolate, and let there be no one to dwell in it.' Moreover, when we pray 'Your kingdom come' (Matt. 6:10) we are, in part, asking that Christ would return and judge the wicked (2 Thess. 1:7-8). So, in light of the Biblical teaching on God's justice, we should have no difficulty singing Psalms which accurately reflect this.

Opposition to singing the curses contained in the Psalter is the effect of Christian's minds being shaped by the ungodly philosophies of this present evil world rather than by the pure word of God (Rom. 12:2). Michael Bushell also observed that 'those who depreciate the imprecatory psalms usually do so on the assumption that the inalienable rights of man have been violated. They forget what the Reformed Christian ought to know full well: that every man born into the world stands condemned already before God as a guilty sinner.' (Ibid., p. 38). People often forget that sinful men deserve nothing, but God's eternal wrath to be poured out upon them, so it should hardly be surprising that God's praise book includes calls for His judgements to be executed upon the enemies of the Lord. Those of us who believe in total psalmody should not consider the imprecatory psalms to be an inconvenient embarrassment, that we would prefer were never there, rather we should point out that they are one of the advantages of using the Psalter as opposed to modern hymns. The book of Psalms displays a proper theological balance setting forth, not only God's love, but also His justice. Man-made songs tend to be intrinsically unbalanced, laying too much stress upon one particular aspect of truth. However, we find no such imbalance in God's own hymnbook.

Psalm Versions are often unfaithful translations

A rather common way of evading the obligation to sing Psalms exclusively is the argument that, since translations of the book of Psalms for singing are not as accurate as those in translation of the English Bible for reading, then singing from a metrical version of the Psalms is no different from singing uninspired hymns. Now it should be admitted that while translation of the book of Psalms for singing are usually not as good as the best modern English versions (ESV, NKJV, NASB and NIV), nevertheless, as far as they reflect the original Hebrew, they are still the word of God. The Greek Septuagint (which the apostles used) was considerably worse than even the best modern English translations today, yet it is still quoted by the authors of the New Testament as inspired Scripture (e.g. Heb. 10:5). So the demand that metrical psalm versions be absolutely brilliant before they can be sung goes beyond the Bible's teaching on the legitimacy of translation out of the original languages. Moreover, Brian Schwertley concludes that those who use this argument to avoid singing only the Psalms 'in order to be consistent, would ultimately require the Scripture reading in public worship to be done in the original languages (Hebrew, Aramaic, and Greek).' (*Exclusive Psalmody: A Biblical Defence*, p. 63). Those who contend that because some translations of the psalms found in metrical Psalters are inaccurate, therefore, we should sing uninspired hymns instead; would also have to argue that because some churches use dreadful paraphrases of the Scriptures (such as the Message, and the Living Bible) it is automatically justifiable to read from uninspired materials in worship. Such reasoning is incoherent; until better translations of the Psalms for singing can be produced we should make the best of what we have got rather than singing entirely man-made hymns.

The Sufficiency and Doctrinal Integrity of the Psalter

Among intellectual Reformed Christians there is a widespread feeling that the book of Psalms is doctrinally insufficient to satisfy the needs of the Church in the New Testament dispensation. However, the fact that God has provided the Church with the book of Psalms, as the exclusive manual of His praise, shows us that the Psalter must be sufficient for the worship needs of the Lord's people. Considering that the psalms were sung by believers in the New Testament also demonstrates that they are adequate for the Church now. But it is argued that the Church needs worship songs written after the completion of Christ's work of redemption. However, if this was true why has God not given us additional inspired songs? The only logical answer is that the book of Psalms is sufficient for New Testament worship and that no additional inspired songs, let alone uninspired hymns, are required. As Michael Bushell says:

Once it is admitted that God through His Spirit has written a divine book of song intended for use in His worship and that this book is fully adequate for the needs of the Church in the present dispensation, the need for a new book of songs, together with its only possible warrant vanishes. (*The Songs of Zion*, p. 11).

This contention might have some basis in reason if the Psalms had little or nothing to say about the Lord Jesus Christ and His work of redemption. However, the Psalter contains much more 'information and doctrine regarding the person and work of Christ than any humanly devised hymnbook.' (B. M. Schwertley, *Exclusive Psalmody: A Biblical Defence*, p. 33). Even a man such as Martin Luther, who was not an advocate of exclusive psalmody (in fact he did not even subscribe to the regulative principle of worship) had this to say about the Christological and doctrinal sufficiency of the Psalter:

The Psalter ought to be a precious and beloved book, if for no other reason than this: it promises Christ's death and resurrection so clearly – and pictures his kingdom and the condition and nature of all Christendom – that it might well be called a little Bible...In fact, I have a notion that the Holy Spirit wanted to take the trouble Himself to compile a short Bible and book of examples of all Christendom or all saints, so that anyone who could not read the whole Bible would here have anyway an entire summary of it, comprised in one little book. (Cited in M. Bushell, *The Songs of Zion*, p. 16).

A through acquaintance with the contents of the book of Psalms will teach us that the Psalter has much to say about Jesus Christ and His work. The Psalms teach us about Christ's deity 'Your throne O God, is for ever and ever' (Psalm 45:6), His eternal Son-ship 'The LORD said to me, "You are my Son; today I have begotten you' (Psalm 2:7); His incarnation and humanity 'Yet you have made him a little lower than the heavenly beings and crowned him with glory and honour' (Psalm 8:5). Moreover, the Psalter teaches us about Jesus' mediatorial offices as our prophet 'I have proclaimed the good news of righteousness in the great assembly; indeed, I do not restrain my lips, O LORD, You Yourself know. I have not hidden Your righteousness within my heart; I have declared your faithfulness and Your salvation; I have not concealed Your loving-kindness and Your truth from the great assembly' (Psalm 40:7-9 NKJV), our priest 'You are a priest for ever after the order of Melchizedek' (Psalm 110:4), and our king 'The LORD says to my Lord: "Sit at my right hand, until I make your enemies your footstool."' (Psalm 110:1). Furthermore, the book of Psalms supplies the Church with 'God-breathed' (2 Tim. 3:16 NIV) details concerning Christ's betrayal 'Even my close friend in whom I trusted, who ate my bread, has lifted up his heel against me' (Psalm 41:9), His agony in the garden 'O my God, I cry by day, but you do not answer, and by night, but I find no rest' (Psalm 22:2); His trial 'Malicious witnesses rise up; they ask me of things that I do not know' (Psalm 35:11), His rejection and mocking by the Jews 'But I am a worm and not a man, scorned by mankind and despised by the people. All who see me mock at me; they wag their heads; "He trusts in the LORD let him deliver him; let him rescue him, for he delights in him!"' (Psalm 22:6-8) and 'The stone which the builders rejected has become the cornerstone' (Psalm 118:22); His crucifixion 'For dogs encompass me; a company of evildoers encircles me; they have pierced my hands and feet – I count all my bones – they stare and gloat over me, they divide my garments among them, and for my clothing they cast lots' (Psalm 22:16-18) and 'They have gave me poison for food, and for my thirst they gave me sour wine to drink' (Psalm 69:21); His burial and resurrection 'For you will not abandon my soul to Sheol, or let your holy one see corruption' (Psalm 16:10); His ascension 'You ascended on high, leading a host of captives in your train and receiving gifts among men' (Psalm 68:18); and His second coming and judgement 'for he comes to judge the earth. He will judge the world with righteousness, and the peoples with equity' (Psalm 98:9). So we can clearly see that the Psalms have much to teach us about the Lord Jesus Christ, and much more than any uninspired hymnbook could ever do. Especially when one considers the sufferings of Christ's soul, set forth in Psalm 22:1 'My God, my God why have you forsaken me?' is something that no uninspired hymn could ever do or has ever done. If you want to learn more about Jesus Christ our Saviour, then sing the Psalms which have so much to say about Him.

However, despite the Christological excellence of the Psalter, the opponents of total psalmody argue that while the Psalms teach us about the Lord Jesus, they use types, symbols and prophecies to describe His work. It is felt that the Church in the New Covenant era should not be restricted to a praise-book which uses shadowy language in light of the "unveiled" nature of the revelation that we now possess in the New Testament. Yet when we keep in mind that the Church now has the completed canon of Scripture, so that we can fully understand and interpret the types, symbols and prophecies contained within the Psalter, this objection has no weight behind it. As Brian Schwertley observed that it is strange 'to suggest that at the precise moment when the Psalter can be fully understood and be even more edifying for the people of God that it is no longer sufficient.' (*Exclusive Psalmody: A Biblical Defence*, p. 36). Considering that the complete revelation of the New Testament enables us to make better use of the book of Psalms (than believers in the Old Testament did) why should we lay aside this praise book that has been 'breathed out by God' (2 Tim. 3:16) in favour of uninspired hymns which very often contradict the teaching of Scripture.

Theological Content of the Psalter

The book of Psalms, being immediately inspired by God, contains a wide range of doctrine which is theologically balanced and fit for edifying and instructing believers in their Christian faith.

Divine Revelation

The Psalms instruct us about how God has revealed Himself in creation (natural revelation) 'The heavens declare the glory of God, and the sky above his handiwork' (Psalm 19:1). Yet they also tell us that while the existence of God may be derived from nature, the only way to obtain a saving knowledge of the Lord is through His word (the Holy Scriptures) 'The law of the LORD is perfect, reviving the soul; the testimony of the LORD is sure, making wise the simple; the precepts of the LORD are right, rejoicing the heart, the commandment of the LORD is pure enlightening the eyes' (Psalm 19:7-8). The Psalter teaches us the inerrancy of Scripture 'The words of the LORD are pure words, like silver refined in a furnace of the ground, purified seven times' (Psalm 12:6); and the infallibility of the Bible 'the sum of your words is truth' (Psalm 119:160). Moreover, the Psalms instruct us that growth in grace in the life of the believer is through memorization of the word of God 'I have hidden your word in my heart that I might not sin against you' (Psalm 119:11 NIV) accompanied by meditation 'Blessed is the man' whose 'delight is in the law of the LORD, and on his law he meditates day and night' (Psalm 1:1-2), through the illuminating grace of the Holy Spirit (Psalm 119:65-69).

The Doctrine of God

In contrast to the Arminianism that taints modern hymnals, the Psalms teach us about God's independence and self-existence 'Our God is in the heavens; he does all that he pleases' (Psalm 115:3). Furthermore, the Psalter provides us with much instruction regarding the attributes of God, such as, His absolute perfection 'Great is the LORD...and his greatness is unsearchable' (Psalm 145:3); the fact that God is spirit, in distinction from the gods of the heathen, 'Their idols are silver and gold the work of human hands' (Psalm 115:4). His eternality 'from everlasting to everlasting you are God' (Psalm 90:2), His omnipresence 'If I ascend to heaven you are there! If I make my bed in Sheol, you are there!' (Psalm 139:8), His omniscience 'all my ways are before you' (Psalm 119:168) 'Even before a word is on my tongue, behold, O LORD, you know it altogether' (Psalm 139:4), His omnipotence 'his eyes see, his eyelids test, the children of man' (Psalm 11:4), his faithfulness 'All paths of the LORD are steadfast love and faithfulness' (Psalm 25:10), His sovereignty 'For the Kingship belongs to the LORD, and he rules over the nations' (Psalm 22:28), His goodness 'The LORD is good to all' (Psalm 145:9), His mercy 'For his mercy endures for ever' (Psalm 136:2 NKJV), His longsuffering 'But you, O Lord, are...slow to anger' (Psalm 86:15), His grace 'the LORD is gracious' (Psalm 111:3), His holiness 'Exalt the LORD our God; worship at his footstool! Holy is he!' (Psalm 99:5), His righteousness 'Righteous are you, O LORD…You have appointed your testimonies in righteousness' (Psalm 119:137-8), and his justice 'surely there is a God who judges on earth' (Psalm 58:11).

The Works of God

The Psalter teaches that God is the creator 'you have created all the children of man!' (Psalm 89:47), and the Saviour 'They forgot God, their Saviour, who had done great things in Egypt' (Psalm 106:21). Also, the Psalms instruct us about God's providence 'the counsel of the LORD stands for ever, the plans of his heart to all generations' (Psalm 33:11), His holy hatred of sin 'For you are not a God who delights in wickedness; evil may not dwell with you' (Psalm 5:4), His punishment of the wicked 'if a man does not repent, God will whet his sword' (Psalm 7:12), and how the Lord chastens and corrects His people 'Before I was afflicted I went astray, but now I keep your word' (Psalm 119:67).

Sin and Salvation

As well as teaching man's original dignity (Psalm 8:5), the book of Psalms contains the doctrines of original sin 'Behold, I was brought forth in iniquity, and in sin did my mother conceive me' (Psalm 51:5), man's total depravity, inability and universal corruption 'God looks down from heaven on the children of man to see if there are any who understand, who seek after God. They have all become corrupt; there is none who does good, not even one' (Psalm 53:2-3). Additionally, the Psalter teaches us about God's Covenant of grace to rescue man out of his sin and misery 'the steadfast love of the LORD is from everlasting to everlasting...to those who keeps his covenant' (Psalm 103:17-18). Moreover, the Psalms teach us about regeneration 'create in me a clean heart, O God, and renew a right spirit within me' (Psalm 51:10), faith 'O my God, in you I trust' (Psalm 25:1), repentance 'Against you, you only, have I sinned' (Psalm 51:4), justification by faith and the forgiveness of sins 'Blessed is the one those transgression is forgiven, whose sin is covered. Blessed is the man against whom the LORD counts no iniquity' (Psalm 32:1-2), sanctification 'How can a youth keep his way pure? By guarding it according to your word' (Psalm 119:9), and the perseverance of the saints 'My help comes from the LORD, who made heaven and earth' (Psalm 121:2) and the glorification of the believer in heaven 'and I shall dwell in the house of the LORD for ever' (Psalm 23:6), and the ultimate salvation of the Church of God 'With joy and gladness they are led along as they enter the palace of the King...therefore the nations will praise you for ever and ever' (Psalm 45:15-17).

In conclusion, obviously this is only the tip of the iceberg, but it is enough to illustrate that the Psalms are a gold mine of doctrine to teach us about the Lord and His great salvation. Why then would we ever want to sing anything else?

CHAPTER 10:

Instrumental Music in the Public Worship of God

When the *Westminster Confession* specifies that 'the singing of psalms with grace in the heart' (Chapter 21: Section 5) is a regulative principle of worship; it is silent on the use of musical instruments in the accompaniment of praise. Clearly the only logical explanation for this is that the Westminster Assembly did not regard the use of instrumental music as a part of New Testament worship. Moreover, the *Testimony of the Reformed Presbyterian Church of Ireland* explains why this is so:

> There is no warrant for instrumental accompaniment to the singing in New Testament worship. In Hebrews 13:15, Christians are called upon to "offer the sacrifice of praise to

God continually, that is, the fruit of our lips giving thanks to His name." It seems clear that the constitution and form of worship of the New Testament Church were patterned after the Synagogue which did not have instrumental music and not after the Temple, which did as part of its sacrificial ritual (2 Chron. 29:27-30). If we are to follow the pattern of worship of the New Testament Church, which is our standard, our praise in worship will consist of psalms sung without instrumental accompaniment. (p. 40).

I shall seek to argue below that this is the Biblical position, by analysing how musical instruments were used in the Old Testament, and by proving that they have been abrogated (done away with) in the New Covenant.

Musical Instruments – Not a Circumstance of Worship

In recent times many Reformed Christians, especially in the Dutch tradition, have contended that musical instruments are merely a circumstance of worship necessary to its performance; and thus falling outside the boundary of the regulative principle. They view instrumental accompaniment as something indifferent such as, buildings, times of meetings, lighting and heating etc. However, an analysis of the Scriptural data concerning the use of musical instruments will show us, beyond all reasonable doubt, that the people in the Bible always regarded the employment of instrumental music as being directly under God's authority. This can be proved by looking at how the trumpet was employed in the worship of the Tabernacle back in the days of Moses. In Numbers 10:10 we read 'On the day of your gladness also, and at your appointed feasts and at the beginnings of your months, you shall blow the trumpets over your burnt offerings and over the sacrifices of your peace offerings.' Notice here that God regulated the specific instrument to be used and the purposes for which it should be used. If the use of instruments was merely a circumstance why would the Lord have given such precise instructions? Moreover, it is worth remembering that Moses was actually divinely guided by the Holy Spirit to invent this particular instrument 'The LORD spoke to Moses, saying, "Make two silver trumpets. Of hammered work you shall make them"' (Numbers 10:1). Moses didn't just pick an instrument at random from the contemporary culture and think that this was acceptable in God's worship; instead he obeyed God's command regarding one specific type of musical instrument. This is highly significant; Pastor John Price observed:

> The trumpet as a musical instrument existed prior to the time of Moses and probably first appeared in ancient Egypt. The Egyptian trumpets of that time were curved like a ram's horn, and, being educated among the Egyptians, Moses would surely have known of them. But Moses was not commanded

to take his trumpet from the Egyptians. For God's worship he was to make a new trumpet that was straight and not curved. (*Old Light on New Worship*, pp 58-9).

The fact that this instrument was not used until God commanded its use, and gave detailed instructions about how and when it was to be used, shows the Bible views the employment or non-employment of instrumental music as under the government of the regulative principle. The trumpet, at this stage in the Church's worship, was the only instrument authorised in God's public worship; the Church never used anything else until the time of David. Then at this point in redemptive history, a very distinct change takes place in the Church's public worship. Israel was no longer a wandering nation, as in Moses' day, they now possessed the land of Canaan and the ark of the covenant was eventually settled in Jerusalem. This led to a change in the role of the Levites, who had previously transported the Tabernacle and its furnishings, but now they were to be used as professional singers and musicians. We read in 1 Chron. 16:4-5 that David 'appointed some of the Levites as ministers before the ark of the LORD, to invoke, to thank, and to praise the LORD, the God of Israel... Asaph was to sound the cymbals.' And in 1 Chron. 23:5 we are further told that '4000 [of the Levites] shall offer praises to the LORD with the instruments that I have made for praise.'

Now, it is worth observing, that the instruments were now to be played only by a certain number of

Levites. Non-Levites, on the other hand, were not authorized to play musical instruments in public worship. It was not simply a matter of somebody saying 'I have a musical gift, therefore, I should be allowed to play an instrument in worship'; quite the opposite. If you were not a Levite, you were not permitted to join in; and the instruments that the Levites played were not the result of an arbitrary man-made choice to use whatever they felt like. Furthermore, David was a prophet who received detailed plans from God concerning the pattern of the Temple which was to be constructed after his death by Solomon (just as Moses had with the Tabernacle); 'All this he made clear to me in writing from the hand of the LORD, all the work to be done according to the plan' (1 Chron. 28:19). Therefore, as Brian Schwertley said 'nothing relating to the temple and its worship originated in man's imagination' (*Musical Instruments in the Public Worship of God*, p. 78), and this includes the use of musical instruments, they were not a mere matter of indifference. Even David had no liberty to change God's worship or fashion musical instruments in line with his own personal preferences. Indeed, the reason why David introduced new musical instruments into God's worship was that he was commanded to by the Lord. Later, when Hezekiah restored the worship of the Temple to its original purity, we read 'And he stationed the Levites in the house of the LORD with cymbals, harps, and lyres, according to the commandment of David and of Gad the King's seer and of Nathan the prophet, for the commandment was from the LORD through his prophets' (2 Chron. 29:25). David's command regarding the introduction and playing of musical instruments in the Church's public worship was the command of the Lord. Consequently, those who would introduce musical instruments into worship today must be able to prove that the use of those specific instruments is mandated in Scripture; otherwise, they are in breach of the regulative principle of worship.

On the one occasion that David did actually employ instrumental music in God's worship, without divine warrant, was when he made his first attempt to bring the ark of the covenant into Jerusalem; 'And David and all Israel were rejoicing before God with all their might, with song and lyres and harps and tambourines and cymbals and trumpets' (1 Chron. 13:8). However, this attempt failed because they merely did what 'was right in the eyes of all the people' (1 Chron. 13:4) and as a result 'the LORD our God broke out against us, because we did not consult Him about the proper order' (1 Chron. 15:13 NKJV). Therefore, the playing of instruments, on this occasion, broke the regulative principle. But when the ark was successfully moved to Jerusalem at the second attempt 'David also commanded the chiefs of the Levites to appoint their brothers as singers who should play loudly on musical instruments, on harps and lyres and cymbals, to raise sounds of joy' (1 Chron. 15:16). This time the instruments were played in accordance with the regulative principle and not according to the imaginations of men, as was the case previously.

If the use of these instruments was merely a circumstance of worship 'common to human actions and societies' (*Westminster Confession* Chapter 1: Section 6) then one would expect the instruments employed in the Temple to have changed with the culture of the day, especially after the exiles returned from the Babylonian captivity, hundreds of years after David's reign had finished. However, Nehemiah restored the service of the Temple 'according to the command of David and his son Solomon. For long ago in the days of David and Asaph there had been directors for the singers and for the songs of praise and thanksgiving to God' (Neh. 12:45-46 NIV). And we are told that they used the 'musical instruments prescribed by David the man of God' (Neh. 12:36 NIV). John Price notices that Nehemiah and the other Old Testament reformers 'did not look to their contemporary culture for what musical instruments to use. Their only concern was to use those instruments God had commanded through David the prophet.' (*Old Light on New* Worship, p. 37). Those who appeal to the worship of the Temple as warrant for the use of instruments today, must be consistent and use the precise instruments that God authorised, and not employ the above texts as an excuse for introducing instruments into worship that are most readily accepted in their present culture. In other words, the worship of the Temple gives nobody any warrant to use drums, guitars, keyboards, bagpipes, pianos, violins, electric organs, accordions etc. However, it will be shown below that these instructions regarding the worship of the Temple have no bearing upon present day New Testament worship.

Musical Instruments and Animal Sacrifices – Abolished in the New Testament

The reason why the playing of musical instruments, in the Old Testament, was the function of the Levitical priesthood is due to the fact that their use was linked with the animal sacrifices which were a part of Old Covenant worship. Indeed, the instruments were only actually played when the sacrifice was being offered; once this had finished the Psalms were sung without instrumental accompaniment. We see this pattern followed in 2 Chron. 29:27-30:

Then Hezekiah commanded that the burnt offering be offered on the altar. And when the burnt offering began, the song of the LORD began also, and the trumpets, accompanied by the instruments of David king of Israel [Notice the instruments began to be played only when the sacrifices began]. The whole assembly worshipped, and the singers sang and the trumpeters sounded. All this continued until the burnt offering was finished, the king and all who were present bowed themselves and worshipped. And Hezekiah the king and the officials commanded the Levites to sing praises to the LORD with the words of David and Asaph the seer. And they sang

praises with gladness, and they bowed down and worshipped [Notice that now they sang unaccompanied because the sacrifice had finished].

Furthermore, on every occasion when the worship of the Temple was restored, the playing of musical instruments and the offering of sacrifice was portrayed as one act of religious worship. This means that it must follow that, in the New Covenant, the instruments are to be set aside as well the use of animal sacrifices.

When talking to the woman of Samaria, Jesus told her that the ceremonial system of worship in the Old Testament Temple was about to be abolished, 'the hour is coming when neither on this mountain nor in Jerusalem will you worship the Father…But the hour is coming, and now is here, when the true worshippers will worship the Father in spirit and truth, for the Father is seeking such people to worship him' (John 4:23-24). With the completion of Christ's work of redemption on the cross 'the curtain of the temple was torn in two, from top to bottom' (Matt. 27:51) symbolising the abolition of the ceremonial worship of the Temple. Anyone, with even a slight knowledge of the New Testament, would know that this is true; the letter to the Hebrews is especially emphatic on this point. The inspired writer describes the ceremonial worship of the Old Covenant was imposed upon the Church 'until the time of reformation' (Heb. 9:10) that came with the Saviour's death. John Owen writes that the Old Testament ceremonies were 'far from being able themselves to perfect the state of spiritual things which God would introduce.' (Cited in Ibid., p. 43). Commenting on the abolition of the Old Covenant's worship (upon the death of Christ) Owen writes 'then did he [Christ] pronounce concerning it and all things belonging unto it, "It is finished".' (Ibid.). Obviously the sacrificial priesthood has now been done away with as a result of Christ's perfect finished sacrifice 'Now if perfection had been attainable through the Levitical priesthood (for under it the people received the law), what further need would there have been for another priest to arise after the order of Melchizedek, rather than the one named after the order of Aaron? For when there is a change in the priesthood, there is necessarily a change in the law as well' (Heb. 7:11-12). So if the Levitical priesthood is now abolished, then so also are the laws of worship that governed their religious duties in the Temple. John Price observed, 'This must include the use of musical instruments as an inherent part of the Levitical priesthood. When the priesthood is taken away, so must be all of its functions including its use of musical instruments (1 Chron. 16:4-6; 23:1-5).' (Ibid., p. 41). It was not just the sacrificial system, which typified Christ's coming, but the whole system of worship employed in the Temple has now been abrogated 'this would necessarily include all the musical instruments that were always considered as part of Temple worship under the Levitical priesthood.' (Ibid. p. 48).

Some might argue that there were instances, in the Old Testament, were musical instruments where used outside of the Temple in public worship; from what is recorded in Scripture, we know this only happened on four occasions:

1. The successful moving the ark of the covenant (1 Chron. 15:14-28).

2. The dedication ceremony held at the completion of Solomon's Temple (2 Chron. 5:11-14).

3. The dedication ceremony held at the completion of the foundation of the second Temple (Ezra 3:10-11).

4. The dedication ceremony held at the completion of the wall of Jerusalem (Neh. 12:27-43). (B.M. Schwertley, *Musical Instruments in the Worship of God*, p. 85).

However, these examples do not prove that musical instruments were used in non-ceremonial or non-Levitical practice, as it was only the Levites who were authorized to play the instruments, and they only employed the specific instruments that God had ordained for them to use. And as the above examples were all closely linked to the worship of the Old Testament sanctuary they are obviously ceremonial and cannot provide modern evangelicals and conservative Presbyterians with a Biblical warrant for pianos, electric organs, guitars, accordions or drums.

New Testament Christians have no more warrant to employ musical instruments in-worship than they do priestly vestments, incense, altars, and a sacrificial priesthood. As Dr John Kennedy of Dingwall put it 'the altar and the sacrifice may be defended as surely as the organ.' (*Hyper Evangelism*, p. 18). The Roman Catholic 'Church' is acting with logical consistency when it employs all of these (now abolished) Old Testament rituals in its worship. John L. Girardeau, a noted 19th century American Presbyterian theologian, wrote:

> Those who have most urgently insisted upon it [musical instruments in public worship] have acted with logical consistency in incorporating priests into the New Testament Church; and as priests suppose sacrifices, lo, the sacrifice of the Mass! Instrumental music may not seem to stand upon the same foot with that monstrous corruption, but the principle which underlies both is the same; and whether we are content with a single instrument, the cornet, the bass-viol, the organ, or go on by a natural development to the orchestral art, the cathedral pomp, and the spectacular magnificence of Rome. We are Christians, and we are untrue to Christ and the Spirit of grace when we resort to the abrogated and forbidden ritual of the Jewish temple. (Cited in B.M. Schwertley, *Musical Instruments in the Public Worship of God*, p. 83).

Moreover, since the designated group which played the instruments in the Temple, the Levitical priests, no longer exists, and since in the New Covenant era there is no specific group of people set apart to play musical instruments, then we can only conclude that the playing of instrumental music is not a part of New Testament worship. And if the command of David concerning the worship of the Temple is no longer relevant, then under what authority are instruments to be brought in? Does the example of Christ provide us with warrant for instrumental music? No, because He and the apostles sang the Psalms unaccompanied after the institution of the Lord's Supper (Matt. 26:30). Furthermore, in the worship of the Jewish Synagogue, which was neither ceremonial nor typical, they also sang the Psalms without musical accompaniment, because they regarded the use of musical instruments as a ceremonial ordinance which belonged to the temporary worship of the Temple. Since the worship of the New Testament is patterned after that of the Synagogue (the word translated 'assembly' in James 2:2 means Synagogue – see AV marginal note) it comes as no surprise that we do not find one single reference to any congregation using instruments. Such a radical change from the Synagogue would surely have been recorded, and no doubt the Jews would have reproached the early Christians for such an innovation, yet the New Testament is silent concerning this. In addition to this silence we find that in the variety of Spiritual gifts, given to the Church in the New Testament there is absolutely no mention of a gift of instrumental music being supplied to anyone for use in New Covenant worship (Rom. 12:6-8; 1 Cor. 12:4-11). In light of the overwhelming Biblical evidence, we may reasonably infer that the playing of musical instruments is not part of New Testament worship.

Musical Instruments in the Psalms and Revelation

One of the most common arguments in favour of the use of musical instruments in public worship is the mention of their use in Psalm 150:3-5 which reads:

> Praise him with trumpet sound; praise him with lute and harp! Praise him with tambourines and dance; praise him with strings and pipe! Praise him with loud clashing cymbals!

Yet, it is worth remembering that the Jews, to whom this Psalm was originally written, never used this as a reason to justify introducing instrumental music into the worship of the Synagogue, so what reason do modern Christians have for thinking that it has any relevance to the public worship of Christian assemblies in the New Covenant? So what then is the Psalm talking about? To determine this we must use Scripture to interpret Scripture. Consequently, Brian Schwertley has summarized the broader teaching of the Old Testament as it relates to this Psalm:

The broad context of Scripture teaches that: dancing and tabaret playing were performed outdoors during festive occasions by women (Ex. 15:20; Jud. 11:34; 21:21; 1 Sam. 18:6; 21:11; 29:5; Jer. 31:4); only priests were authorized to play trumpets in worship (Nu. 10:8, 10; 2 Chron. 5:11-14; 29:26; Ezra 3:10); and, harps, lyres and cymbals were only authorized to be played by the Levites (1 Chron. 15:14-24; 23:5; 28:11-13, 19; 2 Chron. 5:11-14; 20:27-28; 29:25-27; Neh. 12:27). (Ibid., p. 102).

So as the dancing in this Psalm refers to the Old Testament civil celebrations, and was performed only by women, and the instruments mentioned were only played by the priests and Levites, Psalm 150 gives nobody any warrant to introduce these instruments (never mind the ones that are not even mentioned) into New Covenant worship. Moreover, in Psalm 137, which was composed during the Babylonian captivity when the Temple at Jerusalem lay in ruins, the captives cried 'we hung our harps upon the willows' (Psalm 137:2 NKJV) as they were not to be used outside the Temple. So if the Jewish Babylonian exiles did not believe that instruments were to be divorced from the sacrificial worship of the Temple; then why should Christians in the New Testament assume otherwise?

The defenders of instrumental music also appeal to the fact that the book of Revelation mentions the use of musical instruments in heaven (Rev. 5:8; 14:2;

15:2). However, due to the fact that Revelation is apocalyptic literature, which is not meant to be taken literally, it tends to use types and symbols from the Old Testament system of worship to portray the realities of the New Covenant. Brian Schwertley notes:

> John continually refers to Jesus Christ as "the Lamb" (Rev. 5:6, 8, 12-13; 6:1, 17; 7:9-10, 14; 12:11; 13:8; 14:1, 4, 10, etc.) He refers to the Church as "the temple" (3:12; 11:1-2) and the "New Jerusalem" (3:12; 21:2, 10). John mentions the "ark of His covenant" (11:19) and even describes an altar (6:9; 8:3, 5; 9:13; 11:1; 14:18; 16:7). (Ibid., p. 103).

So if we are to use the book of Revelation as a guide for New Testament worship we will have to employ a Temple, an altar, sacrifices, incense etc. And if we do this we will have to join either Roman Catholic or Eastern Orthodox bodies, who use these abrogated ceremonies today. Few evangelical Protestants would consider doing this because they know that these Old Covenant rituals have been abolished by the work of Christ (Eph. 2:13-16). Therefore we must conclude that Revelation only uses this Old Testament imagery in a symbolic way. In fact, this can even be proved from a close reading of the text of Revelation itself:

> The book of Revelation mentions incense (8:4), but John specifically says that the incense is symbolic of the prayers of the

saints. John refers to the use of trumpets (1:10; 4:1; 8:13; 9:14), but in each instance the trumpets symbolise voices or announcements of judgements. (Ibid., p. 104).

In a similar fashion the instrumental music that John apparently heard 'was like the sound of harp is to playing their harps, and they were singing a new song before the throne' (Rev. 14:2-3) this was clearly only symbolic of people singing praise, as they were not literally playing on harps. All of the above evidence proves that it is profoundly unsafe to appeal to the book of Revelation as a pattern for New Testament worship.

CHAPTER 11:

The Sacraments

While a full discussion of the theology of the sacraments is beyond the scope of this particular work, nevertheless, I shall endeavour to analyse the Biblical teaching on the sacraments as it relates to the regulative principle of worship. This means that it is essential, first of all, to consider the institution of the sacraments; by whom, and where they are to be administered, before looking at who is allowed to partake of them and what is the Scriptural mode of their administration.

<u>Instituted by Christ for His Church</u>

In addition to stating that 'the due administration and worthy receiving of the sacraments instituted by Christ' (*Westminster Confession* Chapter 21: Section 5) is part of the ordinary religious worship of God, the *Westminster Confession* also says that 'the sacraments are holy signs and seals of the covenant of grace, immediately instituted by God, to represent Christ and His benefits' (Chapter 27: Section 1). Among the Protestant reformers, and the Churches which have descended from them (Lutheran, Episcopal, and Reformed) there was, and is, universal agreement that the Lord Jesus Christ has only instituted two sacraments to be perpetually observed by His Church in the New Covenant. Hence, the *Westminster Confession*, in line with all strands of historic Protestantism, declares 'there are only two sacraments ordained by Christ our Lord in the gospel; that is to say, Baptism and the Supper of the Lord' (Chapter 27: Section 4). So in order for something to be considered as a sacrament of the New Testament Church, it has to be shown to be something ordained by the Lord Jesus in person, and its observance to be obligatory upon the Church until Christ returns.

The sacrament of baptism was instituted by Christ Himself, prior to His ascension into heaven, when He gave the apostles (and all other ministers of the word) what is known as the 'Great Commission'; Jesus said to them 'All authority in heaven and on earth has been given to me' (Matt. 28:18), including of course, the authority to institute sacraments in the Church, 'Go therefore and make disciples of all nations, baptizing them in the name of the Father and of the Son and of the Holy Spirit' (Matt. 28:19). Here Christ ordained the sacrament of water Baptism, which was to be carried out in the name of the Holy Trinity, not only in the days of the apostles, but it was to be administered until 'the end of the age' (Matt. 28:20) when the Lord will return.

Moreover, 'just as Jesus personally and expressly instituted the sacrament of Baptism...so also He personally and expressly instituted the sacrament of the Lord's Supper.' (R.L. Reymond, *A New Systematic Theology of the Christian Faith*, p. 956). Before His crucifixion, Christ instituted the Lord's Supper, in Matthew's gospel we read:

Jesus took bread, and after blessing it broke it and gave it to the disciples, and said "Take, eat; this is my body." And he took a cup, and when he had given thanks he gave it to them saying, "Drink of it, all of you, for this is my blood of the covenant, which is poured out for many for the forgiveness of sins." (Matt. 26:26-28).

In Luke's account we read that Christ told the disciples to 'Do this in remembrance of me' (Luke 22:19) implying that they were to continually repeat the observance of this ordinance. Furthermore, when instructing the Corinthians about how they were to observe the Lord's Supper, the apostle told them 'as often as you eat this bread and drink the cup, you proclaim the Lord's death until he comes' (1 Cor. 11:26) which means that the Lord's Supper was to be celebrated, by the Church, until Christ should return.

The sacraments ordained by the Lord Jesus Christ for the New Testament Church, are clearly only Baptism and the Lord's Supper. Yet amazingly the Roman Catholic 'Church' has added another five sacraments to the list: ordination, marriage, confirmation, penance and extreme unction. As Robert Shaw observes 'none of these have any divine appointment as sacraments; and the three last, as used by the Papists, have no warrant at all from Scripture.' (*An Exposition of the Westminster Confession of Faith*, p. 336). However, the only way to oppose Rome's additional sacraments is to adhere to the regulative principle of worship, and acknowledge that only what God has appointed in worship is acceptable to Him. This is where our Lutheran, Episcopalian and many modern Evangelical brethren are highly inconsistent. On the one hand they criticise Rome for having sacraments additional to Baptism and the Lord's Supper, while on the other hand they reject the regulative principle. So it is difficult to understand on exactly what grounds they can oppose Rome's five spurious sacraments. G.I. Williamson was certainly correct when he wrote:

> If God may be worshipped any way whatsoever apart from specific Scriptural warrant, then there does not seem to be any good reason why such 'sacraments' may not be added. But if God is to be worshipped within the precise limits of divine commandment, then the position of Rome is overthrown and that of the Confession is invulnerable when it says that there are only two sacraments. It can easily be shown that Christ commanded baptism and the Lord's Supper (Matt. 28:19; 1 Cor. 11:23). And it is impossible to prove

that He commanded any other sacraments. (*The Westminster Confession of Faith: For Study Classes*, p. 201).

So, only Protestants in the Reformed tradition (those who adhere to the regulative principle) can oppose Rome's doctrine of seven sacraments with any degree of logical consistency.

Due to the fact that Christ has entrusted the sacraments to the Church as a visible institution, then it must follow that they should never be administered in private, but only in a public assembly of a congregation of Christ's Church. As Baptism is the sign of membership of the visible Church (Matt. 28:19; Acts 2:38-39) then it would somewhat dilute the meaning of the sacrament to administer it in private. Likewise, Paul rebuked the Corinthians for the manner in which they observed the Lord's Supper when they came 'together as a church' (1 Cor. 11:18) which would imply that they only observed the sacrament as a congregation. Because the sacraments can only be administered in a public assembly of a true Church of Jesus Christ, we must regard the Baptism of the 'Church' of Rome, Eastern Orthodox and Unitarian denominations as invalid. Although Romish and Eastern Orthodox Baptism is performed in the name of the Trinity, these communions are not true Churches of the Lord Jesus Christ because they preach a false gospel, and have even anathematized the true gospel making them 'synagogues of Satan' (Rev. 3:9). Therefore, because they are not true Churches of Jesus Christ we must reject their sacraments as spurious.

Moreover, for the sacraments to be properly administered, they must be dispensed by an ordained minister (teaching elder) of the gospel. Because Roman Catholicism regards grace and salvation as being inseparably linked to the sacraments that no person can be regenerated or saved without them (this is totally un-Biblical as the thief on the cross was saved without receiving the sacraments Luke 23:39-43), they will, in exceptional circumstances, allow a lay person to Baptise infants who are about to die. Louis Berkhof explains:

> Roman Catholics consider baptism absolutely essential to salvation; and because they regard it as cruel to make the salvation of anyone dependent on the accidental presence of a priest, they also in cases of emergency permit Baptism by others, particularly by mid-wives. (*Systematic Theology*, p. 631).

This of course entails a superstitious view of the sacraments, regarding them as grace itself, rather than means of grace, totally confusing the sign and the thing signified. However, Berkhof goes on to explain why those in the Reformed faith have restricted the administration of the sacraments to the ministers of the word:

> The Reformed Churches always acted on the principle that the administration of the Word and of the sacraments belong together, and that therefore the teaching elder or the minister is the only lawful administrator of

Baptism. The Word and the sacrament are joined together in the words of the institution. (Ibid.)

This would appear to be a reasonable inference from Scripture because the 'Great Commission' was given to the ministers of the word whose duty it is, not only to Baptise the members of the visible Church (Matt. 28:19), but also to be 'teaching them to observe all that I [Christ] have commanded you' (Matt. 28:20). Therefore the preaching of the word and the administration of the sacraments are so closely linked that only 'a minister of the Word lawfully ordained' (*Westminster Confession* Chapter 27: Section 4) can be responsible for dispensing them. Hence, we must also regard the Baptism of the various sects, who do not have teaching elders, as also being invalid.

New Covenant Sacraments replace those of the Old Testament

To those thoroughly acquainted with the Old Testament Scriptures it will come as no surprise that the New Testament only authorises two sacraments, this is because under the Old Covenant circumcision and the Passover were the only two ordinary sacraments observed by the Church in that dispensation. These have of course now been superseded by Baptism and the Lord's Supper in the New Testament. As Circumcision and the Passover were ordinances that involved the shedding of blood, symbolising the Redeemer to come, and since Christ has now accomplished our redemption, there is now no need for blood to be shed. So the two bloodless signs of Baptism and the Lord's Supper have to take the place of the two bloody signs of circumcision and the Passover; even though their significance as signs of the covenant of grace remains morally the same in both dispensations. G.I. Williamson in his commentary of the *Westminster Confession* demonstrates this in the following table:

Circumcision — Baptism	Passover — The Lord's Supper
1. Administered once only to each.	1. Administered repeatedly to each.
2. Administered to believers and to their children.	2. Administered to believers only
3. Picture of inception of union with God (cleansing, justification, etc.)	3. Picture of maintenance of union with God (nourishment, growth, sanctification, etc.)
4. Recipient wholly passive (he is circumcised — baptised recieves what another performs).(p. 205)	4. Recipient active (he partakes by his own act).

One clear example in Scripture, of how the New Testament sacrament has replaced its Old Testament counterpart is found in Colossians 2:11-12 were Paul says:

In him also were you circumcised with a circumcision made without hands, by putting off the body of the flesh, by the circumcision of Christ, having been buried with him in baptism, in which you were also raised with him through faith in the powerful working of God, who raised him from the dead.

Here the apostle identifies circumcision and Baptism as both symbolising union with Christ. Meaning that, as William Hendriksen concludes, 'the definite implication, therefore, is that Baptism has taken the place of circumcision. Hence, what is said with reference to circumcision in Rom. 4:11, as being a sign and seal, holds also for Baptism... It is, accordingly, a sign and seal of union with Christ, of entrance into his covenant, of incorporation into Christ's body, the Church.' (*Commentary on the Epistle to the Colossions*, p. 116). Hence, the *Westminster Confession* teaches: 'The sacraments of the Old Testament, in regard of the spiritual things thereby signified and exhibited, were, for substance, the same with those in the New' (Chapter 27: Section 5). As the signs of the covenant of grace in both the Old and the New Testament represent substantially the same thing; then it comes as no real surprise that the apostle Paul:

Sometimes uses the name of an Old Testament sacrament when speaking of those who have literally received only the New Testament sacrament, and vice versa. He says that the Israelites were Baptised (1 Cor. 10:1), whereas, of course they were actually circumcised. He also speaks of the Colossians as circumcised (Col. 2:11), though in actual fact they were baptized. He speaks of the Passover as belonging to the Corinthians (1 Cor. 5:7), though we know that it was the Lord's Supper and not the Passover, that was observed among them. (G.I. Williamson, *The Westminster Confession: For Study Classes*, p. 205).

The relevance of this will become more apparent when we come to examine who are the proper recipients of the sacraments in the New Testament. If the sacraments in the Old Testament represent the same thing as those in the New, then it is reasonable to conclude that the same people are entitled to receive them.

CHAPTER 12:

The Subjects of Baptism

The issue of who are the rightful subjects of the sacrament of Baptism has been a highly controversial one in the recent history of the Christian Church. At the outset I believe it is necessary to commend our Baptist brethren (those who believe that Baptism is for adult believers only) for their sincere desire to take the word of God seriously and not to blindly follow human tradition; some of them, such as, C.H. Spurgeon, John Gill, William Carey, Albert N. Martin, John Bunyan and Andrew Fuller (to name but a few) have made a unique and vital contribution to the Reformed faith and stand shoulder to shoulder with us in their adherence to Calvinistic doctrine and the regulative principle. However, I shall seek to respectfully argue that their position regarding the exclusion of the children of believers from the sacrament of Baptism is not a legitimate application of the regulative principle.

While it is true that there is no specific command to baptise infants in the New Testament, nor is their an unambiguous example of the child of a professing Christian being baptised; nevertheless the baptism of the children of believers may, on the basis of their status in the covenant of grace and membership of the visible Church, be shown to be a reasonable inference from Scripture. While some Baptists may object to this method of Biblical interpretation they have to employ it to arrive at other doctrines. For example, there is not one verse in the Bible that explicitly states that God is three persons in one essence, co-equal and co-eternal; yet from the information we have in Scripture we logically deduce that this is correct. As the *Westminster Confession* says 'The whole counsel of God...is either expressly set down in Scripture, or by good and necessary consequence may be deduced from Scripture' (Chapter 1: Section 6). In fact, the Lord Jesus used this method of making a logical deduction from Scripture to show the Sadducees the truth of the doctrine of the resurrection (Matt. 22:23-33). So for anyone to conclude that infant Baptism is a breach of the regulative principle simply because there is not a specific command to baptise infants in the New Testament is erroneous. If it can be shown to be a legitimate logical deduction from Scripture then we must accept the Baptism of believer's children as a correct application of the regulative principle and as something which is divinely authorised in the Bible.

Adult Baptism

Among orthodox Christians there is little dispute over what is required of un-baptised adults in order for them to receive the sacrament. The *Westminster Shorter Catechism* states 'Baptism is not to be administered to any that are out of the visible church, till they profess their faith in Christ, and obedience to him' (Answer to Question 95). Peter's instructions to the un-baptised adults on the day of Pentecost makes it abundantly clear that repentance, and a profession of belief in the gospel, are what is required of adult converts to Christianity who have not previously received Baptism; 'Peter said to them "Repent and be baptised every one of you in the name of Jesus Christ for the forgiveness of your sins"' (Acts 2:38). Adults are not required to prove they are regenerate, by giving an elaborate testimony narrating their conversion, but they are to receive the sacrament on the basis that their profession of faith is not contradicted by scandalous sin. However, controversy arises over what is to be done with their offspring. I shall seek to argue that not only believing adults 'but [also] the infants of such as are members of the visible church are to be baptised' (*Westminster Shorter Catechism* Answer to Question 95) on the basis of their inclusion in the covenant of grace, membership of the visible church and other Scriptural inferences.

Baptism: Sign and Seal of the Covenant of Grace

Perhaps the leading argument for infant Baptism is the essential unity of God's covenant of grace. While it is true that this covenant has been differently administered in the time of Abraham, Moses, David, and finally in the new covenant, nevertheless there is but one way of salvation throughout (John 14:6), meaning that the different administrations are progressive stages of one over-arching covenant of grace (Gal. 3:17). This covenant was established with Abraham in Genesis 17 when God said to him 'I am God Almighty; walk before me, and be blameless that I may make my covenant between me and you' (v.1-2). Furthermore, at this stage in the history of redemption, a sign was given to demonstrate that the Lord had entered into the covenant with Abraham, this sign was circumcision. This sign was given to Abraham as an adult believer who professed faith in the Lord; the apostle Paul informs us in his letter to the Romans that Abraham 'received the sign of circumcision as a seal of the righteousness that he had by faith while he was still uncircumcised' (Rom. 4:11). Circumcision was the sign and seal of the covenant of grace, as baptism is the New Testament replacement for circumcision (Col. 2:11-12), it now must be the sign and seal of the covenant of grace in the new covenant era.

This is further confirmed by the fact that both circumcision and baptism are continually represented throughout the Bible as symbolic of salvation. Circumcision is most often portrayed as the sign of regeneration, of a person having been given a new heart by the Holy Spirit. Examples include, 'And the LORD your God will circumcise your heart and the heart of your offspring, so that you may love the LORD your God with all your heart and with all your soul, that you may live' (Deut. 30:6); and 'circumcision is a matter of the heart, by the Spirit, not by the letter' (Rom. 2:29). It also represents cleansing from sin 'you were circumcised with a circumcision made without hands, by putting off the body of the flesh' (Col. 2:11), union with the Lord 'my covenant is with you' (Gen. 17:4), justification by faith alone (Rom. 4:11-12), and conversion (faith and repentance) 'Circumcise yourselves to the LORD; remove the foreskin of your hearts' (Jer. 4:4). However, we are not told in the Bible (contrary to popular belief) that circumcision was merely a national sign for the people of Israel; if that were the case then much of the above language, about it being symbolic of salvation, is rendered completely meaningless. Moreover, as Charles Hodge correctly noticed:

> Circumcision was not the sign exclusively of the national covenant with the Hebrews... because it was enjoined upon Abraham and contained in practice hundreds of years before the giving of the law on Mount Sinai, when the people were inaugurated as a nation. It was instituted as the sign of the covenant... made with Abraham. (Cited in R.R. Booth, *Children of the Promise*, p. 100).

How could circumcision merely be a sign of nationality when Israel was not properly constituted as a nation until around four hundred years after it was given to Abraham? It is only rational to conclude that the symbolism of circumcision was first of all spiritual, being the sign and seal of the covenant of grace, and not a mere badge of nationality.

Likewise, Baptism is pictured in the New Testament as symbolic of salvation and pointing to the blessings of the covenant of grace. Rodger M. Crooks, an Irish Presbyterian minister, writes in his book *Salvation's Sign and Seal* that:

> As a sign, baptism tells us what the salvation God offers under the terms of the covenant of grace is like. In Scripture, the symbol of washing with water and the idea of Baptism are linked with:
>
> 1. Cleansing from sin 'I will sprinkle clean water on you, and you shall be clean from all you un-cleanness, and from all your idols I will cleanse you' (Eze. 36:25).
>
> 2. Forgiveness of sins 'Repent and be baptised every one of you in the name of Jesus Christ the forgiveness of your sins' (Acts 2:38).
>
> 3. Union with Christ 'all of us who have been baptised into Christ Jesus were baptised into his death?' (Rom. 6:3).

4. Adoption 'for in Christ Jesus you are all sons of God, through faith. For as many of you as were baptised into Christ have put on Christ' (Gal. 3:26-27).

5. The new birth: Jesus links being 'born again' with being 'born of water' (John 3:3, 5).

6. The gift of the Holy Spirit: 'I will sprinkle clean water on you...I will give you a new heart...I will put my Spirit in you and move you to follow my decrees' (Ezekiel 36:25-27 NIV).

7. The resurrection to eternal life: 'If we have been united with him in his death [something signified by baptism], we will certainly also be united with him in his resurrection' (Romans 6:5 NIV). (p. 33).

So New Testament baptism, like its Old Testament counterpart circumcision, points us to God's salvation in the covenant of grace. As Rodger Crooks also observed, while 'Baptists insist that Baptism is a sign of man's faith. What Scripture stresses, however, is that baptism is a sign of God's grace. Baptism [like circumcision] points to what God has done for us, and not what we have done for God.' (Ibid., p. 35). The sign of the covenant directs us to the salvation that the Lord freely offers to sinners in the covenant of grace; it reminds us of the sovereign grace of God in salvation, and not a mere profession of faith on the part of man.

Yet despite the fact that it symbolised salvation, circumcision was not reserved for adults who could exercise faith in the Lord; we find in Genesis 17 that this spiritual sign was to be applied to Abraham's infant seed because God had told him 'I will establish my covenant between me and you and your offspring ['seed' AV] after you throughout their generations for an everlasting covenant, to be a God to you and to your offspring after you' (Genesis 17:7). This meant that 'Every male among you shall be circumcised. You shall be circumcised in the flesh of your fore-skins, and it shall be a sign of the covenant between me and you. He who is eight days old among you shall be circumcised' (Genesis 17:10-12). While many object to infant Baptism today because an infant cannot exercise faith, and therefore can't understand what Baptism signifies, they would have to be consistent and say that infant circumcision was also wrong, because circumcision was a sign and seal of the righteousness of faith (Rom. 4:11). Yet we read that Abraham circumcised Isaac, though he could not profess faith 'And Abraham circumcised his son Isaac when he was eight days old, as God commanded him' (Genesis 21:4). As R.C. Sproul so prudently observed 'the crucial point is that in the Old Testament, God ordered that a sign of faith be given before faith was present. Since that was clearly the case, it is erroneous to argue in principle that it is wrong to administer a sign of faith before faith is present.' (Cited in R.R. Booth, *Children of the*

Promise, pp 115-6). Therefore, it is no more absurd to administer the sign of the covenant (which is now baptism) to infants, who can't profess faith, nowadays than it was for Abraham to pass on the sign of saving faith to his eight-day year old son Isaac. The bottom line, as Prof. John Murray noticed, is that 'the covenant made with Abraham included the infant seed, and was signified and sealed by circumcision administered by divine command (Gen. 17:9-14).' (*Collected Writings*, vol. 2, p. 374). Just like the children of believers nowadays Abraham's children were included in the covenant of grace because they were the children of a believer. Does this mean that they were automatically saved? No, when they come to years of understanding they had to exercise saving faith in the God of the covenant, or else they would be considered as covenant-breakers (Psalm 25:10; Psalm 78). Circumcision then, as baptism now, acted as a seal of the covenant promises, instructing the covenant children that they must believe on the Lord and if they do they will inherit the full blessing of the covenant – eternal life. Therefore, R.L. Dabney was right to say 'So far as the child himself is concerned, there is no absurdity in giving him the seal in advance of his fulfilment of the conditions. Are not seals appended to promissory covenants? Yea, every covenant is in its nature promissory, including something to be done, as a condition of the bestowment.' (*Systematic Theology*, p. 780).

So far we have established that since both baptism and circumcision symbolise salvation, and since circumcision was the sign of the covenant of grace in the Old Testament, then Baptism, being of substantially the same meaning, must be the sign of the covenant of grace in the New Testament. However, the question that remains to be answered is 'are children still included in the covenant, and should they receive the sign of the covenant in the New Testament era?' For a number of reasons I shall seek to answer the question in the affirmative, demonstrating that the children of professing Christians are still the proper recipients of the sign and seal of the covenant of grace. First of all, if the meaning of circumcision and Baptism is essentially the same (Col. 2:11-12) and God commanded that infants should receive the sign of the covenant in the Old Testament 'then it follows that, unless God expressly forbids infant inclusion, in the new covenant, infants should also be baptised.' (R.R. Booth, *Children of the Promise*, p. 115). Yet we are not explicitly told in the new covenant that the children of believers are no longer in the covenant of grace, and therefore no longer eligible to receive the sign. Far from it, Paul tells us that the Abrahamic covenant is still in force in the New Testament. This covenant was not annulled in the days of Moses 'the law, which came 430 years afterwards, does not annul a covenant previously ratified by God, so as to make the promise void' (Gal. 3:17); and so it remains in operation under the New Testament 'And if you are Christ's then you are Abraham's offspring, heirs according to promise' (Gal. 3:29). If New Testament Christians are the children of Abraham then the obligation to pass on the sign of the covenant to their infant seed must remain in force unless God has specifically revoked it. While the New Testament tells us that the sign of the covenant has changed from the bloody rite of circumcision, to the bloodless ceremony of water Baptism (Matt. 28:19; Col. 2:11-12), it does not tell us that believer's children are no longer entitled to receive the sign of the covenant. Since God has not annulled His commandment, we must assume that it is still obligatory upon us today, because we read that God established the Abrahamic covenant 'as an everlasting covenant' (Gen. 17:7). As Rodger Crooks correctly deduced 'the fact that God's covenant is everlasting and eternal implies that the covenant arrangements God established with Abraham are still the same today.' (*Salvation's Sign and Seal*, p. 46). The only difference in the administration of the covenant sign that we are told about in the New Testament, is that baptism may be applied to females as well as males (Acts 16:15); yet there is not one word about covenant children being excluded from receiving the covenant sign.

Moreover, while some Baptists try and argue that the principle of 'to you and your offspring' (Gen. 17:7) is no longer in operation in the new covenant age, the fact that at the beginning of the new dispensation on the Day of Pentecost, when Peter was emphasising the differences between the administrations of the covenant of grace, he highlights the reality 'that there is one factor that continues on from the old into the new, and it is that the covenant promise is 'unto you and for your children' (Acts 2:39).' (Ibid., pp 47-8). Peter tells his audience, who many of them being Jews would be thinking about whether their children would still be included in the new covenant era, when Baptism, the new sign of the covenant of grace was administered, that the promise of the covenant is not only to adult professing Christians but also to their children as well. Prof. F.S. Leahy remarked on the importance of Peter's statement:

> It is important to consider the meaning which a gathering of Jews would necessarily attach to these words. The 'promise' that they would naturally have in mind, and which Peter's words echoed, was "I will be a God unto you and to your seed." In all ages their children had shared in covenant privileges and blessings. How could Peter's hearers have possibly have understood his words to convey anything different from their patent meaning? (*Biblical Baptism*, p. 27).

To a first century Jewish audience the words 'the promise is unto you and for your children' (Acts 2:39) could only have meant that the obligation of the Abrahamic covenant was still binding in the new dispensation. Considering that Peter says this immediately after instructing adult converts to be baptised (Acts 2:38), it is only logical to conclude that his Jewish hearers would have understood Peter to be indicating that it is their duty to allow their children to receive the new covenant sign of baptism. Any other interpretation involves one wresting the passage out of its historical context and completely disregarding how Peter's original audience would have understood his words. This should not surprise us because the Jews were told that the new covenant would be a better administration of the covenant of grace (Jer. 31:31-34), therefore, as David McKay says, 'it is unimaginable that the place of covenant children within the circle of the covenant would be withdrawn.' (*The Bond of Love*, p. 263). Hence in light of the overall teaching of Scripture, the Baptism of the infants of believing parents is a reasonable deduction from the Biblical doctrine of the place of children in the covenant of grace, and from the unity and continuity of the covenant in all ages.

Infant Baptism and Membership of the Visible Church

The children of believers are baptised, not only on the basis that they are in the covenant of grace, but also because they are members of the visible Church. Hence, the *Westminster Confession of Faith* states that the 'visible Church...consists of all those throughout the world that profess the true religion; and of their children' (Chapter 25: Section 2); in consequence of being members of the visible Church 'Not only those who do actually profess faith in and obedience unto Christ, but also the infants of one or both believing parents are to be baptized' (*Westminster Confession* Chapter 28: Section 4). An analysis of the teaching of both the Old, and the New Testament, will prove that this is a thoroughly Scriptural line of reasoning.

Some of our Baptist brethren have alleged that all the members of the visible Church, in the new covenant era, are regenerate because of Jeremiah's prophecy that in the new administration 'no longer shall each one teach his neighbour and each his brother saying "know the LORD", for they shall all know me, from the least of them to the greatest' (Jer. 31:34). However, such an interpretation of the passage is not sustainable in light of the warnings against hypocrisy and apostasy in the New Testament and especially in the book of Hebrews were this text is referred to (Heb. 8:8-12). If it were true that nobody in the visible Church was unregenerate why would the inspired writers warn professing Christians 'Take care, brothers, lest there be in any of you an evil, unbelieving heart, leading you to fall away from the living God' (Heb. 3:12); 'For if we go on sinning deliberately after receiving the knowledge of the truth, there no longer remains a sacrifice for sins' (Heb. 10:26). If everyone in the visible Church in the New Testament is undoubtedly regenerate why does Paul instruct the members of the Church at Corinth to 'Examine yourselves, to see whether you are in the faith' (2 Cor. 13:5)?; if everyone's regenerate it's a bit of a pointless instruction; and what about John's warning about apostates who 'went out from us, but they were not of us; for if they had been of us, they would have continued with us. But they went out, that it might become plain that they all are not of us' (1 John 2:19). The fact that these apostates departed from the visible Church proves that not all people who make up the visible Church are true Christians.

Furthermore, there are actual examples of apostasy and hypocrisy in the apostolic Church. In Acts

5:1-11 the Lord struck Ananias and Sapphira with death because 'Satan filled your heart to lie to the Holy Spirit' (Acts 5:3); and Simon the Magician, despite professing faith and being baptized (Acts 8:13) was subsequently told by the apostle Peter 'your heart is not right before God...For I see that you are in the gall of bitterness and in the bond of iniquity' (Acts 8:21, 23). Also, Paul lamented over Demas who was 'in love with this present world, has deserted me and gone to Thessalonica' (2 Tim. 4:10). All this means that the (common) Baptist interpretation of Jeremiah's prediction that 'they shall all know me' (Jer. 31:34), as referring to an entirely regenerate visible Church in the New Testament, is absolutely untenable. What Jeremiah seems to be saying is that in the new covenant there would be a greater outpouring of the Holy Spirit so that comparatively more people in the New Testament Church would be truly saved than was the case in the Church under the old covenant. Charles Hodge gives us a number of reasons why the idea of the visible Church being only composed of those that are truly regenerate is beyond the realms of possibility:

> The attainment of such a result in any such society or government administered by men is an impossibility. It would require that the officers of the Church or the Church itself should have the power to read the heart, and be infallible in judgements of character. (*Systematic Theology*, vol. 3, p. 548).

Therefore, those who argue that we can't baptise the children of believers because we don't know if they are regenerate, should be consistent and not baptise anybody, since we cannot infallibly know if anyone is actually regenerate at all. In reference to the parable of the wheat and the tares (Matt. 13:24-30; 36-43 NKJV) Dr. Hodge remarks that Christ instructs the disciples not to make any attempt (beyond the boundaries of ordinary Church discipline for scandalous sin) to purge the visible Church of secret hypocrites:

> Our Lord expressly forbids the attempt the attempt, being made [v.28-30]. He compares his external kingdom, or visible Church, to field in which tares and wheat grow together. He charged his disciples not to undertake to separate them, because they could not, in all cases, distinguish the one from the other. Both were allowed to grow together until the harvest. (Ibid.).

It will only be at the last day, when the Lord returns, that the Church will be entirely pure 'The Son of Man will send his angels, and they will gather out of his kingdom all causes of sin and all law-breakers, and throw them into the fiery furnace' (Matt. 13: 41-42). On that day 'the wicked will not stand in the judgement, nor sinners in the congregation of the righteous' (Psalm 1:5). This is even consistent with Christ's own example, because as Dr Hodge observes 'Christ, to whom all hearts are known, admitted Judas to the number of his most favoured disciples, and even made him an apostle' (Ibid.); even though he was to ultimately die the death of an apostate. Little wonder then that:

> All attempts to make a Church consisting exclusively of the regenerate, have failed. So far as known, no such Church has ever existed on the face of the earth. This is of itself proof that its existence did not enter into the purpose of God. (Ibid.).

Having established that the doctrine of a mixed visible Church, consisting of regenerate and unregenerate members, is Biblical; we now have to examine whether or not the children of professing Christians are included in this body.

The children of believers were most certainly considered a part of the Church in the Old Testament. While it is true that Israel was a nation state, it was also the visible Church of the Lord. That is why Stephen calls it 'the church in the wilderness' (Acts 7:38 AV). As a Church, Israel was 'entrusted with the very words of God' (Romans 3:2 NIV); to them belonged 'the adoption, the glory, the covenants, the giving of the law, the worship, and the promises' (Romans 9:4) just like the Church in the new dispensation. Indeed, the usual English translation of 'congregation' in the English Old Testament, such as 'the congregation of Israel' (Ex. 12:3), it is actually referring to the Church (see Psalm 22:22; Heb. 2:12 AV). The sign of entrance into the visible Church,

God's covenant community, in the Old Testament was circumcision. Not being circumcised was equivalent to being outside the Church of God 'Any uncircumcised male who is not circumcised in the flesh of his foreskin shall be cut off [i.e. excommunicated] from his people; he has broken my covenant' (Gen. 17:14). So circumcision marked the boundaries of who was, and who was not, in the visible Church. It was not simply an ethnic or national sign, because as Randy Booth observes:

> In Israel, many who were uncircumcised received temporal blessings. For example, the resident alien was a foreigner who lived in the midst of Israel. He was a free man who could hire out his services (Deut. 24:14). Israelites were to show him charity and compassion (Ex. 22:21; 23:9). Aliens could glean with the rest of the poor in Israel (Lev. 19:10; 23:22), and they were under the protection of God (Deut. 10:18). Israelites were to love aliens as they loved themselves (Lev. 19:34). The alien could share in the poor tithe (Deut. 14:29) and in the Sabbatical year (Lev. 25:6). He was entitled to the protection of the cities of refuge (Num. 35:15) and the same rights as Israelites (Deut. 1:16). However, aliens were not to partake of the Passover unless they had been circumcised (Ex. 12:48-49). (*Children of the Promise*, pp 104-5).

Why were heathens allowed to partake in so much of the civil life of Israel, yet they were excluded from the Passover? The only reasonable answer is that because the Passover was an ordinance of the Church, and not the state of Israel, so to partake of it a heathen had to join the Church by submitting to the circumcision not only of himself but also of his children as well. Thus we read in Exodus 12:48 'If a stranger shall sojourn with you and would keep the Passover to the LORD, let all his males be circumcised. Then he may come near and keep it'. As circumcision was the sign of entrance into the visible Church and it was given, not only to adult believers, but also their children, then it is only logical to conclude that God has placed the offspring of believers within the bounds of the visible Church.

The big question we now have to answer is 'are the children of believers still regarded as part of the visible Church in the New Testament?' First of all we, must keep in mind the fact that it does not tell us anywhere in the New Testament that God has excommunicated (cut off) the infants of believers from His Church; as Charles Hodge put it 'If the Church is one under both dispensations; if infants were members of the Church under the theocracy, then they are members of the Church now, unless the contrary can be proved.' (*Systematic Theology*, vol. 3, p. 565). If the Lord has put the children of believers outside the covenant community in the New Testament, then surely He would have told us, but there is no indication in the New Testament to say that God now wants Christians to treat their children 'like a heathen and a tax collector' (Matt 18:17 NKJV) i.e. as one outside the Church. As God has not told us to exclude believer's children from His covenant community, we must conclude that the Lord still looks upon the children of Christians as part of His Church. Who are we to excommunicate those who God has not excluded from His own Church? Sadly, Randy Booth observes that our Baptist brethren, 'rather than including the children of believers in God's visible covenant community, Baptists place their children in the pagan community.' (*Children of the Promise*, p. 128). This led the Puritan John Owen to comment that the Baptist deprives:

> The children of believers of a privilege once granted them by God, never revoked, as to the substance of it, assigning nothing in its room; which is contrary to the goodness, love, and covenant of God, especially derogatory to the honour of Jesus Christ and the gospel. (Cited in Ibid.).

So if the covenant children have not been excluded by God, from the visible Church which He put them into (Gen. 17), what reason have we from withhold the sacrament of Baptism from them which has replaced circumcision as the sign of entrance into the visible Church (Matt. 28:19; Acts 2:38, 41)? There is no reason whatsoever, absolutely none, if they were fit to receive the sign of Church membership in the Old Testament, then why not in the New when there is no evidence to suggest that they have been excommunicated from God's covenant community?

Furthermore, not only is the New Testament silent on the excommunication of the children of believers from the Church, but it actually contains positive evidence that children form part of the visible Church. The Lord Jesus Christ clearly regarded believer's children as part of his kingdom; we read in Luke's gospel:

> **People were also bringing babies to Jesus to have him touch them. When the disciples saw this, they rebuked them. But Jesus called the children to him and said, "Let the little children come to me, and do not hinder them, for the Kingdom of God belongs to such as these..."'** (Luke 18:15-16 NIV).

If Christ considers infant children to be part of the eternal kingdom of God, it is only logical to conclude that they are also included in the outward expression of 'the kingdom of heaven' (Matt. 19:14) which is the visible Church. Many Baptists would argue that Jesus is merely saying that those who are like children belong to God's kingdom because the Lord goes on to say 'Truly, I say to you, whoever does not receive the kingdom of God like a child shall not enter it' (Luke 18:17). However, Rodger Crooks responds by saying:

That line of reasoning is invalid because consistently in the New Testament, he Greek word which is translated 'such as' introduces a category and not a comparison. For example, it is used in Galatians 6:1 to refer to the person who is caught up in a sin; in Titus 3:11 to those who cause divisions among Christians; and in 2 Corinthians 10:11 to those stirring up trouble for Paul in Corinth. When Jesus uses the phrase 'such as' in connection with the children of believers in Luke 18:16, he is saying that this category belong to God's kingdom. If Baptism is the right of all who belong to the kingdom of God, then believer's children have the right to Baptism. (*Salvation's Sign and Seal*, pp 49-50).

While it is true that this passage is not an explicit command to baptise infants, nevertheless, it does prove that infants may belong to God's eternal kingdom and thus be saved, and in consequence, be part of the visible expression of the kingdom of heaven – namely the Church. If the children of believers are part of the visible Church then they must be eligible to receive the sacrament of membership into that community. As J.C. Ryle said 'It is allowed on all sides that infants may be elect and chosen of God unto salvation, may be washed in Christ's blood, born again of the Spirit, have grace, be justified, sanctified and enter heaven. If these things be so, it is hard to see why they may not receive the outward sign of Baptism.' (Cited in F.S.

Leahy, *Biblical Baptism*, p. 35). Those who say that an infant covenant child cannot be baptised (receive the sign and seal of salvation) because it can't profess faith, if they were consistent, would have to say that such a child cannot be saved. Thankfully, however, they are not consistent, as it is clear from Scripture that covenant children, dying in infancy, are saved and go to the eternal kingdom (2 Sam. 12:15-23). As *The Canons of Dordt* say:

> Since we are to judge of the will of God from His Word, which testifies that the children of believers are holy [1 Cor. 7:14], not by nature, but in virtue of the covenant of grace in which they, together with the parents, are comprehended, godly parents have no reason to doubt of the election and salvation of their children whom it pleases God to call out of this life in their infancy (Head 1: Article 17).

If there was to be such a radical change between the composition of the visible Church in the Old Testament and that in the New Testament, would it not be reasonable to assume that Christ would have positively commanded the exclusion of covenant children from the ordinance of Baptism when He gave the apostles the Great Commission on the institution of the sacrament as the sign of initiation into the Christian Church? However, no mention at all is made of excluding the children of believers from the ordinance, all Jesus said to them was 'Go therefore and make disciples of all nations, baptizing them in the name of the Father and of the Son and of the Holy Spirit' (Matt. 28:19). Would the apostles, who made up the original audience, have understood this as meaning that the new sign of Church membership was not to be administered to children? Charles Hodge does not think so:

> It was inevitable, therefore, when Christ commanded his apostles to disciple all nations, baptizing them in then name of the Father, of the Son, and of the Holy Spirit, that they should act on the principle to which they had always been accustomed. When under the Old Testament, a parent joined the congregation of the Lord, he brought his minor children with him. When, therefore, the apostles baptized a head of a family, it was a matter of course, that they should baptise his infant children. (*Systematic Theology*, vol. 3, p. 556).

When one considers that nations are made up of families this seems like a pretty fair conclusion to reach. In the New Testament it is not just Jewish families who are included in the covenant of grace, because we are told 'that in Christ Jesus the blessing of Abraham might come to the Gentiles' (Gal. 3:14), thus fulfilling the promise made to Abraham 'in you all the families of the earth shall be blessed' (Gen. 12:3).

Moreover, the fact that Paul addresses children in his epistles as members of the Church is highly significant. In Ephesians 1:1 he writes 'To the saints who are in Ephesus and are faithful in Christ Jesus'; yet later he says 'Children obey your parents in the Lord' (Eph. 6:1) so Paul obviously considered covenant children as among the saints. Likewise, in Colossians 1:2 he addresses 'the saints and faithful brothers in Christ at Colossae'; and then gives the instruction 'Children, obey your parents in everything, for this pleases the Lord' (Col. 3:20). Obviously if Paul regarded the children of believing parents as members of the Church, then they must have been baptised, as baptism is the sign of entrance into the visible Church. If covenant children were now outside the boundaries of the visible Church, and to be regarded as heathens (Matt. 18:17 NKJV), then why would Paul address them as 'saints' in letters that he wrote to Churches where presumably the members would have received the sign of baptism to signify their admittance into the covenant community? The only rational answer is that Paul regarded the offspring of professing Christians as part of the visible Church and consequently the recipients of the sacrament of Baptism. In light of the overwhelming evidence we are forced to conclude that if covenant children are members of the visible Church, then they must also be the proper subjects of Baptism.

Biblical Inferences in favour of Infant Baptism

In addition to the inclusion of the children of believers in the covenant of grace and in the visible Church, there are other things in Scripture from which we may reasonably deduce that the practice of infant Baptism is Biblical. While some of our Baptist brethren may feel a little uncomfortable with relying upon inferences as a means of determining what the Bible is teaching, nevertheless, they must use this method of interpretation if they are to justify keeping the first day of the week as the Lord's Day. As David L. Neilands writes:

> Most Christians in the world keep Sunday, which is the first day of the week, as the Sabbath day or Lord's Day. What New Testament commandment established this new day? There is none. The day has been changed by inference. The inference has been deduced from such passages as John 20:19, 26; Acts 20:7 and 1 Corinthians 16:2. All immersionists [Baptists], except Seventh Day Baptists [people who still keep the Sabbath on the seventh day of the week], have agreed with us in drawing this inference. (*Studies in the Covenant of Grace*, p. 152).

Most Calvinistic Baptists are happy enough to observe Sunday as the Lord's day, despite the fact that it is not specifically commanded, on the basis of either continuity with the Sabbath in the Old Testament or of inferences drawn from the New Testament; so if it is legitimate to employ this method of interpretation for that issue, why not when it comes to the subjects of Baptism?

Perhaps one of the strongest inferences in favour of infant Baptism is actually the silence of the New Testament on the subject. If Christians had been baptising their children, and the apostles had disapproved of it, then surely this would have been recorded in the New Testament writings. We cannot simply assume that because the New Testament does not explicitly refer to infant Baptism that the practice did not take place in its day. Hence, J.G. Vos wrote:

Anti-pedobaptists [Baptists] interpret the silence of the New Testament...on the question of infant Baptism as evidence that the practice did not exist in their day. But the silence may equally well be interpreted as implying that infant Baptism was prevalent and unchallenged by opposition or controversy in their day. People do not write in defence of doctrines or practices which are generally accepted. Paul argued in favour of the resurrection in his First Epistle to the Corinthians because a party in the Church of Corinth denied the resurrection. His lack of argument about the resurrection in the Epistle to the Galatians does not indicate that Paul thought the resurrection unimportant, far less that he doubted or denied it, but only that there was no occasion to argue with the Galatians about it, for they fully accepted it. Similarly, the lack of explicit reference to pedo-baptism in the New Testament does not necessarily imply the absence of the doctrine and the practice. The anti-pedobaptist, in other words, fails to take the occasional character of the New Testament writings into account. (*Baptism its Subjects and Modes*, pp 7-8).

Since the place of believer's children in the covenant of grace and in the visible Church was so clearly taught in the Old Testament (Gen. 17; Joel 2:16) there would be no need for the apostles to defend infant Baptism (which symbolised the covenant child's place in both) unless the practice was being objected to by some new converts, or even false teachers, in the apostolic Churches.

Furthermore, while Baptists challenge Presbyterians to explain why there is not a single unambiguous example of an infant being baptised in the New Testament, Vos answers:

We might reply by challenging them to point out a single case of adult Baptism being administered to a person born of Christian parents. On the Baptist assumptions there must have been many hundreds of such cases before the end of the New Testament. Yet there is no instance of it, nor a word of instruction about it in any part of the New Testament. If it was the practice for children of Christian parents to receive adult Baptism on reaching maturity or adolescence, is it not passing strange that in the Pastoral Epistles there is not a word of instruction as to the proper age and qualifica-

tions for the administration of the ordinance.
(Ibid., p. 9).

How can we explain the silence of the New
Testament regarding the Baptism of people brought
up in Christian homes? We can only answer this in
a satisfactory way by deducing from their place in
the covenant of grace and in the visible Church, that
the children of Christian parents in New Testament
times were baptised in infancy. If the New Testament
taught such a radical distinction between the status
of covenant children in the old administration and
the new, that they were no longer entitled to the sign
of the covenant, then surely it would have given us
an example of someone growing up in a Christian
home and being baptised in adulthood and given us
instructions about at what age we should baptise such
people. The fact that the New Testament is silent about
these matters presents the Baptist with an innumer-
able number of difficulties which they cannot answer
from Scripture. However, the Presbyterian can logically answer these difficulties by concluding, in light
of the standing of believer's children in the covenant
of grace and the visible Church, that the offspring
of professing Christians in the New Testament must
have been baptised in infancy.

Timothy is a New Testament example of a covenant child who was brought up 'in the training and
instruction of the Lord' (Eph. 6:4 NIV). Paul was
only to happy to acknowledge how God had worked
covenantally through the family to bring Timothy
to faith 'I am reminded of your sincere faith, a faith

that dwelled first in your grandmother Lois and your mother Eunice and now, I am sure, dwells in you as well' (2 Tim. 1:5). Would Paul have employed such language if he regarded the offspring of Christians as little heathens who were now shut out from the covenant of grace and the visible Church? Highly unlikely, the only reason Paul has for using this type of language is that he viewed Timothy as a covenant child who had kept the way of the Lord. Moreover, he seems to indicate that Timothy, like many covenant children today, was regenerated either in infancy or in very early childhood, when he says 'from infancy you have known the holy Scriptures, which are able to make you wise for salvation through faith in Christ Jesus' (2 Tim. 3:15 NIV). Unlike Paul, Timothy did not have a dramatic conversion experience (Acts 9), but probably could not remember a time when he did not know the Lord. This is not something which should surprise us, as God is pleased to work through covenant families which He has ordained to produce 'Godly offspring' (Mal. 2:15) and He tells us that 'his righteousness' is 'to children's children, to those who keep his covenant and remember to do his command-ments' (Psalm 103:17-18). While it is true that not all covenant children are saved, many end up becoming a 'godless person like Esau' (Heb. 12:16 NASB), yet we should realise that it is often the purpose of the Lord to 'pour out my Spirit upon your offspring, and my blessing on your descendants' (Isa. 44:3). Yet isn't it interesting that while we read of Timothy being circumcised in later life (Acts 16:3), because he was working among the Jews yet was uncircumcised himself despite having a mother of Jewish descent, we never read about him being baptised. Perhaps Timothy's mother didn't have him circumcised as an infant, because, as a convert to Christianity, she believed it would be more appropriate to have him baptised. While this is not explicitly stated it nevertheless appears to be a logical inference.

Another problem for the Baptists is that when Paul explains what Baptism symbolises in his epistles (e.g. Rom. 6:3-4; Col. 2:11-12) he never says 'do you remember when you were baptised?' Why does he not do this? After all, if they all had been baptised as adults they would have remembered their baptism. However, if they had been baptised as infants then Paul could not have used such language because at least some of the people he addressed were baptised in infancy.

Moreover, if Christian parents are now to regard their children as little pagans, why does Paul say 'the unbelieving husband is sanctified by the wife, and the unbelieving wife is sanctified by the husband; otherwise your children would be unclean, but now they are holy' (1 Cor. 7:14 NKJV). While Paul is not saying that the children of believing parents are regenerate, nevertheless, he is saying that they are distinct from the world. Whereas an unbelieving marriage partner is sanctified through the influence of their believing spouse; the children of Christians are constituted 'holy' by their place in the covenant of grace and membership of the visible Church. Prof. Leahy explained that in 1 Cor. 7:14 'the apostle says literally what he says figuratively in Romans 11:6, although in a different context, "If the root be holy, the branches are too"...There is, therefore, a wide distinction between the children of unbelieving parents and the children of parents, one of whom is a believer in Christ.' (*Biblical Baptism*, p. 28). Since there is such a radical distinction between the children of the ungodly, who are 'unclean', and the children of Christians, who are 'holy'; is it really so unreasonable to acknowledge this by administering to the believer's offspring the sacrament of Baptism which signifies their distinction from the world?

Furthermore, if the New Testament no longer regards children as part of the covenant of grace and the visible Church, and views each person as an individual, rather than regarding families covenantally; why then do we read about household baptisms? Surely if the New Testament is now as individualistic as Baptists maintain, then it should only speak about people individually, and not as members of a household. Furthermore, the existence of household baptisms becomes even more important when we consider just how few baptisms are actually recorded in the New Testament. The book of Acts is a brief history of the apostolic Church covering a period between A.D. 30 to A.D. 63. During this period of intense missionary activity thousands of people came into the Church, therefore it is hardly surprising that we read about adult baptisms. Just as if you were to read a biography of a Presbyterian missionary you would read about the Baptism of adult converts. Examples in the New Testament include the apostle Paul (Acts 9:18) who was unmarried and had no children (1 Cor. 7:7), the Ethiopian eunuch (Acts 8:38) considering that a eunuch is a person who has been castrated it seems fair to assume he had no children, Simon the Magician (Acts 8:13) yet there is no indication he had children, and Gaius (1 Cor. 1:14) again there is no suggestion that he had a family. So, none of these examples, of only a handful of individuals being baptised, is any obstacle to infant Baptism. This is further substantiated by the fact that in remaining cases of Baptism recorded in the New Testament we read of entire households being baptized. While we aren't specifically told that here were children in these households, John P. Sartelle comments that 'to assume that these homes along with other households baptized in the Mediterranean area, had no children is a presumption bordering on prejudice.' (Cited in R.R. Booth, *Children of the Promise*, p. 143). Let's examine the term household as it is used elsewhere in Scripture to see if it encompasses infants. Joshua said 'as for me and my house, we will serve the LORD' (Josh. 24:15) are we to believe infants were excluded and that Joshua went round each individual waiting to see whether they would agree to serving the Lord before making this declaration? Not very likely. When stating the qualifications for eldership Paul said that a man 'must manage his own household well, with all dignity keeping his children submissive, for if someone does not known how to manage his own household, how will he care for God's church' (1 Tim. 3:5). Are we to believe that Paul excluded infants from these households? Such a conclusion would be most strange. Clearly there is no Biblical reason then for thinking that a household cannot include infants. Therefore when we read about the apostles baptising the head of a family we must assume that they also administered the sacrament to his whole family. An analysis of household baptisms in the New Testament appears to bear this conclusion out.

In the account of the conversion of Lydia we are told that 'The Lord opened her heart to pay attention to what was said by Paul...she was baptized, and her household as well' (Acts 16:14-15). Notice that the text only says that the Lord opened Lydia's heart so that she would respond to Paul's message, it doesn't say this about the rest of her household, so they must have been baptized an account of Lydia's faith which rendered them holy (1 Cor. 7:14). As we are not told that Lydia had a husband (if she did the house would not have been called 'her household' as the husband is the head of the home Eph. 5:23) the other members of the household who were baptized are most likely to have been young children. Later in the same chapter of Acts we read about the baptism of the Phillipian Jailer and his household. After Paul and Silas told him 'Believe in the Lord Jesus, and you will be saved, you and your household' (Acts 16:31) we read that 'he was baptized at once, he and all his family' (Acts 16:33). Notice again that the text does not explicitly tell us about anyone else believing except for the jailer, although it is entirely possible that some in his household did believe 'they spoke the word of the Lord to him and to all who were in his house' (Acts 16:32), yet we can't be sure as the passage doesn't say so. However, Randy Booth observed that the statement 'you shall be saved, you and your household' (Acts 16:31) 'was made before anything was said to the other members of his household.' (Ibid., p. 144). Why did Paul and Silas say this? Booth answers 'perhaps Paul and Silas were prophesying about the individual members of the jailer's household – but that seems implausible. More likely, Paul and Silas were referring to the practice of including whole households in the covenant of grace.' (Ibid.). The reason why Paul and Silas could use such terminology, when speaking to the Phillipian jailer, is because they knew that the Lord had promised believer's 'to be a God to you and to your offspring after you' (Gen. 17:7) and that this promise applied to Gentile converts (Gen. 22:18; Gal. 3:14). Another example of household baptism occurs in Acts 18:8 were we read 'Crispus, the ruler of the synagogue, believed in the Lord, together with his entire household. And many of the Corinthians hearing Paul believed and were baptized' [cf. 1 Cor. 1:14]. At face value, many would conclude that this verse indicates that not only Crispus, but all his family, personally professed faith and were subsequently baptized. However, Randy Booth gives us some reasons why we should not jump to this conclusion:

> Since Cripsus was the leader of the synagogue, his entire household, including his children, would have belonged to the synagogue. It seems likely, then, that Crispus, as the head of the house, would have brought

his entire family for household baptism. We should expect that a first century Jewish family would similarly have followed the lead of its covenantal head. This text should be interpreted in accordance with the Jewish culture of the times, not the individualistic assumptions of our own culture. The New Testament culture arose from the Old Testament culture, and therefore it is not surprising to find whole households believing because the head of the household believes. (Ibid., pp 147-8).

Household baptisms were clearly a normal event in the life of the early New Testament Church; so much so that Paul could just mention in passing that he had 'baptised the household of Stephanus' (1 Cor. 1:14 NKJV) as an ordinary occurrence. If the apostles had believed in such a radical difference between the status of children in the covenant of grace and the visible Church, in the Old and New Testaments, would the inspired writers not have made it abundantly clear that infants were not included in these households in case anyone got the idea that they still were? The only rational answer to this, and other similar questions, is that the children of believers are still the proper recipients of Baptism as the sign and seal of the covenant of grace and membership of the visible Church.

CHAPTER 13:

The Mode of Baptism

Regarding the correct mode, by which the sacrament of Baptism is administered, the *Westminster Confession* says: 'Dipping of the person into the water is not necessary: but Baptism is rightly administered by pouring or sprinkling water upon the person.' (Chapter 28: Section 3). However, our Baptist brethren, on the other hand, believe that the regulative principle demands that the subjects of Baptism be fully immersed in water; otherwise their 'Baptism' is invalid even though it is done in the name of the Trinity, by a lawful Christian minister, and within the jurisdiction of a true Christian and Protestant Church. Thus the *Baptist Confession of Faith* (which is a mild revision of the *Westminster Confession*) states 'Immersion, or dipping of the person in water, is necessary to the administration of this ordinance.' While again commending our Baptist brethren for their commitment to the regulative principle, I shall endeavour to demonstrate from Scripture, that while immersion is still a valid mode of Baptism (because water and the name of the Trinity are used), the best way to administer the sacrament is by sprinkling or pouring.

The meaning of the Greek word *baptizo*

Many Baptists argue that the Greek verb *baptizo*, that is often used in the New Testament to denote Baptism, always, and can only mean, to immerse. So, every time this verb is used in the New Testament, Baptists assume that the inspired writer is talking about an act of immersion. Therefore, when we read that after his conversion Paul 'rose and was baptised' (Acts 9:18) Luke is supposed to be telling us that Paul was immersed in water. However, while it is true that the word *baptizo* can and may refer to an act of immersion, it is going too far to say that this is the only usage of the word in the Bible. One case were *baptizo* cannot refer to immersion is found in 1 Cor. 10:2 where Paul says that the children of Israel 'all were baptized into Moses in the cloud and in the sea.' As Rodger M. Crooks explains:

> Paul's statement cannot mean that the Israelites were immersed in the Red Sea. Neither did the Israelites immerse themselves in the cloud. The cloud came upon them. Whatever the verb means in 1 Corinthians 10:3, it does not mean to immerse. (*Salvation's Sign and Seal*, p. 59).

So according to Paul's logic the Israelites were baptized though they were not immersed, while the Egyptians were immersed but they were not baptized (Exodus 14). Another place were the word *baptizo* cannot refer to the dipping of a person into water is in Luke 11:38 when Jesus was dining with a Pharisee. Luke tells us that 'the Pharisee was astonished to see that he did not first wash before dinner' (Luke 11:38). In his *Expository thoughts on Luke* J.C. Ryle observes:

> The Greek word literally translated would be rendered, "that he had not first been baptized" before dinner. It is clear that the washing spoken of cannot be a washing of the whole body, but a partial washing, as of the hands and feet, or a sprinkling of water on the hands, after the manner of Eastern nations (2 Kings 3:11). The opinion held by some Baptists that the Greek word to "baptize" is never used except in the sense of a total immersion of the body, is one that cannot be reconciled with the expression used in the text. (*Expository thoughts on Luke*, vol. 2, p. 47).

Was the Pharisee shocked because Christ did not dip himself in water before He 'went in and reclined at the table' (Luke 11:37) or because He didn't first of all pour or sprinkle water over His hands? The latter of the two seems much more probable.

Furthermore, in the New Testament a word closely related to *baptizo* is used to refer to sprinkling i.e. the 'various ceremonial washings' in Hebrews 9:10 (NIV). These 'various ceremonial washings' included Moses sprinkling the people (Heb. 9:19; Ex. 24:6-8), the sprinkling of defiled persons (Heb. 9:13; Num. 19:17-18), the sprinkling of the tabernacle (tent) and the vessels used in the worship (Heb. 9:21; Lev. 8:19, 16:14). Rodger Crooks notes that 'the significant feature about all these was that the mode employed was sprinkling, not immersion. So the New Testament, in at least one place, actually links *baptizo* with sprinkling.' (*Salvation's Sign and Seal*, p. 60). Clearly we must conclude that the argument that to baptise means to dip or to immerse, is going way beyond, and is indeed contrary to the usage of the word in Scripture.

Historical Accounts of Baptism Could Not Have All Been By Immersion

An analysis of some of the instances of Baptism being administered, which are recorded in the New Testament, makes it extremely difficult to accept the contention that Baptism was always carried out by immersion as being a reasonable one. First of all, it is extremely unlikely that mass baptisms which took place in the days of John the Baptist or on the Day of Pentecost were administered by immersion. Many have assumed that the baptisms carried out by John were by immersion because Mark tells us that the people 'were being baptized by him in the river Jordan' (Mark 1:5). However, this may only mean that John had to use the water of the river Jordan due to the meagre water supply in the towns in that region. The necessity of John doing this is confirmed by the fact that 'Jerusalem and all Judea and all the region about Jordan were going out to him' (Matt. 3:5). Therefore, multitudes were coming to be baptized, so when it says that the crowds 'were baptized by him in the river Jordan' (Matt. 3:6) it may well mean that he stood in the Jordan and sprinkled or poured water on the multitudes that presented themselves to him for Baptism. Nowhere in the accounts do we read that John submerged the multitudes under the waters of the river Jordan. For him to have done this would have been practically impossible, as it would have taken an enormous amount of time to have baptized hundreds and thousands of people individually by full immersion. Whereas if John had sprinkled them with a rod of hyssop (Psalm 51:7), while he stood in the Jordan, these baptism could have been administered fairly quickly and would not require John to have super-human strength to dunk thousands of people in water one after the other. Even if it could be proved that John did baptize by immersion this would not necessarily mean that we would have to be immersed, because the Baptism of John is not the same as New Testament Baptism. Indeed, John's Baptism would seem to have origins in the ritual washings of the Old Testament which were carried out by pouring or sprinkling (remember that John himself was a priest Luke 1:5), and not by immersion. Moreover, John predicted that his water Baptism looked forward to the Baptism of the Holy Spirit that the ascended Christ would pour out upon

His Church; 'I have baptized you with water, but he will baptize you with the Holy Spirit' (Mark 1:8). The Baptism of the Holy Spirit cannot possibly be thought of as an act of immersion because Acts 2:17 (fulfilling Joel 2:28) tells us that the Spirit of God was poured out upon them 'I will pour out my Spirit on all flesh.'

The last point leads us on nicely to the baptisms carried out on the Day of Pentecost (recorded in Acts 2); this was, of course, the very first time that this sacrament of the new covenant was administered. After Peter preached the word we read that 'those who received his word were baptized, and there were added that day about three thousand souls' (Acts 2:41). Are we really to believe that the apostles dipped three thousand people in the public baths of Jerusalem? Princeton scholar J.A. Alexander comments:

> To the supposition that these converts were baptized by immersion, it may be objected, besides the greatness of the number and the shortness of the time, that Jerusalem has always been remarkably destitute of water, the fountain of Siloam being its only constant source. That the three thousand went out in procession to this fountain, or that many were baptized in the swimming-baths or cisterns belonging to public establishments or to private dwellings, or that these difficulties were miraculously overruled for the occasion, are conceivable hypotheses; but whether they are probable or preferable to the simple

supposition that the water, like the Holy Ghost in spiritual Baptism, and the blood in the ceremonial purification, was poured or sprinkled – every reader must determine for himself. (*A Commentary on the Acts of the Apostles*, p. 89).

The probability that the apostles baptised by immersion, on the Day of Pentecost, appears to be very slim. It is extremely doubtful that the apostles would have even been physically capable of dipping three thousand people in one day, nor is it likely that the Jewish authorities who 'crucified the Lord of glory' (1 Cor. 2:8) would have permitted His followers to use Jerusalem's pools to baptise their new converts en masse. However, it is much more reasonable to assume that the apostles baptised these new converts (and their children) en masse by sprinkling, just as Moses had sprinkled the whole nation of Israel en masse at Sinai (Ex. 24:8).

Many Baptists are of the opinion that Philip baptized the Ethiopian Eunuch by full immersion; because we are informed in the record of his baptism that 'they both went down into the water, Philip and the eunuch, and he baptized him. And when they came up out of the water, the Spirit of the Lord carried Philip away' (Acts 8:38-39). They infer that the phrases 'went down into the water' and 'came up out of the water' imply Baptism by immersion. However, there are serious logical problems with this view. When Luke says that they 'went down' and 'came up' from the water, he is merely saying that they moved towards the water and then moved away from it, he is not saying that they went beneath the surface of the water and then emerged from it. Moreover, it is worth keeping in mind that 'if this movement implies immersion, then Philip immersed himself as well as the eunuch' (R.M. Crooks, *Salvation's Sign and Seal*, pp 61-2). because the text says that 'they' went down and came up from the water. So if Baptists are going to point to this passage as a proof-text for immersion then they should be consistent and immerse, not only the candidate for baptism, but also the administrator of the sacrament as well. Also, considering that they were in a desert it is highly unlikely that there would have been enough water for Philip to dip the Eunuch into. It is much more probable to conclude that Philip and the Eunuch walked into a stream of water and there Philip poured or sprinkled water upon him. As Thomas Vincent said:

> When we read of some that were baptized, we do not read that they were dipped or plunged over head and ears; they might be baptized by pouring or sprinkling the water upon their faces; yea, in some places where, the Scripture tells us, persons were baptized, travellers tell us that they were but ankle-deep, in which it was impossible they could be plunged all over. (*The Shorter Catechism Explained From Scripture*, p. 247).

And it is highly unlikely that the Eunuch would have 'went on his way rejoicing' (Acts 8:39) if he had just been immersed in water, surely he would have to have waited until he and his clothes had dried out. Also, when one considers that Cornelius and his companions (Acts 10:47) as well as the Phillipian jailer's household (Acts 16:30-34), were actually baptized indoors, in a day and age when private baths were in short supply, then it is almost impossible to believe that these baptisms were administered by full immersion. Since then, there is no clear and unambiguous evidence that any of the baptisms recorded in the New Testament were performed by dipping the candidate in water; then it is most unreasonable to assume that immersion is the only valid form of Baptism.

Theological Argument for Immersion

It has been asserted by many Baptists 'that going down into and coming up out of water is an analogy portraying going down into the grave with Christ in His burial and rising again in His resurrection.' (*Testimony of the Reformed Presbyterian Church of Ireland*, p. 65). They have two passages on which they base this assertion; Romans 6:3-6:

Do you not know that all of us who have been baptized into Christ Jesus were baptized into his death? We were buried with him by baptism into death, in order that, just as Christ was raised from the dead by the glory of the Father, we too might walk in newness of life. For if we have been

united with him in a death like his, we shall certainly be united with him in a resurrection like his. We know that our old self was crucified with him in order that the body of sin might be brought to nothing, so that we would no longer be enslaved to sin.

And Colossians 2:12:

Having been buried with him in baptism, in which you were also raised with him in the powerful working of God, who raised him from the dead.

The Baptist interpretation of the above passages is highly erroneous for a number of reasons. First of all, if immersion is supposed to symbolise burial with Christ then our Baptist brethren have forgotten that 'Christ was not lowered into a grave but placed on a ledge in a cave-like sepulchre. Thus immersion in water is not a proper symbol of Christ's burial.' (Ibid. p. 66). So culturally lowering into a pool of water could not have had the symbolism then that it has now. If you are going to plunge somebody in water, in order to symbolise burial with Christ, then it would be necessary to baptize them in a fish-tank with a locked door on the side in order to imitate Christ's burial in a locked tomb. Secondly, in these passages Paul is not discussing the mode of Baptism at all; he is primarily talking about our union with Christ, an in Romans 6 his main objective is to demonstrate 'that our union with Christ has secured not only our justification, but also our sanctification.' (J. Pipa in G. Strawbridge (ed), *The Case For Covenantal Infant Baptism*, p. 113). In his epistles Paul often describes believers as being 'in Christ', 'in the beloved', 'in him' etc. So when he says that Christians were 'buried with him in baptism' (Col. 2:12), he is merely saying that Baptism is an outward sign of union with Christ. Elsewhere in his letters Paul uses Baptism to illustrate the idea of union. Joseph Pipa explains:

> In 1 Corinthians 10, he uses the figure of Baptism to show the union of the Old Testament Church with Moses, the covenant head. In verses 1 and 2 he says, "I do not want you to be unaware, brethren, that our fathers were all under the cloud and all passed through the sea; and all were baptized into Moses in the cloud and in the sea" [NASB]. The "baptism into" teaches that they were in union with Moses, the mediator of that old covenant. In a sense he was their covenant head. This union is expressed a little differently in Galatians 3:27, "For all of you who were baptized into Christ have clothed yourselves with Christ" [NASB]. Paul again expresses the concept of union, this time using the covering of clothing to picture union. So to be baptised into Christ brings one into union with him. Consider one other example in 1 Corinthians 12:13, "For by one Spirit we were all baptized into one body, whether Jews or Greeks, whether slaves or free, and we were all made to drink of one

Spirit" [NASB]. Here Baptism expresses the unity of the body of Christ. Immersion as a mode fits none of these illustrations. (Ibid., p. 119).

Baptists are very arbitrary in their selection as to what aspects of our union with Christ are symbolised by Baptism, putting an inordinate emphasis upon burial and resurrection in order to justify immersion. In similar vein, Prof. John Murray exposes the inconsistency of the immersionist argument:

> The union signified by Baptism includes more than union with him in his burial and resurrection. It signifies union with him in his death and crucifixion. The burial must not be equated with either. Paul in Romans 6 speaks of being baptized into Jesus' death (v.3), of being planted together with him in the likeness of his death (v.5), and of being crucified with him (v.6; cf. Gal. 2:20). It is apparent that immersion and emergence do not resemble these. But they are as germane to union with Christ as burial and resurrection. In the Baptist argument, therefore, the burial and resurrection are accorded the exclusive relevance in the plea for symbolism.
>
> Other passages likewise prove the arbitrariness of preoccupation with the analogy of burial and resurrection. Paul also writes: 'For as many of you as were baptized into Christ did put on Christ' (Gal. 3:27). It would be as

legitimate to argue for the mode of Baptism from this passage as from Romans 6:4. But the figure here is that of putting on a garment, to which immersion bears no resemblance. In 1 Cor. 12:13 the figure is that of making up one body, which is foreign by way of analogy to immersion. The fact is that Baptism signifies union with Christ in the whole range of his ministry, and other aspects are as integral as burial and resurrection. It is prejudicial to the completeness of the union signified to limit the symbolism to any one phase of Christ's redemptive accomplishment. (*Collected Writings*, vol. 2, pp 372-3).

As it is through regeneration that we are brought into union with Christ 'he saved us…by the washing of regeneration and renewal of the Holy Spirit, whom he poured out on us richly through Jesus Christ our Saviour' (Titus 3:5-6); and regeneration is often symbolised by the pouring or sprinkling of water 'I will sprinkle clean water on you…And I will give you a new heart' (Eze. 36:25-26); 'unless one is born of water and the Spirit, he cannot enter the kingdom of God' (John 3:5) and 'I will pour out my Spirit on all flesh' (Acts 2:17). Therefore it is only logical to infer that Baptism by pouring or sprinkling is sufficient to symbolise union with Christ, because 'as Baptism brings us in contact with water, it expresses union.' (J. Pipa, in G. Strawbridge (ed), *The Case For Covenantal Infant Baptism*, p. 118). So as the washing of the Holy Spirit brings us into union with

Christ, so the washing of water upon us, by sprinkling or pouring, is entirely adequate to symbolise that union. Hence Baptism by immersion, while still a legitimate mode of administering the sacrament, is not necessary.

CHAPTER 14:

The Lord's Supper

As the Scriptural warrant for observing the Lord's Supper has been dealt with earlier, it would be superfluous to go over it again. Rather, my purpose is to investigate how we should observe the Lord's Supper in a manner consistent with the regulative principle of worship.

Elements used in the observance of Communion

When observing the Supper of the Lord the only elements authorized by Scripture are bread and wine. This is evident from the accounts of the institution of the sacrament by Christ recorded in the gospels. In Mark's gospel we read:

And as they were eating, he took bread, and after blessing it broke it and gave it to them, and said "Take; this is my body."

And he took a cup, and when he had given thanks he gave it to them, and they all drank of it. And he said to them, "This is my blood of the covenant, which is poured out for many." (Mark 14:22-24).

The bread represents Christ's broken body and the wine His Shed blood. While the bread that was used at the institution of the sacrament was unleavened bread, I would not agree with G.I. Williamson that we are obliged to use this today. This is because when 'Christ instituted the Supper at the Passover... the only bread at hand was unleavened.' (A.A. Hodge, *The Confession of Faith*, p. 358). Hence the use of unleavened bread was clearly something circumstantial, so that it is perfectly acceptable to use an ordinary loaf when we observe the Lord's Table. A common practice, among Fundamentalists, has been to substitute alcoholic red wine in favour of grape juice. This decision has not been based upon Biblical considerations, but out of deference to the Temperance Movement that arose in the 19th century, and in order to appease those who continue to believe that the use of alcohol is sinful. Since the consumption of alcohol is clearly permitted by Scripture (Matt. 9:17; John 2:3-10; Rom. 14:21; 1 Tim. 5:23 etc.), G.I. Williamson is right when he says:

If the decision to use grape juice instead of wine is based on the influence of the Temperance Movement, we must regard this as seriously unbiblical. It is a false doctrine, a legacy from the ancient Gnostics, to locate sin or evil in material things. The cause of the sin of drunkenness was located by Christ in man's depraved heart (Mark 7:14-23), not in wine. It is not Biblical to locate evil in the handiwork of God [Psalm 24:1] rather than in the heart of man. Nor can the sacrament of the Lord's Supper be rightly administered on the basis of deference to such error. (*The Westminster Confession of Faith: For Study Classes*, p. 223).

Some Fundamentalists have argued that the Lord didn't use real wine when He instituted the sacrament, however, if this is true why did Paul rebuke the Corinthians for having a drunken party at the Lord's Table (1 Cor. 11:20-22)? And notice that Paul condemns them for being 'drunk' (1 Cor. 11:21), not for drinking alcoholic wine. Another reason why we should use alcoholic wine is because the alcohol serves to kill bacteria, whereas grape juice doesn't, meaning that we can all hygienically drink from one cup. This is why the use of grape juice leads to the use of mini-glasses because of the fear of someone picking up an infection. Yet, if we adhered to Christ's appointment of one common cup ('This cup' Luke 22:20) and alcoholic wine, then this problem wouldn't arise.

Sacramental Actions Involved in the Administration of the Lord's Supper

It is essential to the proper observance of this ordinance that the proper sacramental actions are observed. The *Westminster Confession* tells us that:

> The Lord Jesus has, in this ordinance, appointed His ministers to declare His word of institution to the people; to pray, and bless the elements of bread and wine, and thereby set them apart from a common to a holy use; and to take and break the bread, to take the cup, and (they communicating also themselves) to give both the communicants but to none who are not then present in the congregation. (Chapter 29: Section 3).

First of all there is the consecration of the elements. This consists of repeating the words that Christ used in the institution of the sacrament (Luke 22:17-20), a prayer of thanksgiving and blessing upon the elements (Matt. 26:26-28) which sets them apart, from ordinary to sacred use. The minister after praying is to break the bread and then distribute it to the other communicants, thus following Christ's example that 'after blessing it broke it and gave it to them' (Mark 14:22). Likewise, the same is to be done with the cup of wine because Jesus 'took a cup, and when he had given thanks he gave it to them, and they all drank of it' (Mark 14:23). This last point refutes Rome's practice of withholding the cup from the laity (only allowing the priests to drink from it). Rome's custom is intimately connected with her doctrine of transubstantiation, in which the Papists believe that the elements are magically transformed into the actual body, blood, soul and divinity of Christ. As a result of this doctrinal error 'there arose the natural fear lest some of the...person of the Lord should be spoiled of lost from the crumbling of the bread or the spilling of wine. Hence the bread is prepared in little wafers which cannot crumble, and the cup is denied to the laity and confined to the priests.' (A.A. Hodge, *The Confession of Faith*, p. 361). Hence, Rome totally ignores the command of the Lord Jesus that all who partake of the sacrament should drink of the cup.

Moreover, Reformed Christians have generally believed that it is wrong for communicants to kneel at the Lord's Table, as this implies a veneration of the elements as objects of worship. Horton Davies wrote 'all Puritans rejected the Sacrifice of the Mass, and the posture of kneeling at Communion, which they believed lent colour to that doctrine.' (*The Worship of the English Puritans*, p. 204). Episcopalians, on the other hand, usually kneel when they partake of the Lord's Supper believing that kneeling before the elements is an act of divine worship given by the sign to the thing signified, so they claim to be worshipping Christ by kneeling to receive the elements that represent Christ. George Gillespie spotted the danger of kneeling out of reverence for the elements, comparing it to the Roman Catholic usage of images as means by which God is worshipped. He therefore writes:

> He that will say that it [kneeling] is not idol-
> atry must acquit the Papists of idolatry also
> in worshipping before their images; for they
> do in like manner profess that they…give no
> more to the image but relative or respective
> worship. (*English Popish Cermonies*, Works:
> 2, p. 93)

Although it is true that the Lord and the disciples
did not sit around the table on chairs (they reclined
on couches), since it is the ordinary way that we eat
meals in our culture, then it is a suitable posture to
adopt when receiving the sacrament.

Much controversy arose among Reformed
believers in the 17th century as to whether or not the
ordinary people should receive the elements sitting
at a table, along with the elders, or sitting in the pews
on their own. The Independent Puritans favoured the
latter view, whereas, the Presbyterians (especially
the early Scottish Covenanters) held tenaciously to
the belief that all communicants should sit around a
table. According to Horton Davies this was because
'they believed it was an accurate attempt to repro-
duce the circumstances of the Last Supper, whilst it
had symbolic value as a declaration that the Lord's
Supper was a Feast, at which the Lord was Host and
the communicants the guests, rather than a sacrifice.' (*The Worship of the English Puritans*, p. 214).
Although this issue was debated vigorously by the
two parties at the Westminster Assembly, neither
method was officially adopted.

The practice of private communion in which the minister takes the elements to a single person, or small group of persons, apart from the rest of the congregation, finds no support in Scripture. Paul gave the Corinthians instructions about how to observe the Lord's Supper 'when you came together as a church' (1 Cor. 11:18); therefore the sacrament is only to be administered in a public assembly and not in private. G.I. Williamson gives us a number of reasons why private communion, which is now so common among Protestants, is un-Scriptural:

> First, the example of Christ is not consistent with such practices. He instituted the sacrament in a gathering of believers. They were commanded to divide the cup and to partake together of a common loaf. Manifestly, this example cannot be followed where there is no assembly of believers. Second, every New Testament reference to the observance of this sacrament shows us that is was an ordinance of the visible Church, administered when and where there was a gathering together of the members (Acts 4:42; 1 Cor. 11:18-20, etc). Third, the Lord's Supper is an expression or representation of communion between believers. But this cannot be unless there are at least "two or three…gathered together" in his name. Finally the sacraments are not to be severed from the preaching of the Word and the administration of Church discipline. Christ is our prophet and king as well as our

priest. As our prophet he teaches us the will of God by his Word and Spirit. As a king he rules us by his Spirit and Word. As our priest he offered himself a sacrifice to satisfy divine justice and to reconcile us to God. But private administration of the sacrament obscures or even denies that these are necessarily inter-related and inter-dependent. (*The Westminster Confession: For Study Classes*, p. 224).

However, this does not mean that the sacrament can't be administered in a private house for those that are unwell, but in order for that to be legitimate, the public assembly must meet there and conduct an ordinary Church service.

How Frequently Should the Sacrament be Observed

The question of how often the Lord's Supper should be observed in Christian congregations is not specifically stated in Scripture. However, one may infer from the words 'Do this, as often as you drink it, in remembrance of me' (1 Cor. 11:25), that the sacrament should be frequently observed in Christian congregations at the times appointed by the Session. The Independent Puritans, however, favoured weekly communion, while the Baptist Puritans, in a number of their congregations, believed that the Lord's Supper should only be celebrated in the evening because that was the original time that Christ had instituted the sacrament at. While there is nothing in Scripture against weekly Communion, the argument that it should only be observed in the evening is going too far. Should we only observe it on a Thursday because the Lord instituted the Lord's Supper on a Thursday? No, because that was only a circumstance, that is why we read that the Church at Troas 'On the first day of the week' was 'gathered together to break bread' (Acts 20:7). Moreover, Paul's directions to the Corinthians, as to how they should observe the Lord's Table, were applicable when they 'came together as a church' for the purpose of observing the sacrament, regardless of what time it was. Presbyterians have generally tended only to observe the Lord's Supper a few times a year; many have thought the sacrament will be observed more solemnly if it is observed less frequently. John Brown of Haddington was a notable exception arguing 'why not pray seldom, preach seldom, read God's Word seldom, that may become more solemn too?' (*Systematic Theology*). Furthermore, John Calvin and Richard Baxter were strongly in favour of weekly communion. Baxter said:

> This Sacrament in the primitive Church was celebrated every Lord's day; yea, and often, even ordinarily on every other day of the week when churches assembled for communion. And might be so now without any hindrance to preaching or prayer, if all things were ordered as they should be. (Cited in H. Davies, *The Worship of the English Puritans*, p. 214).

Even if you are not in favour of weekly communion perhaps you should consider if a more frequent observance would be helpful.

Recipients of the Lord's Supper

In order to be admitted to the Lord's Supper one must be a baptized professing Christian (Ex. 12:48; Acts 2:41-42) who is able to examine himself as to whether or not he is a true believer living in a manner consistent with his profession. Hence Paul gives us the warning:

> **Whoever, therefore, eats the bread or drinks the cup of the Lord in an unworthy manner will be guilty of profaning the body and blood of the Lord. Let a person examine himself, then, and so eat of the bread and drink of the cup. For anyone who eats and drinks without discerning the body eats and drinks judgement on himself.** (1 Cor. 11:27-29)

This requirement of self-examination obviously excludes infant covenant children from the sacrament, as self-examination is something that they are not capable of doing. Some have contended that this should not be the case as infants partook of the Passover. However, this is not true as infants are incapable of digesting the meat that is part of the Passover meal (Ex. 12:8). Furthermore, it would also appear that Jesus Himself did not partake of the Passover until He was twelve years old (Luke 2:41-42). Despite the requirement for self-examination, a Church Session still has the duty of forbidding the openly ungodly and professing Christians who indulge in scandalous sin, to sit at the Lord's Table. Therefore, when instructing the Corinthians to discipline the man who was having an affair with his step-mother, Paul said 'expel the wicked man from among you' (1 Cor. 5:13 NIV). This meant that he was to be excommunicated from the Church, and debarred from its ordinances. Also, a professing Christian 'who stirs up division' (Tit. 3:10) over foolish controversies or promotes serious doctrinal error (Rom. 16:17), or behaves in a disorderly way (2 Thess. 3:6-14) is to be barred from the sacrament until there is repentance and reformation.

CHAPTER 15:

The Christian Sabbath

It is essential to a proper understanding of the regulative principle of worship that we acknowledge that God 'has particularly appointed one day in seven, for a Sabbath, to be kept holy unto Him' (*Westminster Confession* Chapter 21: Section 7). Reformed believers have historically maintained that Christians are to observe the first day of the week as the Lord's Day which the *Westminster Confession* says 'is to be continued to the end of the world as the Christian Sabbath.' For the duration of the Sabbath the whole time is to be taken up 'in the public and private exercises of His worship, and in the duties of necessity and mercy' (Chapter 21: Section 8), see Isaiah 58:13-14. Sadly this position, which was almost universally held among professing Christians, has been rejected by many Evangelicals in recent years; so it will be my endeavour to demonstrate that first day Sabbath observance is in full conformity to the word of God.

Even though there is no explicit command in the New Testament for the first day of the week to be kept as the Christian Sabbath, nevertheless, it is something which 'by good and necessary consequence may be deduced from Scripture' (*Westminster Confession* Chapter 1: Section 6) in the same way that other doctrines, such as, the Trinity, the hypostatic union of Christ's two natures, infant baptism and female admittance to the Lord's Supper can.

The Sabbath is a Creation Ordinance

Though it is a fact which is often overlooked, the Sabbath was actually established at Creation, prior to the fall of man into sin. After completing His work of creating the universe we read 'And on the seventh day God finished his work that he had done, and he rested on the seventh day from all his work that he had done. So God blessed the seventh day and made it holy, because on it God rested from all his work that he had done in creation' (Gen. 2:2-3). Therefore, the principle of six days of labour and one day of sacred rest is patterned after God's sequence in His work of creation. As Prof. John Murray said:

> The sequence of six days of creative work and the seventh of rest is an irreversible fact in the transcendent sphere of God's relation to this universe which he has made. (*Collected Writings*, vol. 1, p. 207).

If we are no longer required to observe the Sabbath (as anti-Sabbatarians believe) then God's pattern of creation has ceased to be relevant to us! Moreover, the fact that the Sabbath was instituted at creation proves, beyond a shadow of a doubt, that it is not merely a Jewish ordinance inseparable from the ceremonial law (which is the Dispensationalists favourite argument). God instituted the Sabbath long before the emergence of the Jewish nation; thus Walter Chantry commented 'it is evident that when at creation week God made the Sabbath for man, his reference was not to Jewish man alone. It was for Adam and all his posterity that the Sabbath was made.' (*Call the Sabbath a Delight*, p. 56). This explains why Jesus said to the Pharisees 'The Sabbath was made for man' (Mark 2:27) i.e. it is made for the good of the whole of mankind, not simply the Jews. Clearly the Dispensationalist argument, that the Sabbath was only a Jewish ordinance, is entirely without a Scriptural foundation. As Pastor Chantry further writes:

> Anyone who claims that the Sabbath is uniquely Jewish is arguing against Moses, the founding prophet of Judaism, who wrote Genesis. He is also plainly contradicting the express teaching of our Lord Jesus Christ. It is simply not a defensible position...It is true that Jesus was speaking to Jews in Mark 2 and other gospel passages. But he was not discussing a matter unique to Jewish ceremony or Jewish law. The Sabbath is an issue

of morality which touches all mankind from the time of creation. (Ibid.).

The Sabbath is part of God's Moral Law

Furthermore, the permanence of the Sabbath is confirmed by the fact that it is included in God's moral law (which has been summarised in what we know as the Ten Commandments). The fourth commandment reads:

Remember the Sabbath day, to keep it holy. Six days you shall labour, and do all your work, but the seventh is a Sabbath to the LORD your God. On it you shall not do any work, you, or your son, or your daughter, your male servant, or your female servant, or your livestock, or the sojourner who is within your gates. For in six days the LORD made heaven and earth, the sea, and all that is in them, and rested the seventh day. Therefore the LORD blessed the Sabbath day and made it holy (Ex. 20:8-11).

The command to keep the Sabbath day holy was based, not on circumstances unique to the Jewish nation, but on God's institution established at creation and thus obligatory upon all mankind. In a somewhat lengthy quotation John Murray argues:

The Sabbath commandment is comprised in the Decalogue. The fourth commandment is not an appendix to the Decalogue, nor is it an application of the Decalogue to the temporary conditions and circumstances of Israel. There were ordinances in Israel, regulating the observance of the Sabbath, which were peculiar to the circumstances of the people of Israel at that time, and we have no warrant to believe that they are of permanent obligation. But the fourth commandment itself is an element of that basic law which was distinguished from all else in the Mosaic revelation by being inscribed on two tables of stone. The fourth commandment belongs to all that is distinctive and characteristic of that summary of human obligation set forth in the Decalogue. It would require the most conclusive evidence to establish the thesis that the fourth command is in a different category from the other nine. That it finds its place among the ten words written by the finger of God upon tables of stone establishes for this commandment, and for the labour and rest it enjoins, a position equal to that of the fifth or the seventh or the tenth. (*Collected Writings*, vol. 1, p. 207).

Is there any evidence then that the New Testament declares the fourth commandment null and void? Certainly not! In the Sermon on the Mount, Christ proclaimed:

Do not think that I have come to abolish the Law or the Prophets; I have not come to abolish them but to fulfil them. For truly, I say to you, until heaven and earth pass away, not an iota, not a dot, will pass from the Law until all is accomplished. Therefore whoever relaxes one of the least of these commandments and teaches others to do the same will be called least in the kingdom of heaven, but whoever does them and teaches them will be called great in the kingdom of heaven. (Matt. 5:17-19).

While this refers to more than the actual words of the Decalogue (the Ten Commandments), it most certainly includes them; and if the Ten Commandments have not been abolished, then the fourth commandment continues to bind men and woman to observe the Sabbath today. However, Dispensationalists would argue that unless an Old Testament commandment is repeated in the New Testament it is no longer relevant for Christians today. Not only does such an approach contradict the passage quoted above, but if taken to its logical conclusion it would mean that a Christian would have to ignore the moral instructions found in the book of Proverbs as being utterly irrelevant. Do you think it would be a wise idea to ignore almost a whole book of wisdom, placed in the middle of our Bible's, simply because the vast majority of its ethical directives are not repeated in the New Testament? Such an approach to the word of God is utterly foolish; God has given us the whole Bible to guide us, not just the New Testament. That is why Paul writing to Timothy, primarily about the books of the Old Testament, said 'All Scripture is breathed out by God and profitable for teaching, for reproof, for correction, and for training in righteousness, that the man of God may be competent, equipped for every good work' (2 Tim. 3:16). Contrary to the teaching of Dispensationalism, the truth is, that unless an Old Testament commandment is abrogated in the New Testament (Acts 15:10), it continues to be morally binding. The fourth commandment has not been abrogated in the New Covenant; therefore, the observance of the Sabbath is still morally binding. As Richard B. Gaffin put it 'The fact, then, that the fourth commandment is not explicitly quoted in the New Testament is far from being a presumption for its cessation. To the contrary, its inclusion in the Decalogue carries the presumption that it continues in force, unless abrogation be made explicit.' (Cited in J.L. Dugan (ed), *The Westminster Confession into the 21st Century*, p. 141).

If Christ had really came to abolish the Sabbath, why would He have referred to Himself as 'the Son of Man' who is 'Lord of the Sabbath' (Mark 2:28 NKJV). Is it really logical to think that 'the Son of Man' would actual come to abolish an ordinance that had been instituted for the good of man, and go so far as to call Himself 'the Lord of the Sabbath' which, according to Dispensationalist thinking, He was about to abrogate? Such a conclusion is so contrary to sound reason that it cannot be entertained for a single moment. John Murray explained that Christ is Lord of the Sabbath:

> Not for the purpose of depriving men of that inestimable benefit which the Sabbath bestows, but for the purpose of bringing to the fullest realization on behalf of men that beneficent design for which the Sabbath was instituted. If the Sabbath was made for man, and if Jesus is the Son of man to save man, surely the lordship which he exercises to that end is not to deprive man of that which the Sabbath institution involves. Jesus is Lord of the Sabbath – we dare not tamper with his authority and we dare not misconstrue the intent of his words. (*Collected Writings*, vol. 1, p. 208).

Since we have established, beyond any reasonable doubt, that the fourth commandment is to be observed by people living in the New Testament age the question which remains to be answered is what day should we keep the Sabbath on?

The Sabbath Changed to the First Day of the Week

Although we are not specifically told in the New Testament that we are now to observe the Sabbath on the first day of the week; this can be shown to be a reasonable inference from the example of Christ and His apostles. Our Lord rose from the dead on the first day of the week to signify the end of His humiliation and the completion of His work of redemption on behalf of His people. Mark tells us that Christ rose 'very early on the first day of the week' (Mark 16:2), which indicates that the Sabbath is to be kept from midnight to midnight. Not only did Jesus rise from the dead on the first day of the week, but He also appeared to His disciples 'On the evening of that day, the first day of the week' (John 20:19). However, Thomas was not with the other disciples when Christ appeared to them, and he continued to doubt that the Saviour had risen, even though they told him 'we have seen the Lord' (John 20:25). To this declaration Thomas protested 'Unless I see in his hands the mark of the nails, and place my finger into the mark of the nails, and place my hand into his side, I will never believe' (John 20:25). Significantly the Lord did not appear to Thomas, in order to resolve his doubts, until 'eight days later' (John 20:26) which happened to be the next first day. William Hendricksen comments 'employing the inclusive method of time-computation...John states that eight days later the event of the previous Sunday-evening was repeated.' (*Exposition of the Gospel According to John*, p. 464). On seeing the risen Christ, Thomas worshipped Him saying 'My Lord and my God!' (John 20:28). But the question we need to answer is why did the Lord not just appear to Thomas on any other day, why did he wait until the next first day? To this question Hendricksen answered 'did the Lord wait until Sunday evening in order to encourage his disciples to observe that day – and not some other day – as the day of rest and worship? That would seem probable.' (Ibid.). From Christ's appearances on the first day of the week we may infer that the 'Lord of the Sabbath' (Matt. 12:8 NASB) changed the day of the Sabbath from the seventh day to the first, in order to commemorate His resurrection from the dead and His completion of the work of redemption on behalf of His people.

Furthermore, the assertion that the day set apart for worship is now the first day of the week, and not the seventh, is confirmed by the example of the apostolic Churches. In Acts 20 we are told that Paul 'stayed for seven days' (v.6) at Troas, delaying his journey to Jerusalem for an entire week so that he could join with the believers there in public worship. Hence we are told 'on the first day of the week, when we were gathered together to break bread, Paul talked with them, intending to depart on the next day, and he prolonged his speech until midnight' (Acts 20:7). Why did Paul wait until the first day of the week? The only rational answer is that the first day of the week is the day set apart for the worship of God in the New Testament. Luke did not record this for no reason, J.A. Alexander noted:

> It is not a simple date or chronological speci-fication of the day on which this meeting happened to be held; for such a circumstance was too minute to be recorded for its own sake, and is never given elsewhere. The only satisfactory solution is, that the observance of the first day of the week, as that of our Lord's resurrection, had already became customary,

so that the assembling of the church at that time for the purposes here mentioned, was a matter of course, with or without special notice and arrangement.' (*A Commentary on the Acts of the Apostles*, p. 227).

Moreover, the fact that Paul instructed the Churches of Galatia and Corinth to present their offerings 'on the first day of the week' (1 Cor. 16:2) indicates that it was on the first day of the week that they gathered for worship.

Some might be inclined to argue, okay the apostolic Church met for worship on the first day of the week, but does that mean that they considered it to be a Sabbath day set apart from the other days of the week? This is a most reasonable question, but it can be answered in a number of ways. First of all the fourth commandment hasn't been abrogated in the New Testament, so we can deduce from the apostles worshipping on the first day of the week that they now applied the fourth commandment to Sunday rather than to Saturday. Christ, by His resurrection, had 'sanctified' (Gen. 2:3) the first day of the week. This can be inferred from the fact that the apostle John referred to the New Testament Sabbath as 'the Lord's Day' (Rev. 1:10); it was the Lord's Day because it was distinct from other days due to the fact that it was now the weekly Sabbath. The change of the weekly Sabbath, in light of the resurrection of Christ, had in fact been predicted in Psalm 118:24 'This is the day that the LORD has made; let us rejoice and be glad in it.' John Gill considered this day to be remarkable because it was the day of Christ's 'resurrection from the dead; when God gave him glory, and was a matter of joy to those for whose justification he rose; or the Lord's day, kept in commemoration of it.' (*An Exposition of the Old Testament*, vol. 3, p. 330). If John believed every day was the Lord's Day (as some anti-Sabbatarians maintain) then his designation of a particular day by that title would have been meaningless. By this time all Christians would have understood that the Lord's Day was the day set apart for worship – the Christian Sabbath. Moreover, why would the author of Hebrews have said 'there remains a keeping of a Sabbath for the people of God' (Heb. 4:9 AV margin) if the weekly Sabbath had been abolished? Christ's resurrection from the dead meant that He had finished His work of redemption and 'has also rested from his works as God did from his' (Heb. 4:10). As Walter Chantry explained 'Christ's ceasing from his works occurred on the first day of the week, just as God's ceasing from his was on the seventh day.' (*Call the Sabbath a Delight*, pp 94-5). On the New Covenant Sabbath we not only commemorate God's work of creation, but also Christ's finished work of redemption, and in anticipation of the future renovation of the universe when God's people will enjoy an eternal Sabbath with the Lord at the consummation of the kingdom (Rom. 8:21-24; Heb. 4:11). While some anti-Sabbatarians have appealed to texts such as Rom. 14:5; Gal. 4:10; Col. 2:16-17 to claim that weekly Sabbath observance is no longer obligatory it is abundantly plain, from the context in which all these passages are written in, that they apply to the non-weekly Sabbaths of the ceremonial law that have ceased to be obligatory with the completion of Christ's work. They have nothing whatsoever to do with the weekly Sabbath with its basis in creation, its place in the moral law, and its additional sanctity as the 'Lord's Day' in the New Covenant era.

Should we have Holy-days outside the Sabbath?

The question of whether or not the Church, in the New Testament era, should have extra-biblical holy days, apart from the weekly Lord's Day is an issue which has historically divided Protestants; while the Reformed Churches, especially those descended from the Puritans, have regarded them as illegitimate because they are not appointed in the word of God. Other Protestants, such, as Lutherans, Episcopalians, and most Evangelicals, who reject the regulative principle, have argued for the lawfulness of extra-biblical festivals (like Christmas, Easter, Ascension Day etc.).

While it is true that there were festival days outside of the Sabbath in the Old Testament, these were divinely appointed by God, and have been abrogated with the coming of Christ 'let no one judge you in food or in drink, or regarding a festival or a new moon or Sabbaths, which are a shadow of things to come, but the substance is of Christ' (Col. 2:16-17 NKJV). These, now abrogated, holy days provide no warrant for those who wish to invent their own festivals on a pretext of religious devotion. In the Old Testament, whenever men sought to devise their own holy days, without any commandment from God, they were met with divine displeasure. For example, when Israel made the golden calf in the wilderness 'Aaron made proclamation and said "Tomorrow shall be a feast to the LORD"' (Ex. 32:5). However, the Lord did not accept this unauthorized festival as being in any way legitimate; He said to Moses in His righteous anger that 'your people, whom you brought up out of the land of Egypt, have corrupted themselves. They have turned aside quickly out of the way that I commanded them' (Ex. 32:7-8). Notice that God was so enraged at their impiety, in presuming to invent for themselves a holy day, that he calls them 'your people' i.e. people who belonged to Moses and not to Himself. This was repeated by Jeroboam, the first king of Israel after the separation of the northern tribes from Judah; when he decided to place golden calves in Dan and Bethel he also 'appointed a feast on the fifteenth day of the eighth month like the feast that was in Judah' (1 Kings 12:32). Jeroboam did not do this at the command of the Lord but concocted it in his own heart, and God viewed it as an act of serious declension which set Israel on the road to apostasy. Thus when Nadab his son succeeded him, we read, 'He did what was evil in the sight of the LORD and walked in the way of his father, and in his sin which he made Israel to sin' (1 Kings 15:26). Jeroboam's festival day was not based on the commands of divine revelation and thus unacceptable to the Lord. As Dale Ralph Davis said 'worship either rests on the prescriptions of divine revelation or on the preferences of the human heart.'

(*The Wisdom and the Folly: An Exposition of the Book of First Kings*, p. 145). So unless a holy day can be proved to be appointed by the Lord, it must be rejected as a breach of the regulative principle. Therefore, man made holy days such as Christmas and Easter etc. are not consistent with the Scriptural law of worship.

Although the ceremonial festivals were abolished by the work of Christ, during the period of transition from the Old to the New Covenant (which ended with the destruction of Jerusalem in A.D. 70) Jewish converts to Christianity, who had weak consciences, were allowed to observe them until the transitional period had ended. This is why Paul wrote to the Gentile Christians at Rome not to despise their weaker Jewish brethren 'One person esteems one day as better than another, while another esteems all days alike...The one who observes the day observes it in honour of the Lord' (Rom. 14:5-6). Though they were no longer obliged to keep them, the Jews were allowed to observe these (divinely appointed) holy days, outside of the Sabbath, until they had adjusted to the different circumstances of the New Covenant. However, when the Judaizers tried to enforce the observance of these Jewish festivals upon the Gentiles, Paul took a very different line indeed; saying 'You observe days and months and seasons and years! I am afraid I may have laboured over you in vain' (Gal. 4:10-11). As James Bannerman observed, Paul includes holy-days, outside of the weekly Sabbath, as 'among the number of the things belonging to the bondage of a former dispensation, not to be considered binding upon those who had entered into the freedom of the Gospel.' (*The Church of Christ*, vol. 1, p. 413). If Paul used such strong language to condemn those who were unlawfully enforcing the observance of holy days that God had originally appointed (although now abrogated) one wonders how much more strongly he would condemn those today who enforce the celebration of man-made festivals that God has never appointed?

Although the Puritans acknowledged that there could and should be 'solemn fastings [Joel 2:12], and thanksgivings upon special occasions [Psalm 107; Esther 9:22]' (*Westminster Confession* Chapter 21: Section 5). Nevertheless, as Horton Davies said 'the Sabbath retained its lonely splendour as the sole red-letter day of the Puritan calendar.' (*The Worship of the English Puritans*, p. 75). The Lord's Day is the only holy day we need; God has been exceedingly generous in giving us fifty-two holy days a year. Moreover, we have no cause to appoint certain days to commemorate Christ's birth, death, or resurrection, because, in the Puritan view, when we observe the Christian Sabbath 'the mighty acts of God in the creation, redemption and sanctification of man, through the life, death and resurrection of Christ, were celebrated. The whole drama of salvation was rehearsed each Sunday in its entirety. What need was there, then, for separate festivals which celebrated only one scene of the divine drama at once?' (Ibid., p. 76).

Conclusion

Although this book has not covered all aspects of the regulative principle of worship exhaustively; I hope it will be of some benefit to the reader and provoke them to further thought, study, and prayer upon the subjects which have been analysed. If this work in some small way helps to stem the tide of anarchy in worship, and turn the Church back to the battle cry of the Protestant Reformation: 'Scripture Alone' and simple Biblical and Reformed worship it will have been of no small benefit. While it would be unrealistic to expect even every Reformed Christian to agree with all that has been written; I do hope that those of you in the Reformed faith will have a greater concern about the purity of our worship. Who knows what great things the Lord may do through modern day reformers!

Ascribe to the LORD the glory due his name;
worship the LORD in the splendour of holiness
(Psalm 29:2)

Bibliography

Alexander, J.A.*A Commentary on Mark*. Edinburgh: Banner of Truth, 1960

Alexander, J.A.*A Commentary on the Acts of the Apostles*. Edinburgh: Banner of Truth, 1963

Bannerman, James*The Church of Christ*, 2 vols. Edmonton: Still Waters Revival Books, 1991

Baxter, Richard*A Christian Directory*. Morgan: Soli Deo Gloria, 2000

Berkhof, Louis*Systematic Theology*. Edinburgh: Banner of Truth, 1958

Boettner, Lorraine*Roman Catholicism*. London: Banner of Truth, 1966

Booth, R.R.*Children of the Promise*. Phillipsburg: Presbyterian and Reformed, 1995

Brown, John *Hebrews*. Edinburgh: Banner of Truth, 1961

Brown, John *Systematic Theology: A Compendious View of Natural and Revealed Religion.* Fearn: Christian Focus Publications, 2002

Bushell, Michael *The Songs of Zion: A Contemporary Case for Exclusive Psalmody.* Pittsburgh: Crown and Covenant, 1999

Cairns, Alan *Dictionary of Theological Terms.* Belfast: Ambassador Publications, 1998

Calvin, John *Commentary on the Epistle of Paul the Apostle to the Hebrews* in vol. 22 of *Calvin's Commentaries*, 22 vols. Grand Rapids: Baker Book House, 1993

Calvin, John *Institutes of the Christian Religion.* London: James Clarke, 1949

Calvin, John *The Necessity of Reforming the Church.* Edmonton: Still Waters Revival Books, originally published in 1544

Chantry, Walter *Call the Sabbath a Delight.* Edinburgh: Banner of Truth, 1991

Clark, Gordon H.*What do Presbyterians Believe?* Phillipsburgh: Presbyterian and Reformed, 1965

Crooks, Rodger M.*Salvation's Sign and Seal.* Fearn: Christian Focus Publications, 1997

Dabney, R.L *Discussions: Evangelical and Theological*, vol. 2. Edinburgh: Banner of Truth, 1967

Dabney, R.L. *Systematic Theology.* Edinburgh: Banner of Truth, 1985

Davies, Horton *The Worship of the English Puritans.* Morgan: Soli Deo Gloria, 1997

Davis, Dale Ralph *The Wisdom and the Folly: An Exposition of the Book of First Kings.* Fearn: Christian Focus Publications, 2002

Dickson, David *A Brief Exposition of the Evangel of Jesus Christ According to Matthew.* Edinburgh: Banner of Truth, 1981

Duncan, J.L. (ed)*The Westminster Confession into the 21st Century*, vol. 1. Fearn: Christian Focus Publications, 2003

Durham, James *A Practical Exposition of the Ten Commandments.* Dallas: Naphtali Press, 2002

Frame, John *Worship in Spirit and Truth.* Phillipsburgh: Presbyterian and Reformed, 1996

Gill, John *An Exposition of the Old and New Testament* in 6 vols. London: William Hill Collingridge, 1852

Gillespie, George *A Dispute Against the English Popish Ceremonies Obtruded on the Church of Scotland* in *The Works of George Gillespie*, vol. 1. Edmonton: Still Waters Revival Books, 1991

Hendricksen, William *An Exposition of the Gospel According to John.* Grand Rapids: Baker Book House, 2002

Hendricksen, William *Commentary on the Epistle to the Colossians.* Edinburgh: Banner of Truth, 1962

Henry, Matthew *Commentary on the Whole Bible* in 6 vols. United States: Hendricksen Publications, 1991

Hodge, A.A. *The Confession of Faith.* Edinburgh: Banner of Truth, 1998

Hodge, Charles *A Commentary on Romans.* Edinburgh: Banner of Truth, 1972

Hodge, Charles *Systematic Theology* in 3 vols. London: James Clarke, 1960

Kennedy, John *Hyper Evangelism.* No date or place of publication available

Leahy, Fredrick S. *Biblical Baptism.* Belfast: Cameron Press, 1992

Murray, Iain H. *The Psalter – The Only Hymnal.* Edinburgh: Banner of Truth, 2001

Murray, John *The Collected Writings of John Murray*, vols. 1 and 2. Edinburgh: Banner of Truth, 1976

Murray, John and Young, William *Minority Report of the Committee on Song in the Public Worship of God submitted to the Fourteenth General Assembly of the Orthodox Presbyterian Church* (1947) available at: http://members. aol.com/RSICHURCH/song3.html

McKay, David*The Bond of Love.* Fearn: Christian Focus Publications, 2001

McNaughter, John (ed)*The Psalms in Worship.* Edmonton: Still Waters Revival Books, 1992

Neilands, D.L.*Studies in the Covenant of Grace.* Phillipsburg: Presbyterian and Reformed, 1980

Olyott, Stuart *Preaching – Pure and Simple.* Brytirinan, Brytirinan Press, 2005

Owen, John *A Brief Instruction in the Worship of God and Discipline of the Churches of the New Testament* in *The Works of John Owen*, vol. 15. Edinburgh: Banner of Truth, 1965

Owen, John *A Discourse Concerning Liturgies and their Imposition* in *The Works of John Owen*, vol. 15. Edinburgh: Banner of Truth, 1965

Owen, John *An Exposition of the Epistle to the Hebrews*, 6 vols. Edinburgh: Banner of Truth, 1991

Price, Greg L.*A Brief Introduction to Head coverings*. Edmonton: Still Waters Revival Books, 2004

Price, John *Old Light on New Worship*. Texas: Simpson Publishing, 2005

Protestant Reformed Church *The Three Forms of Unity*. Ballymena: Protestant Reformed Church, 1999

Puritan Reformed Church of Edmonton *The Practice of Head coverings in Public Worship*. Edmonton: Still Waters Revival Books, 2001

Reformed Presbyterian Church of Ireland *The Testimony of the Reformed Presbyterian Church of Ireland*. Belfast: Reformed Presbyterian Synod, 1990

Reymond, Robert L.*A New Systematic Theology of the Christian Faith*. Nashville: Thomas Nelson, 1998

Ryle, J.C. *Expository thoughts on Luke*, vol. 2. Edinburgh: Banner of Truth, 1986

Schaff, Phillip (ed) *The Creeds of Christendom*, 3 vols. Grand Rapids, Baker Book House, 1998

Schwertley, Brian M. *Exclusive Psalmody: A Biblical Defence*. Haslett: American Presbyterian Press, 2002

Schwertley, Brian M. *Musical Instruments in the Public Worship of God*. Haslett: Reformed Witness, 2003

Schwertley, Brian M.*Sola Scriptura and The Regulative Principle of Worship*. Southfield: Reformed Witness, 2004

Shaw, Robert *An Exposition of the Westminster Confession of Faith*. Fearn: Christian Focus Publications, 1998

Strawbridge, Greg (ed)*The Case for Covenantal Infant Baptism*. Phillipsburg: Presbyterian and Reformed, 2003

Swinnock, George *The Christian Man's Calling* in *The Works of George Swinnock*, vol. 1. Edinburgh: Banner of Truth, 1992

Vincent, Thomas V.*The Shorter Catechism Explained from Scripture*. Edinburgh: Banner of Truth, 1986

Vos, J.G.*Baptism its Subjects and Modes*. Pittsburgh: Crown and Covenant, undated.

Vos, J.G.*The Westminster Larger Catechism: A Commentary*. Phillipsburg: Presbyterian and Reformed, 2002

Ward, Rowland S.*The Psalms in Christian Worship*. Melbourne: Presbyterian Church of Eastern Australia, 1992

Watson, Thomas*Heaven Taken By Storm*. Morgan: Soli Deo Gloria, 1992

Watts, Malcolm H.*God's Hymnbook for the Christian Church*. Aberdeen: The James Begg Society, 2003

Westminster Divines*The Westminster Confession of Faith*. Glasgow: Free Presbyterian Publications, 1997

Williamson, G.I.*The Singing of Psalms in the Worship of God*. Belfast: Cameron Press, 1998

Williamson, G.I.*The Westminster Confession of Faith: For Study Classes.* Philadelphia: Presbyterian and Reformed, 1964

Williamson, G.I. *The Westminster Shorter Catechism: For Study Classes.* Philadelphia: Presbyterian and Reformed, 1964

Wilson, Geoffrey B. *New Testament Commentaries*, 2 vols. Edinburgh: Banner of Truth, 2005

CPSIA information can be obtained at www.ICGtesting.com
Printed in the USA
LVOW11s1017130416

483433LV00001B/1/P